MW00784397

THE JOYS OF
BEING AND
BECOMING

The Secret of Joy Revealed

Dear David + Kathy!
Joy is a Gift!
Felicity
Ps 94:19

Rosemarie Page Yerka

Rosemarie Page Yerka

ISBN 979-8-88616-861-7 (paperback)
ISBN 979-8-89345-014-9 (hardcover)
ISBN 979-8-88616-862-4 (digital)

Christian Faith Publishing
832 Park Avenue
Meadville, PA 16335
www.christianfaithpublishing.com

Printed in the United States of America

Testimonials

I have known Rose Yerka for many years now, and she is a Proverbs 31 woman for sure. If she is not caring for her grandchildren, she is writing a book or running for mayor of the town where she lives in. In her book *The Joys of Being and Becoming*, you will see the steps that lead to joy and are easily followed. Rose breaks down her life into its various seasons with excerpts from her diary cleverly interwoven into each season. The book is written so that every person can find the blessings in each season of their life. The Bible tells us that our steps are ordained of the Lord, and in this book, you will find the rhythms of each season that lead to accomplishing your assignment!

—Dr. Andrew P. Surace
Senior Pastor of Christ Fellowship Church
Ocean View, New Jersey

I am finding *The Joys of Being and Becoming* quite good and deeply personal, sometimes painful. (It took a great deal of courage to put it out there.) I want to compliment Rose on her fine knack for vivid detail descriptions of family members (red lipstick and all), shopping excursions in Camden, travels in Europe, dates with Bob, 70s memories (which resonated with me as well!), and pulling off a wedding on a budget really kept my interest. This attention to fine detail so a reader lives, sees, smells, and hears what you have put on paper is the gift of a good writer. Bravo!

—Joni Scanlon
Author of *A Sacrifice of the Heart: The Biography
of Irish Patriot Gearoid O'Sullivan*

The Joys of Being and Becoming: The Secret of Joy Revealed by Rose Marie Page Yerka

I am extremely honored that Rose has asked me to do a testimonial on this book. While reading it I have come to know Rose better. She has shared her life through her journaling her story is so amazing. It shows how God is in control of our lives, if we just let him. I am so glad that her journaling has turned out to be this wonderful testimonial of her life.

I believe it can be a guide on how to journal and the importance to leave a written legacy for your family, friends and others. I tried journaling when I was a little girl. I didn't think I had anything very interesting to say or write down. This book has changed my mind about that, I should've written everything down to share with my daughter, my son and my family. Our lives are unique and different. And should be recorded for our future families to read and meet us even when we are gone. I am so honored to call Rose my friend. Thank you Rose for sharing the story of your life.

—Mary T. Wood

Rose, captivates the reader by bringing them into the most intimate parts of her life. Whether joy, heartache, struggle or success the reader will find Jesus in all of it!

—Rita Reyes
Executive Director
Choices of the Heart

The Joys of Being and Becoming is a treasure trove of life events that spiritually birthed a woman of God, Rosemarie Page Yerka.

Rose sought truth and faith found her. Rose dug deeply and faith healed her. Rose followed her heart and leads others to revival, redemption and reconciliation.

On the pages of TJOBAB, Rose leaves a legacy of truth for her children, grandchildren, great grandchildren and her friends. She forgives selflessly, stays steadfast and focuses on Jesus. TJOBAB is based on facts of Rose's life told truthfully and joyfully, to save souls.

"She is clothed with strength and dignity; she can laugh at the days to come. She speaks with wisdom, and faithful instruction is on her tongue. She watches over the affairs of her household and does not eat the bread of idleness." Proverbs 31 NIV

—Cynthia L Gallenthin, AIPS-CP

This Book is for anyone who needs to be reminded that God uses every person, every heartache, and every situation to mold us and shape us into who we were created to be. Rose shares powerful stories from her childhood to adulthood of how God has directed her life from the time she was created in her mothers womb. Saving her own life from the very beginning!

This book reminds us of the importance and power of a praying mother who would see God's miraculous protection over her life, the life of her baby and generations to come. I love how Rose takes us through her own journey and shows us that we can put our faith in a God who loves us unconditionally. She teaches us there is no shame or condemnation in our past mistakes. Only love.

This book is a testimony to a powerful truth in Proverbs 16:9 "We can make our plans, but the Lord directs our steps."

—Pastor Gina Kulikowski
Discipleship Pastor
Gloucester County Community Church
Ministry Director/Fearless Women Ministries

DEDICATION

Rose and Her Mother Agnes

I have loved you with an everlasting love.
(Jeremiah 31:3 NIV)

This work is dedicated to my mother, Agnes, who was always
my biggest supporter. My mother was a strong woman of faith—gra-
cious, kind, and softened by a hard life. She was my hero.

In honor of my mother and women like her who need love and
support, I give to Choices of the Heart, a women's resource center
that speaks for those who cannot speak. I learned that I am not a mistake but an answer to prayer. I was saved from the abortionist's knife!

This is the journal of the journey of an insecure princess, the story of the grace to live soberly, righteously, and godly in this present age.

Dear Lord, teach me to love.

Time[1]
(One of my favorite anonymous poems about time)

Time is too slow for those who wait.
Too swift for those who fear,
Too long for those who grieve,
Too short for those who rejoice.
But for those who love, time is eternity.
—Author Unknown

---

[1] *"Time"*, Author Unknown, n.d.

CONTENTS

INTRODUCTION

The most important legacy a person can leave for the next generation is a written record of the many interesting and memorable events of one's life. *The Joys of Being and Becoming*, is a braiding together of stories: my grandmother's, my mother's, and mine—character studies of the family tree and love letters that shaped the unique moments of my life. God has answered prayers for generations in our family, and it is my prayer that this book encourages the next generation of storytellers to give God the honor in each family tree in spite of any painful memories. I was an illegitimate child, not a mistake, God knew me before I was born. My mother chose life and I pray you choose life—and not death... I am an answer to my mother's prayers, and my children, grandchildren, and great grandchildren are God's answer to my prayers. Bitterness and unforgiveness can rob joy for the next generation unless someone reverses its curse through forgiveness.

This book is based on my diary that was a journal I started to understand myself and my circumstances. This journal became the story of my struggle to overcome grief and insecurity and find answers to my questions about the meaning of life. The Lord told me my journal would be a book. He gave me the title and all chapter headings. I was amazed as I knew nothing about writing a book. The title spoke to my heart every time I was growing to do something new. Even now as I write, this is me Becoming a writer for the first time. This is the journal of the journey that started fifty years ago.

It's a Wonderful Life

My mother asked me to tell our story, so what follows is an account of lives lived—hers, mine, and my grandmother's—braided together into a multigenerational family's historical narrative. This unique generational perspective brought into focus the way the past is truly a window into the future of the next generation. The weaving together of these dramatic stories helped me to understand myself and share the timeless secret of being joyful and becoming more mature. I am forever grateful for such a godly mother, who chose to give me the gift of life.

I am thinking, *This feels like* 'It's a Wonderful Life!'[2] All my complaining about things that I thought were important have all left my aching mind. My life is sad and small with three babies at home and two school-aged children. My husband had a $10,000 pay cut from his job, and I found myself applying for food stamps. God told me, "Do not trust the system, trust me!" They had denied me until a woman from church saw my tears and asked if she could look into it for me—it turned out that she was a supervisor at Social Services.

---

[2] Frank Capra (director), *It's a Wonderful Life* (USA: Paramount RKO Pictures, 1946).

I am feeling very blue because it is Christmastime, and I have no money. So I decided to make Cabbage Patch dolls for my kids. They were very expensive and hard to find at this time.

So I am in my family room with a mountain of laundry to fold. Also, it looked like a doll hospital with doll heads, arms, and legs to be stuffed with filling. I flipped the channels to find a Christmas movie while my babies were napping, and the other kids were in school.

I found a black-and-white movie called *It's a Wonderful Life*, from 1946 by Frank Capra. I have never seen it before, and it caught my attention—I was glued to my TV set with a rabbit-ear antenna on top. It was the first time I had seen a movie about the flu epidemic of 1918 when my grandmother had died. It also showed wartime and the depression. Jimmy Stewart is the star, and Donna Reed plays his wife with four children in a big old house in Bedford Falls.

I related to the discouragement of George Bailey, the main character, as he is about to jump from a bridge. He has so many problems, he is thinking about ending it all—and on top of everything else, it's Christmas. However, he is rescued by his guardian angel, who then shows George what life would be like if it had not been for his good deeds over the years. By the end, George realizes that he wants to live, and it *is* a wonderful life. What the intensely moving film does is shows the value of friendship and love. I wound up watching it with tears running down my face and sobbing so loudly that my mother came to check on me. "Are you all right?" she asked. She told me this was one of her favorite Christmas movies too. It would later become one of my whole family's favorite movies. It showed the historic perspective of my mother's generation and helped me to understand her and the real value and meaning of Christmas. This is the Christmas that my family remembered the most. Homemade gifts and a real tree were given to us and strangers that came to our house bearing gifts for my children from a local group home.

My friend Mary Lou tried to encourage me to start a daycare in my home. I told her, "I already have a daycare with five children. I do *not* want more! Two days later my friend Carol came to ask if

I could watch her baby Corinne while she went back to work. She punctuated the plea with "You are the only one I would trust with my baby, please…" And so my daycare business began. I would have up to ten children or more in the summer and had to hire my cousin Mary Beth, who was a college student, to help.

I became known as the Family Day Care in the neighborhood and even had a bumper sticker that said "I play for a living." This became one of the happiest jobs I ever had, and the best part was that it allowed me to stay home with my babies.

My heart was touched by that movie and God used it to remind me that He knew my circumstances. Still, I needed some encouragement and God planned to provide it for me through a life changing experience that coming year.

Here is what happened, I had the opportunity to go away for a weekend with my daughter Tara and I was thrilled! Little did I know that it would become one of the most dramatic weekends of my life. Like a sail in the winds of change, it swiftly unfurled into a life altering crisis that could have been straight out of a white-knuckle page-turner that forever rewrote the story. It seemed surreal…

This is my day to die! I felt happy and sad. I will never see my kids again. Will they be okay? They are only babies. "Lord, Your will be done," I prayed. I could no longer speak or open my eyes. I heard people yelling to each other, "We're losing her! BP 60/40!" As I heard them speaking of crash carts and hemorrhaging, I thought, *God, are they talking about me? Why can't I answer? Am I really dying?* Oh no! I prayed an SOS prayer. "Lord, please help them help me. I want to see my kids again!" Then I saw a bright light and felt myself being wheeled once again to the operating room. I felt the life leaving my body… "Is this it? Lord, if it is my time, I am ready. But if you can change this, please help me. I want to live again. It *is* a wonderful life, please hear my prayer…"

PART 1

WINTER

**The Journey of an Insecure Princess
Surmounting the Cinderella Complex, the
Triumph of Faith Over Grief and Denial,
Finding True Love**

CHAPTER 1

Being a Child and Becoming a Daughter

The Insecure Princess Character: Recognizing
It Is Okay to Be Different
My Journey Begins at Age Eighteen

I was saved from the abortionist's knife. I do not know anyone with such a dramatic birthday story as mine, and I am forever thankful for a Godfearing mother who could hear God's voice. I can't imagine the fear and heartache she felt that day when her God answered her prayer. In my search for meaning and answers to my life's questions, I spent time learning to listen for the voice of my heavenly Father. This account is from my journal of the joys in being and becoming more joyful. My most memorable birthday was when I turned eighteen years old.

February 18, 1972

Today is my eighteenth birthday. Now I will be able to drink with my friends, and I will graduate this year. I can't believe how fast time has gone. My high school years seemed to go by quickly and now I would have to decide what I want to do. I think I want to help people as a nurse—I hope I can do it.

I was now considered an adult. It seemed both exciting and scary, but the best part would be that I could order a beer. I was surprised by the salty bitter taste, which I spit out and did not like. But when I was introduced to mixed drinks, they tasted good and made me feel happy, less shy and more confident. This is wonderful. Now I experienced why my family drank so much. It seemed to help me deal with life better. In hindsight I realize looks are deceiving and family secrets are kept so no one knows the true cost of alcohol and its effects on a family. I learned of one family secret firsthand that changed my life forever, but I don't want to talk about that again. As a matter of fact, I decided to forget it and get over it! The world seems to be going crazy with the Vietnam War. There are protests in the streets that they say are part of a "peace movement," but there are riots and it is a scary time. The top song of 1970 was "Bridge Over Troubled Water"[3] by Simon and Garfunkel.

My birthday wish is that the Vietnam War will end and that my boyfriend, Bob, would not have to go to Thailand for six months. I am afraid I will never get to see him again, and I think he may be the one for me—at least that is what he is saying. I want to wait until after he comes home to see how things go. I am not ready to settle down, I have too much living to do. This is my senior year, and I plan on having lots of fun. I am even getting to go on a dream trip to Europe and am so excited and thankful to my mom and stepfather for sacrificing so that I can go. I am blessed and I know it. Thank you, God! What a wonderful year!

Being and Becoming Journal

My favorite teachers made an impact on me. Sister Anne was my eighth grade teacher. I saw such joy in her face. I wonder how can

---

[3] Paul Simon and Art Garfunkel, *Bridge Over Troubled Water* (New York: Columbia Records, 1970.)

you be happy living the life of a nun? She shared that it was Jesus who gave her joy. I wanted what she had. One Saturday she came to visit my mother and told her that I should go to Catholic high school. My mother kindly declined the offer and explained that we could not afford this. She told my mother she would pray and the Lord would provide for my education. I was amazed by her faith and that the Lord was thinking about my education. My mother was a little offended by the nun's visit. But my mother started to think creatively, and she also prayed. So she and my cousin Dottie came up with an idea for a summer job. The Lord provided a summer job at the shore with my cousin Dottie. I worked there five years, and it provided for high school and my first year of nursing school. I was amazed at how my life changed because a teacher took special interest in one of her students. I am thankful as I remember Sister Anne.

Gloucester Catholic Education

I was touched by a teacher Leonard "Lenny" Smith. He was a singer, songwriter, and music publisher. Smith is best known in Christian music circles for writing the international worship standard "Our God Reigns"[4] in 1973. According to Wikipedia, in 1970, he taught religion at Gloucester Catholic. Instead of sticking to the standard curriculum, he brought his guitar to class, sang, prayed, and read the Bible, having "little" revivals at times in the classroom. Once a month, Lenny held a prayer gathering for his students in an auditorium. Smith thought it was a huge success, but the priests were worried he was starting a cult. At the end of the year, Smith was let go. During that time, I was one of the seekers. I wanted what he had found. I went to the mall to buy a Good News for Modern Man New Testament. I was like a sponge. The book read like a story. The greatest story ever told. It came alive in my heart. I started to talk to Jesus like my personal friend. I even started a journal to Jesus every day.

---

[4]   Leonard Smith, "Our God Reigns" (Great Comfort Record, 1973).

February 23, 1972

As I ponder another year of my life, I hope I can become more mature this year. There is so much to learn and so much to experience, and I think this is going to be my best year ever! So I decided today to start a journal to write for the daughter I will have one day. I write every day on the public bus I take to Gloucester City to my high school, Gloucester Catholic. It gives me time, and I truly want to become a good mother someday. I want to be honest with my daughter, no secrets—secrets make you sick. My journal will help me remember how joyful I feel now at age eighteen.

May 1972

The last couple of days I have been a stranger to myself. The more I thought about it, the worse my thoughts became. I knew something was wrong, but I could not place my finger on what it was. I looked into the mirror, saw my reflection, and thought, *Who is she?* I'm eighteen years old, and I don't know who I am. I don't even recognize my own reflection. I am a complete stranger to myself. How can this be? I feel afraid. Where do I begin? How do I fit the pieces of my life together? How do I discover the world that awaits me? Help, I'm lost...

Two years before this time, at age sixteen, I learned the secret of my birth. Secrets can make you sick! I found the circumstances of my birth hard to understand and felt angry with my mother. My mother thought it best to keep the truth about my father a secret from me, so I was told he died of a heart attack when I was a baby. I thought a father who died suddenly still loved me even though I had never seen a photograph of him. I had a wonderful stepfather; he was old enough to be my grandfather. I loved him very much, and he loved me as his own. He was not one to show affection or his feelings, but I still knew he loved me even if he did not say it.

The Harsh Truth

I found out the harsh truth about my real father from a drunken aunt. She had a slip of the tongue and told me she saw my father that day. She was my favorite aunt, the life of the party, who always seemed to be a happy drunk. I loved her bleached-blond platinum hair that was up on her head in a French twist. She wore high heels and red nail polish and lipstick. She had a son four years younger than me who was born when she was thirty-five-years-old and unmarried also. She went to the Children's Home Society of New Jersey in Trenton. They encouraged her to put the baby up for adoption, however, she refused and decided to keep him. I remember driving to Trenton to pick her and the baby up in a snowstorm, we had chains on the tires to make sure we would not get stuck. I sat in the backseat with my aunt and the little baby boy. She told me he would be my little brother and I was thrilled! My mother helped my aunt care for her baby. They seemed close even though they fought sometimes, usually when my aunt had been drinking.

My aunt did not marry the child's father, however, she made sure her son knew who his father was, and two years later she did marry and had another son.

So, anyway, on this one particular night, my mom was babysitting my aunt's two boys when she came to pick them up at my house drunk. As I heard her arguing with my mother, she blurted out, "She is old enough now to know the truth." The truth, as it turned out, was very hard to hear. I can still remember the feeling of shock, fear, and hurt as my Aunt Marge said to me, "Rosemarie, I saw your father tonight." The questions hit me in one salve after another: Why did my mother lie to me? Who is this unknown father? If he is alive, why did he never come to see me? Was he so horrible that my mother told me he was dead? And who does that make me? Who am I anyway?

Love's Beginnings

In the beginning, we know only love… "I ran into the bathroom, crying hysterically. I locked the door, and my sobs filled the room. I was hurting and in extreme emotional pain. This was the first time I started to experience what love is."

As my mother explained her story to me, I tried to understand what my mother tried to protect me from. She had wanted to shelter me from the painful truth of a married man with three children taking advantage of a single woman, aged thirty-five, waiting for the right man to come into her life. She loved him very much and then found herself pregnant with me—she was certain that he was my father. I am a mistake, I thought to myself!

Being a single Catholic woman in 1953, struggling with an out-of-wedlock pregnancy, created a serious dilemma for my mother. She had no one to talk to and no one to help her make this life-changing decision—a decision that was between her and God. My father had already decided on the easy way out; an illegal abortion which he had arranged and scheduled in New York City. The plan was for him to pick my mother up after work and take her to have the procedure. My mother, for her part, was devastated and afraid.

My Mother's Answer

My mother prayed and asked God for a sign and an answer to her dilemma. After God showed His will concerning this pregnancy (by allowing her to feel my life within her body at an especially early gestational age), she heard His quiet voice say, "I will be a father to this baby and care for you and your child. Do not be afraid."

She now had little time to prepare to talk to my father and refuse the offer for the abortion. She told my father that day that he was off the hook. She told him that God would be the father to this baby and take care of both of us. She gave a firm, "No" to the abortion that was driven by an even firmer, "Yes" to my life. I am forever thankful for a God-fearing mother who could hear His voice—I was rescued from the abortionist's knife!

Little Support

The hardest part was telling her family about the pregnancy and unfortunately, they disapproved of the pregnancy so strenuously, that they disowned her. In fact, many of them wanted her to go through with the abortion. Only her younger brother, who knew my father and her cousin, was supportive.

She would also need a two-bedroom apartment and someone to watch me so she could go back to work. We moved to the top apartment in the "Mansion House," and my mom's cousin, Jeanette, who was out of work, lived with us and provided daycare for me.

My Aunt Jeanette was like a sister to my mother, as they had grown up together. She was also one of my most favorite aunts and used to work at the Rex-all Drugstore in Woodbury. Like many drugstores back then, they carried an ample supply of cosmetics so unsurprisingly, Aunt Jeanette almost always wore makeup, nail polish, and red lipstick. She also curled her hair, wore nice clothes accented by high-heeled shoes, and even had a mink coat!

My mother had five half-sisters and one half-brother, but they all lived with her father in Gloucester City. She lost her mother in the flu epidemic of 1918 when she was 8-months-old. So she was raised by her father's family in Woodbury with Aunt Jeanette.

Jeanette had been abandoned by her father in Florida when he left her mother and brother for another woman. My grandfather and his brother, Robert, went down to pick them up. Unfortunately, her mother had a nervous breakdown after she found her husband had left her and her children for another woman causing her to be placed in a psychiatric hospital in Philadelphia for the rest of her life. So Jeanette was raised by her grandmother along with my mother.

Mental health was not talked about back then, just as sex was a topic that was off-limits. It was hushed and kept in silence as people believed that dirty laundry should not be "aired," that is, spoken of in public. Because of these attitudes, unwed mothers also endured a painful stigma as well.

Sadly, Aunt Jeanette struggled with alcoholism and mental health related problems after a difficult divorce from her sick husband. He had to move to Florida for his health but Jeanette did not want to live in "The Sunshine State" and came home to live in New Jersey. She ended up having a nervous breakdown and was put into a sanitarium where she endured shock treatments and was eventually given a lobectomy as the shock treatments were unable to stop the bad memories.

Grief Father Unknown in Latin

I was born February 18, 1954, at Our Lady of Lourdes Hospital in Camden, New Jersey. I was named after both my grandmother Rose and my mom's best friend Marie; hence Rosemarie. I took my mother's maiden name as "Father Unknown," which was written on my baptismal certificate in Latin. I ordered the official birth certificate and broke down in tears when I saw his name in English. It was what I needed to know to clear the record as an adult. My mother had gone to court, as suggested by her father and brother, to request child support from my father. She learned from the judge that since my father would deny me, I would need a blood test to establish paternity through DNA. She did not want to put me through that, so once again my father was off the hook.

Although my father denied me, his wife did not. She came to visit my mother to see me. My mother said, "You have no business here." She replied, "Please, I just need to see her." She looked at me and said, "Yes, I can see for myself. She looks like my youngest daughter." My mother apologized to her, saying, "He did not tell me he was married with children. I would have never been involved with him." My father's wife said, "It is not your fault." My mother felt her pain because she felt her own. They never spoke of the visit or saw each other again. I found out just recently that my father's wife divorced him.

Apartment Life

We lived on the third floor of a huge apartment building. As a small child, I remembered being loved and well cared for by my mother and Aunt Jeanette. I was afraid of the mice and can remember the sound of the traps going off in the middle of the night. I wonder how they climbed all those steps. But I could hear them in the walls.

One time I remember pretending to be asleep because I was too tired to climb the steps. My uncle carried me. He always told me I was his little girl. Later he told me he knew my father and that he was a nice guy. I wondered why he never came to see me. My mother would bring me to work once in a while and Aunt Jeanette would work part-time at a drug store and toy factory to help make extra money. I love Woolworth's, where my mother was the bookkeeper. She had gone to Taylor's School of Business in Philadelphia. I loved lunch time and sitting at the counter having hot soup and a grilled cheese sandwich with chocolate milk. Sometimes I would pretend to be sick just to go there. I had to go to a neighbor's house after school. I remember getting stung by a swarm of wasps that were under the cushion on her swing on the porch. I was so afraid. I never wanted to go back there.

My New Stepfather and My New Room

In the spring of 1958, my mother met Marko Mudrinic. He was an immigrant from Yugoslavia who spoke broken English. He fell in love with my mother and I both. He was a sweet older man. He told my mother that he would take care of my mom and her baby, as he called me. He had a two-bedroom bungalow in Verga. I remember being dressed up for the wedding and my mother was wearing a corsage of flowers that smelled so pretty! We went out to dinner with family and friends and then we went to my new home. I had my own bedroom. They painted it pink, and my mom gave me her vanity dresser and I was thrilled! It had three big mirrors.

Everything seemed better to have a stepfather. But when it was time to go over my family tree at school, I felt anxious. I did not know my real father's name. My mother said it did not matter. But I felt different than my friends. I began to understand the idea that it was bad not to have a real father. But I felt happy to have a stepfather.

Believe That Fairy Tale Life Is Possible
The Fairy Tale Begins

I felt like a princess, finally! Even though I was a little insecure, I believed in fairy tales and I knew someday my prince would come! And I will live happily ever after.

Theirs was a marriage of convenience and platonic love. My mother helped my stepfather learned to read and write in English and to become an American citizen. I remember being at the service. He was so proud. And he took good care of us.

The home had a fenced yard and a big garden and pear trees and a chicken coop and grape vines. I asked for a puppy. My stepfather reluctantly agreed. We went to the pound. Brownie was scratching my foot as I looked up at all the cages. He captured my heart and was my best friend. I was a lonely only child, even though I had twelve cousins. They came occasionally to play.

My stepfather was handicapped but I did not view him as such. He had one arm and one eye from an accident on the tugboat that he worked on. When he would take me into the city to shop in Philadelphia, I felt secure with him. He told me to hold onto his back pocket while he carried the bags with the other arm.

Then we got new neighbors, Sandy and Len. They became like second parents and role models to me. They had three children and I became the babysitter, and I loved to be a part of their family. They would even bring me on vacation with them to the shore, my favorite place. We also went to the shore to visit my mother's cousin, Dottie. She had four children. I would babysit for her the whole summer to earn money for the parochial school tuition I needed each year for high school. She and her husband Ray became my summer parents.

Only Child Syndrome

I always felt different being an only child. But I felt the love of the people around me. I felt surrounded by love all around me. It is okay to be different. It helps you feel special. My stepfather had only one arm. He worked for the dredging company on the Delaware

River. He had an accident on a tugboat on his way to America. That is how he was able to stay here to work. He had been at the Wills Eye Hospital, where he had lost his eye and his arm. I never thought of him as a disabled person. He did everything himself and was very strong and confident. He inspired me that I could do everything too.

He loved me very much and I knew it. I wrapped him around my finger. He gave me almost everything I ever wanted. He was very proud to have helped pay for me to go on a trip to Europe in high school. He called it "the old country."

An Answer to One Question

I understand that on one trip to the grocery store, we met my father. I was riding in the cart. My father spoke to my mother about me. My stepfather took him aside. He told him to stay away from my mother and I. He said that he was taking care of us now and we did not need him or want him in our lives. That day my stepfather made a boundary for my mother and I. I was beginning to understand why I had never met my father.

Unknown Father, Denial, and a Seed of Bitterness

So I had never seen or met my father my whole life. I had no desire to meet the man who had hurt my mother, his wife and children by living a lie. By suppressing my desire to know my real father, I planted a seed of bitterness. And I experienced the first stages of grief, which are denial and anger. There are five stages of grief: denial, anger, bargaining, depression, and acceptance. I said, "I do not want any part of him." With that, came suspicion of all men. "Be careful not to trust them," I said to myself.

Stages of Grief Research

As per Wikipedia, grief is a strong sometimes overwhelming emotion for people; regardless the sadness stems from the loss of a loved one or a terminal illness. The grief process is active or passive depending on how you choose to respond. Ken Doka coined the phrase *disenfranchised grief*,[5] thirty years ago, 1989. This is deep grief that a person experiences when they incur a loss that is not or cannot be openly acknowledged, socially sanctioned or publicly mourned. The loss of a typical family structure or recognized relationship. Samples can be the death of a person you haven't been in touch with for years, feeling abandonment by family or friends, not having a relationship with parents or siblings, grieving someone still living, a dream that never comes to fruition. This shows up in five ways: One, considered less significant. Two, surrounded by stigma. Three, involving concealed relationships. Four, excluded because of other family members. Five, expressed in ways that do not conform to society's rules.

Growing Pains Lesson in Godliness

As a child, I was loving and loved. Being Loved helped me to become lovable. Mark Hughes said, "Our life today is a result of our decisions and choices in the past."

Faith in Hearing God's Voice

My mother had faith to believe that God had answered her prayer. I was her child and she loved me before I was born. And God knew me before I was born. Jeremiah 1:5 says, "I knew you before you were in your mother's womb." My Heavenly Father had a plan for my life before I was born. I am a loved daughter. Love is many different things. Love is a beautiful experience, a fulfilling, learning, growing experience and sometimes a hurting experience. Love is worth going through the pain. God is Love. He will meet you when you walk in Love and show you the way you should go. I have an amazing love story. And this is where it begins.

---

[5]   Wikipedia, "Disenfranchised grief."

CHAPTER 2

Being a Daughter Becoming a Young Lady

My Mother's Dilemma

Who Am I? Conflict Problems and God's Answer
My Mother's Real Story Taught Me
About Becoming a Woman

My mother, a single Catholic woman in 1953, faced a dilemma with being pregnant out of wedlock. With virtually no one to aid her in making life-changing decisions, her internal disputes were between her and God. My father had already decided on the easy way out, an abortion. My mother had to make the decision herself.

To understand what it was like to be an unwed pregnant woman in the fifties, I did some research:

By definition, Wikipedia says, "An unwed mother is a girl or woman (13–35 years) who is not legally married to a man by whom she has conceived a child."

Here are some books that talk about unwed pregnancies in the 1950s:

My Mother's Shadow, by author Nikola Scott

In a Family Way, by Jane Robinson. An overview of illegitimacy and unmarried mothers in the 1950s, sets individual stories against the devastatingly harsh moral canvas of the times.

Sixty Years a Nurse, by Mary Hazzard with Connie Sweet. An enjoyable look at 1950s society with interesting insights into the treatment of women, the woeful lack of sexual education, and maternity wards.

The Girls Who Went Away, by Ann Fessler. Two decades before *Roe v Wade* made abortion legal in 1973, parents hid the shame and sent pregnant children off to maternity homes.

The *Washington Post* article by Diane Bernard and Maria Bogen-Oskwarek.

November 19, 2018, *Retropolis*, "The maternity homes where mind control was used on teenage moms to give up their babies." Explains the process to encourage adoption instead of keeping their children.

In the 1950s, professionals said that the problem with unwed mothers was a psychological one, making them unfit to raise children. By the 1950s, the Florence Crittenton Association of America, the Salvation Army, Catholic Charities, and other organizations operated more than two hundred maternity homes in forty-four states.

The last mother and baby institution closed in 1990, and the last Magdalene Laundry in 1984 in the United States. There are still over four hundred maternity homes in the United States, ranging in size and criteria for admittance. The three major staff models are house parents (e.g., a married couple), live-in staff, and shift staff.

For more information on Magdalene Laundries in Ireland, watch the Irish documentary film *Sex in a Cold Climate* from 1998, directed by Steve Humphries. It details the mistreatment of "fallen women." It was a source for the 2002 film, *Magdalene Sisters*. From 1922 until 1996, pregnant or promiscuous women could be incarcerated for life in Magdalene Laundries.

It explains the causes and reasons of unwed mothers as psychiatric illness, broken homes either by death or divorce, necessity for both parents to work, lack of parental devotion, loss of security by the girl, rebellion of the girl against her parents, her mother particularly, masochistic trends by both mother and daughter.

(*VC Reporter*, May 10, 2017, Alicia Doyle cover story, "Ending the Shame of the Baby Scoop Era Opens Up about Giving Up Their Babies.")

An estimated 2.5 million women in the United States were victims of the Baby Scoop Era which occurred from 1945 to 1975. During this period, unwed mothers were "coerced" into putting their babies up for adoption, against their own free wills.

These women are now sixty-five to ninety years old. Many are still in the closet and are still ashamed and humiliated. That's why they kept it a secret, even though it is a different world now and unwed motherhood is totally accepted. It was not accepted back then.

Historical reference to understand abortion was illegal in the United States from the 1820s. Laws reflected the difference between the "quick and nonquick fetus," (referring to movement and life). As long as the abortion was performed prior to quickening, it was legal. During the later stages of pregnancy, abortion was a crime, but distinct from other forms of murder and punished less harshly.

The 2004 film, *Vera Drake*,[6] tells the story of working-class women in London in 1950 who perform illegal abortions on local women with unwanted pregnancies. The film is based on a study of imprisoned abortionists conducted from 1959 to 1962. The film depicts the procedure in exact detail. It involves a bulb and syringe to introduce warm, diluted solution of soap into a woman's uterus.

Doctors who performed illegal abortions would use medical instruments for dilation and curettage to induce the abortion. Side

---

[6] Mike Leigh (director), *Vera Drake* (UK: New Line Cinema)

effects from such abortions include incomplete abortion, hemor-rhage, (heavy bleeding), infection, septic shock, uterine perforation, (caused when the uterus is pierced by a sharp object) and damage to internal organs.

"The Impact of Illegal Abortion," by *Our Body, Ourselves* Contributors, March 23, 2014. Updated February 22, 2019. Historically, women around the world have tried to end unwanted pregnancies whether abortion was legal or not, often jeopardizing their safety and health by self-inducing or seeking a dangerous illegal abortion. Each year around 7 million women are admitted to the hospitals for complications of unsafe abortions, and between 4.7%–13.2% of maternal deaths can be attributed to unsafe abortion.

Psychology Wiki: *Post-abortion syndrome* is the term used to describe psychological characteristics that have been observed in women following an elective abortion. Characterized as being sim-ilar to post-traumatic stress disorder (PTSD). Symptoms include "repeated and persistent dreams and nightmares related to the abor-tion, intense feelings of guilt, and the need to repair."

Questions on Google: What is the meaning of PAS? Some people suggest abortion is a traumatic experience that can result in "post-abortion syndrome," which refers to intense distress that has a lasting impact on mental health. June 11, 2020.

"What is PASS?" (Aastra Woman's Center, Fort Lauderdale Abortion Clinic). May 21, 2021.

"It is similar to PTSD. They also share the same symptoms that can last for months and even years afterward. Many women expe-rience heightened feelings of anxiety or depression at the anniver-sary months of the abortion procedure. Unfortunately, many doctors and mental specialists fail to recognize the symptoms of PASS. Also, many people don't know anything about it, and they usually ask if it is even real. But it is more than real, and many women experience it nowadays. Mostly, it's the same scenario with a patient's friends and family, and these are all the reasons why it is so hard to understand it."

Symptoms of Post Abortion Stress Syndrome

"Depression is the most common after abortion symptom. Some of the signs of depression are losing interest in some things you love. You would stay home instead, and it will be more and more until you are cut off from society. It will surely start to affect your daily life, your work, family, friends, and you can end up suppressing all your emotions. Then you'll need someone to help you."

Anxiety and Guilt

"After the abortion, it's impossible to stay totally cold without emotion. Many women are scared of abortion, maybe because it is one of the most significant decisions in their life. Anxiety is a typical symptom of PASS. You can experience it if you see a mother and father with the newborn or visit friends who have a baby. Also, there is something called "anniversary anxiety." It is similar to depression when you try to act, it is just another day, but your mind is not functioning like that. When talking about the traumatic event, you can experience anger, flashbacks or guilt too."

Sadness and Regret

"Sometimes, abortion can be the only possible solution. Many women feel relief at first, but later it turns out some guilt and sadness are involved. It's completely normal to question your decisions, mainly important ones. There are some extreme cases of regret and sadness in combination with suicidal thoughts. In that case you should definitely talk to someone."

Why Should You Talk About It

Dealing with PASS alone could indeed affect your mental health. If you are around a lot of babies or pregnant women, you can experience flashbacks or normal feelings of sadness and grief, it lasts for a couple of months or longer, so maybe you should talk to your doctor at the abortion clinic.

The first step in recovering is confessing to yourself that you have a problem. Do not feel embarrassed to reach out for support or even join a support group. These groups are designed to help you finally heal and be happy again. You will probably feel better if you share your abortion story with other women who know the pain you are going through."

The Lord Provided for Me Through My Stepfather

So I had never seen or met my father in my whole life. I had no desire to meet the man who had hurt my mother, his wife, and his children by living a lie. I was loved and had a stable environment provided by my stepfather.

I thank God that he provided what I needed through a man, my stepfather, who adored me and treated me like a little princess. He taught me how to be loved by a father. As a child, I was loving and loved. Loving God helped me to become lovable and you can see how He reached into my heart just as the Scripture says He will, the following are but two of many similar passages.

The Second Letter to Corinthians 6:18: "And I will be a Father to you and you shall be my sons and daughters to me, says the Lord Almighty." Philippians: 4:19: "And my God shall supply every need according to his riches in glory in Christ Jesus."

Childlike Impressions and Searching for Me

Psalm 139:16: "You saw me before I was born" (NLT).

I wish I were a child again, for the world was beautiful then. I was being sheltered from the dark and surrounded by love when hurt broke my heart. All hurt was kissed away and forgotten within minutes. Grownups were infallible and strangers were never strange. Dreams always came true and fantasy time came at least once a day. The rainbow was at my fingertips and God was someone I could call on with no questions asked because I believed and my belief so real. Smiles were a penny a dozen, and happiness was a way of life. New experiences awaited me every day.

Then one day, childhood passes away and you find yourself a young adult facing down intimidating fears that glare at you defiantly and block your path—and everything changes. Childhood dreams fade like smoke on the winds of change, and young adult fears become a menacing reality as you're confronted by the dread of what are called tween and teenage self-doubt these days. I faced the world alone. New times, new faces, a new road leads to a new world of young adulthood. What good will it be if it is still the old me who is afraid of the dark and the unknown? I want someone to hold my hand again, to face my fears. I wish I were a child again. For I have never known the world a child envisions.

Proverbs 3:13 tells us, "Joyful is the person who finds wisdom, the one who gains understanding" (NLT).

Lord, help me have faith and be and become a young lady who loves you. You said in Luke 18:16: "Let the little children come to me" (NIV). And Paul said, "When I was a child, I spoke as a child, I understood as a child, I thought as a child; but when I became a man, I put away childish things (1 Corinthians 13:11). Please help me be teachable so I can become wise. Proverbs 9:9 said, "Give instruction to a wise man, (or woman in my case) and he will be still wiser; Teach a just man, and he will increase in learning."

Concept of Being and Becoming

The concept of being and becoming is not new at this stage of my life. I am looking for someone who will help me become the person I want to be. This becoming process is an exciting possibility for a dreamer like me, but there seems to be too many questions and too few answers.

Where is Love? God Is Love

Is it only behind closed doors? It seems to be missing, so maybe that is my purpose, to find true love. Jesus said, "Love one another." I am so hung up on finding myself; how could I love someone else? Maybe I cannot see myself until I find my other half—someone who I can love and share with and feel complete. I feel like something is missing in me, maybe there's a path to be found in 1 John 4:19, "We loved him…because he first loved us."

Growing Pains Together with Taking off the Mask

I am finding the "real me," the person that God knows inside and out yet still loves—me, with weakness and anger and hang-ups, the me that only God can set free. God help me take off the masks and be genuine and honest with You. I am becoming real like the Velveteen Rabbit who was loved so much that his fur was rubbed off. I need to be honest with myself about my strengths and weaknesses. Let me have faith in God and the grace to become who He has created me to be. I am searching for the real me…

The Second Book of Corinthians 4:2 tells me to, Renounce the "…secret and shameful ways; we do not use deception, nor do we distort the word of God. On the contrary, by setting forth the truth plainly we commend ourselves to everyone's conscience in the sight of God" (NIV).

My mother was the saint, and my unknown father was the villain in my story. There needed to be someone to blame for all the pain and it was easy to hate someone I didn't know. But it was also hard to love with hate in my heart—the only thing that came out was anger. More critical was the unfinished business of my mother and her distrust of men. That distrust rubbed off onto me making it hard for me to trust any man. I learned to enjoy relationships with other female friends, but I was very suspicious of boys, especially men. I need to forgive this unknown man and give him the benefit of the doubt. I didn't know what I didn't know so maybe there were some things that I did not understand. Perhaps he was a nice guy like my uncle said, and I would want to know him or my half-sisters some-day? What do they look like, I wondered? Like me? I still appreciate that he was my biological father who helped God create me.

Can I love him because Jesus loves him? Can I forgive him because Jesus forgives him? Can I forgive him because Jesus forgave me? Yes, Lord, help me forgive and live a life that pleases you. I know that the love of God helps me to forgive and in Catholic school I had learned the Lord's Prayer which pointed out the need to forgive, it tells us to "forgive us our debts, As we forgive our debtors (Matthew 6:12). And do not lead us into temptation" (Matthew 6:12–13a). Forgiveness is a choice, not a "feeling" so please help my mother and I choose forgiveness and forgive the man. Later I would attend my father's funeral to find closure to this chapter of my life.

Learning to Be a Young Lady/Woman

Saturday was a shopping day. There were no malls back then, so we rode a bus to Camden for fresh produce, fish, and tobacco. We also went clothes and shoe shopping at Sears, Strawbridge, and Penny's department stores. Then the highlight of the trip for me would be the Chinese Restaurant for dinner. I loved the wonton soup and egg noodles and of course, the fortune cookies.

One night as we were leaving, a man tried to open and hold the door for me, but I jumped in front of him and did it myself. I felt more than capable, and it seemed like the kind thing to do—so I thought. I was always polite and helpful but apparently this move didn't fall into either of those categories. My mother's face turned red and sour as she took my hand and pulled me back. The man held the door for my mother and my one-armed stepfather, who was over-loaded with packages. My mother acknowledged his thoughtfulness, saying, "Thank you, sir," to which he replied, "My pleasure Madam."

On the way to the bus stop, my mother explained the impor-tance of learning proper etiquette, formalities, manners, and the pro-tocols of being a young lady. A young lady allows a gentleman to hold the door, offer a seat on the bus, and let her go first in line. I was fascinated at all the rules and yet practical benefits there was to being a young lady. I felt privileged to be of the female gender—I was teachable and hungry to learn more. I wanted to learn how to become a beautiful, graceful young lady. And though my beginnings were small, I learned to be a loved daughter and become a young lady!

Impressions

Footprints leave impressions in the sand. This is nature. It is God's plan. How about society's impression on people's minds? Is this the nature of God's plan as well? I hope someday I can understand the complexity of this plastic society, so maybe I will eventually fit in. On that day, I hope to realize that I do not need to fit in. Rosemarie Page is honest. No unfeeling society will not satisfy the hunger and expectations of my heart. I do not live by the standards of this world. Being free to be me is a dream worth following. As a young lady, I will continue to dream bigger, better plans and live inside my mind with hopes for happiness. I have always been a dreamer.

I will build a wall that will allow me to survive in the future. It will protect me from the plastic society waiting to swallow me and my dream. I will keep reaching for the joy I need in my heart to keep dreaming.

Yes, I believe there is hope for everyone, even those with restless longing hearts such as mine. For this, I pray, the ocean moves according to the moon's pull. The moon revolves around the sun, just like the earth. All a part of the universe with specific movement and purpose, each represents a tiny spec of creation following its course. Why is it so difficult for creation's most intelligent form of life to find its purpose? One can look at all of nature and see beauty, tranquility, and balance. But where is love? It's the only thing missing. Since this can only be seen by and through people, maybe love is man's purpose, to impress this cold society with love. Is this God's plan?

New Thought from the 1970s

Concept of Nirvana, a state of perfection, happiness. A blowing out and becoming extinguished, a peaceful state. Is this what I am looking for?

My Dysfunctional Family Life and Scary Times with Family Alcoholics

I remember my aunts with all their problems, my mom was the caretaker and rescuer. She was the helper and I watched and learned—sometimes I found it very scary. Once when my aunt was home from the hospital for the weekend and visiting, I heard her conversations of abuse at the hospital. It sounded far-fetched, so I tried to avoid her, but it was impossible in a two-bedroom bungalow.

I went to the kitchen and saw every butcher knife we owned lined up on the kitchen counter. I went into the bathroom and locked the door. I looked up and saw a noose tied above my head on a hook on the wall with my stepfather's tie and before I knew it, I was infested with goosebumps. I felt something evil with me in the room, so I opened the door to get out of there and my aunt pushed open the door and cornered me in the bathroom, screaming at me about being raped by a Black man. Her pitch was fevered as she screamed, "If it happens to me it will happen to you!" Her eyes pierced me like a hot iron, filled with hatred. Panicked, I wondered, "Who is this woman?" And I cried out for my mom to help me.

The craziness from her home that I had experienced many times before, had now infested my house. Though I had seen fights and bloodshed in the past, I was always happy to go home—it was my safe zone. But now it seemed evil had come to roost in my home and sink its claws into my life, causing me nightmares after that horror show. I thought when I grow up, I will have none of this in my home. I felt sorry for my cousins who had to live with this distress. *God, will you help my family?*

Chapter 3

Being a Young Lady Becoming a Bride

God Knew Me Before I was Born
Despite the Crisis My God Knows Me and All My Dreams
Self-Talk... Is This All There Is?

Dreams Coming True
New Year's Eve Adventure Flashback
December 31, 1969

I just turned sweet sixteen this year! And though I planned to reconnect with an old boyfriend for New Year's Eve, God had a different plan for me. The old boyfriend did not show up to the party, so I had to look around me. I noticed a tall, dark and handsome man smiling and looking at me. He was funny and got my attention—His name was Bob.

When it was time to ring in the New Year, my friend matched us together for a New Year kiss. I felt my face turn red with embarrassment, but Bob made me laugh and feel comfortable with him. It was our first "Magic Moment." I remember thinking this was a magical moment! I did have the "Cinderella Complex, "so maybe

---

[7] Elizabeth Haines, "What are the signs you have Cinderella Complex?" Health Grade.com (September 9, 2020).

this was my new Prince Charming? Hopefully, he does not have Peter Pan Syndrome…

Peter Pan Syndrome is a colloquialism hung on a person who can't seem to grow up and remains trapped in their childhood or youth. While not recognized as a mental illness, it does have symptoms that include social inability, lack of career interest, and the inability to handle adult situations.

Cinderella Complex, on the other hand, contains the idea of a women's fear of independence. It radiates with an unconscious desire to be taken care of by others and, as you might have guessed, is named after the fairy tale character Cinderella.

Free Dictionary.com says, "Cinderella is the heroine of the fairy tale who is mistreated by her stepmother but achieves happiness and marries a prince through the intervention of a fairy godmother. She receives recognition and sudden success after obscurity and neglect."

Health grade.com, mental health and behaviors, by Elizabeth Hanes, RN, September 9, 2020. "What are the Signs you have Cinderella Complex?"[7]

The Cinderella Complex was coined by Agatha Christie, in a murder mystery by this title written by Colette Dowling[8] in 1981. Psychological condition secretly expecting a "knight in shining armor" to come along to take care of her. This is not recognized by the American Psychiatric Association as a diagnosis.

Symptoms include:

1. Defers life choices to a partner.
2. Feels anxious to live alone.
3. Difficult making life decisions.
4. Difficulty supporting yourself and holding a job.
5. Prefer traditional homemaking or mother role.
6. Prefer a strong person in your life.
7. Rarely operates outside the emotional comfort zone.
8. Secretly or openly expresses a strong desire to be taken care of.

---

[8] Colette Dowling, "Cinderella Complex" (New York: Harper, 1981).

Our Love Story Begins with a Movie Called the Same, "Love Story"

We talked, and I learned he was in the Air Force and was home for the holidays. So I gave him my number, and he asked me to watch a movie that I wanted to see. It was called "Love Story."[9] It just came out at the Ritz in Philadelphia—so it was a date.

We took the bus with another couple. The first thing I noticed was that he smelled so good. I think it was English Leather, and it mixed well with my Wind Song. We had to walk a few blocks to get to the theater. He held my hand and I felt safe in the big city. The movie theater was huge, but packed, so we ended up on the balcony. He went with the other guy to get popcorn. My friend Mary Jane asked, "How do you like this guy?" I answered, " So far, so good!" We both cried at the sad movie. The guys laughed at us. What I took away from that movie is, "Love means never having to say you're sorry." I would later find out that is not true...

Our week was like a whirlwind; it went so fast. We went ice skating and out for ice cream and dinner at the Brooklawn Diner; it is shaped like a boat! I also took him for the "Girlfriend Test." They would let me know if he was good for me. My head was in the clouds, but they agreed that he was a keeper! I was in love! Then as quickly as it started. It was over. I promised to write, but I thought to myself, "I will probably never see him again."

Love Letters and Sweet Nothings

I would write letters on the public service bus to school. Then I would run to the mailbox to check for a love note when I got home. As soon as I received one, I would write back to him. We were getting to know each other. They started to seem like love letters that arrived every other day. But I made it clear that I was a senior in high school, and I planned to have fun! I had plans to go to Europe and the Prom

---

[9]   H. Minsky (producer), A. Hiller (director), *Love Story* (Paramount Pictures, 1970).

with my friend's brother. He did not seem to mind. He seemed to understand that I was still young. He was four years older than me.

Europe, the Old Country and a Whole New World

I worked three jobs and scrimped and saved for the trip to Europe. My mom and Mike, my stepfather, had put in money and my cousin Dottie too. After working all summer at the shore, I also worked after school every day at Gino's and then babysitting on the weekends in the evening. At Gino's I worked with my friend Linda**.** We wore red-and-white-striped uniforms and looked a little like candy strippers from the hospital but ours were wider. It was a fun job as it was mostly people my age, but it was hard to be on my feet all day. I remember the pain in my calves at the end of the day and aching feet. It took a while for my savings to add up, but I was learning the value of a dollar even though I only stared at about eighty-five cents an hour.

One day I remember there was an accident out front of the store. I was early and not clocked in yet. So as a member of the future Nurses Club, I found myself running out to see if I could help. I climbed into the front passenger seat on my knees to check on the driver. I talked and helped the person stay calm. When help arrived, I got out and blood was pouring down my legs through the white stockings. There was glass on the seat. I had to call my mom to bring a new pair of stockings for me.

The night had finally come, and we went by bus to JFK Airport in New York. We went through customs and had to walk through something that was like tunnels. So I never did see the airplane, but I heard it was a 747.

After we were in the air, I decided to go for a walk. I walked and walked and walked, then suddenly, I felt sick and scared and found myself praying, "Lord, how is this staying in the air. It must be at least three city blocks long and all these hundreds of people?!" Goosebumps covered my skin with fear and excitement, and I felt so grown up—my friend Linda and I sat together.

Munich Germany was one of the first stops. They were preparing for the Olympics; it was a beautiful stadium but would quickly become a scary time when hostages were taken, and snipers were killing people. It was very frightening, and I had seen it firsthand—it made me feel that the world was a smaller place after this trip. The Bras Haus was a fun night of singing and German dancing and good food. The sausages and sauerkraut with Birch Beer in Frosted Mugs were all so much fun, with locked arms we swayed to the music... When we went out to lunch, I ordered a steak sandwich and was shocked to see a sirloin steak between slices of hard bread. "What is this?" I queried? "It is what you asked for," the server replied. "I do not think so. This is not how it looks in America." We all laughed. One girl just kept asking everywhere we went for a "Panzerotti," and no one knew what it was. That is when I knew we really were far away from home.

In Venice, Italy, the men make an unusual sound with their lips like a clicking sound and not a whistle. But I gathered it meant the same thing when the nuns hurried us girls along the sidewalk—it was very strange. We went to an amusement park with a huge Ferris wheel. We met some Middle Eastern guys there. They spoke broken English and said, "American girls are fast, yes?" I was not sure what they meant, but it did not sound good. So I said, "You heard wrong, we are Catholic! We have to go back to the hotel," and we walked fast! We could not drink the water there, it was too dirty, and it even smelled bad. So we all got to drink wine which was exciting to us Americans who had to wait till age eighteen. We enjoyed the Italian food; it was a fan favorite.

A funny moment was when we were on a gondola ride. The boys rocked the boat and overturned it into the canal with the priest in it too. The water was so yucky that I was really glad the girls did not get that idea, we stayed in the boat! In a city called Graz, a mountain island city in Italy, it was just beautiful. The houses were built into the side of the mountain. We walked up to the top on the rooftops, and there, we sat and watched the stars. They shimmered like jewels set in a black velvet crown and it looked like you could reach out and touch them... It was so beautiful.

Switzerland was my favorite country. We went to clock shops with music boxes, the craftsmanship was amazing. I could only afford a small music box that played a song about a flower called an "Edelweiss." We saw fields filled with them and I got a real one preserved in a little frame to bring home. As we drove in the tour bus, we saw where they filmed, "The Sound of Music," including the gazebo and abbey that were used in the Oscar-winning movie, it was just magical. We all sang the songs on the bus and took a train ride up the Alps to meet a cable car to take us to the top. We were above the clouds with a view so breathtaking and so magnificent, that I felt the presence of God. It was such a beautiful place.

In Mt Pilatus, overlooking Lucerne, Switzerland, I couldn't help but wish my mom and stepfather Mike, and Bob could be here to share this with me. But Bob, who I prayed for as the Lord brought him to mind, was in Thailand. I didn't storm the heavens but was faithful to lift my heart to heaven and pray, "Lord, please bring him home safely. Amen." I made sure to write a postcard from each city to all of them and stayed up late squeezing my adventures into the limited space on my postcards. My world had become much bigger after seeing the "Old Country," as my stepfather called Yugoslavia, where he was from.

We did not get there but Austria was beautiful. I was amazed and enchanted with just how old everything was there. They treasure their centuries of history; America is less than two hundred years old now while Austria was established in AD 976.

The trip birthed a love for travel that I embrace to this day. I knew someday I would be back—and I was three times! My mother used to say I was born with roller skates on because I always loved to go somewhere. It makes me think of the number one hit song from late 1971, "Brand New Key," by Melanie Safka.[10]

I was working hard to lose my shyness, especially with my friend Linda, who was from a big family. I knew that I couldn't be shy if I was going to nursing school in the fall. Nurses are courageous and bold and that was what I wanted to become.

---

[10] Melanie Safka, "Brand New Key," *Gather Me* (New York: Allegro Sound, 1971).

Wildwood Days

We would see each other three more times before Bob came home for good. It was fun in the summer at the shore in Wildwood. We would go early in the morning to see the sunrise and I felt romantic that early in the morning. We stayed on the beach all day. I wore a one-piece powder-blue bathing suit and he said, "You look beautiful and sexy!" I worked to keep his hands in the right places as the nuns in the Catholic school had taught me—I am a "good girl." He bought me ice cream, though I was saving my calories for the Blue Hawaiian Restaurant. I got home and showered and dressed up in my new sundress and put my lipstick and heels on. I was so hungry but there were no reservations available, so we had to wait in line. Finally, it was our turn next and… That is all I remembered, I fainted onto the floor. Bob said, "Put your head between your knees and take deep breaths." *Oh no!* I thought, *How embarrassing!* Now we had to go home.

Dottie posed a question to me that I was not ready for. "Are you pregnant?" she asked. "What do you mean, I am a virgin!" I replied highly insulted. "Why did you say such a thing?" She answered, "It is because pregnant women faint when they are hungry. Let me get you some orange juice; your blood sugar must be low."

So instead, we went to the boardwalk and got a burger, fries, zeppoles, and ice cream. We got a sketch done to remember this special day. I wore a high neck reddish-orange chiffon blouse with Juliette sleeves and jeans. I wore pink granny glasses and peace earrings. Bob wore jeans and a shirt with a brown suede fringed leather vest. He had long hair and long sideburns and wore black granny glasses. We make a "cute couple" is what everyone told us. We walked and walked and laughed every time we heard, "Watch the tram car, please!"

It was a Summer of Love for us. Beach combing for treasures hand in hand was one of my favorite things to do. The radio station WIBG[11] was playing love songs all day. The Beach Boys, "Under the Boardwalk," The Bee Gees, The Association, and of course, The Turtles, "Happy Together." We were happy. It seems like fate.

---

[11] *WIBG Greatest Hits* (Post Records, 1968).

THE JOYS OF BEING AND BECOMING

Jesus Christ Superstar

Bob took me to see Jesus Christ Superstar[12] at the Wildwood Convention Center. I cried, and I realized that Jesus had brought us together and died for our sins. He was giving me my heart's desire. Bob brought me the vinyl album and we still have it fifty-years-later. We would listen to it as a family every Good Friday. I even made the kids come in from outside from 12:00 p.m. to 3:00 p.m. to remember what Jesus had done for us. It reminds me of His presence in our marriage from the very beginnings of our relationship.

Atlantic City Miss American Beauty

September came quickly. Bob took my mom and I to see the Miss America competition in Atlantic City. One of my classmates, named Suzanne, who rode the bus with me, was in it. We were cheering for her as she beautifully played the grand piano. She had long blonde hair and wore a stunning long pink gown. In the meantime, Bob could not keep his hands off of me. He said, "You are the only beauty I am looking at!" I felt happy to feel beautiful in his eyes. I need to remind myself of that to be true for me because I do not always feel beautiful inside and outside. I feel thankful to have Bob in my life.

Myrtle Beach, South Carolina

Bob is stationed in Myrtle Beach, South Carolina but that will be changing soon. He is to be deployed to Thailand for the last six months of his service. So he invited me to come and visit him with his mother, brother, and sister. I did not think my mother would agree, but she did since his mother would be our chaperone. He had sent me a bottle of beach sand with a black shark tooth in it and I could not wait to go.

The base looked like a country club, just beautiful, and he had his own little house—we had a fun visit. It is getting harder to

---

[12] Andrew Lloyd Webber (music), *Jesus Christ Superstar* (1970).

resist his sexual advances, but we agreed to wait. We plan to wait six months after he returns to travel cross country, and then six months later, at least a year to consider marriage.

Christmas Wish 1971

The song this Christmas is "Merry Christmas Darling"[13] by Karen Carpenter. I cried when I heard it. Bob was in Thailand, and I was praying for his safe return. It's true, absence makes the Heart grow fonder and I missed Bob so much. I was sending love letters, but we were an ocean away. So I planned to send "Love Boxes" with homemade cookies and goodies. I also planned to make him a new shirt. It was navy blue and white paisley crepe material and a pattern with puffed sleeves like the Beatles, his favorite music. My teacher was an old nun named Sister Gertrude Mary. She was always grumpy, but she seemed to like the idea of me making this shirt for my boyfriend. She would watch as I struggled with the crepe material getting stuck in the sewing machine. She reminded me that this was not shirt material, but I was making him something I liked. It seemed every part of it was a struggle. The buttonholes were especially hard, and I was not very good at it. But finally, I would have time to get it in the mail for Christmas.

When it came back with the grade written on it, I was angry—I got an A-minus! I thought I would fight this grade; my teacher saw how hard I worked on the project, and I thought I deserved an A and I planned to fight for it. As I gave her my complaint about the unfair grade, she looked at me with puzzlement. She said, "You told me this was a man's shirt, right?" "Yes, it is," I replied. "Okay then, your buttons are on the wrong side," she pointed out. "That is the reason for the minus." I began to cry out of frustration. "I am sure he will like it because of all the work you put into it for him." She reassured me. She was right, and he loved it even though it confused him as he

---

[13] Richard Carpenter, "Merry Christmas Darling" (A&M Records, 1970).

tried to button it. He was happy and proud of me for making it for him. That is true love!

Time Flies

Love takes time, and each day seems like an eternity or a year. The world seems like a jungle, and I am in an ant hole. It is a lonely place that I do not want to face alone, like the words from the hymn, "In the Garden." (I thought she was talking about God). All of a sudden, I am no longer alone. He holds my hand, and I am no longer afraid. He walks with me and talks with me and helps me with every step. At first, I was scared of him for no apparent reason—I do not trust. Then he tells me he loves me. I am afraid, but he proved himself steadfast and trustworthy. I find that he is all that matters in my life. Is this love? And this is love, two souls that meet and have no need to prove anything to each other, only that they love each other forever. This is the kind of love that Jesus showed to me, and I pray I will find it, the type of love that lasts a lifetime.

Growing Pains

June 9, 1972
Graduation Day

Today is the first day of the rest of my life. The time of decision is here—time to go out and make my way in the world and pick a profession. I picked nursing and will go to school at Thomas Jefferson University School of Practical Nursing. At the graduation, I met a cousin I went to four years of school with and did not know she was my cousin on my mother's side. My mother also told me my half-sisters also went to my school. It was strange that I did not know them, and it made me feel sad and a little angry again, but I would not let it ruin my special day. My Cousin Mary Pat and I had spent four years hearing people ask us if we were sisters or related—we just laughed. So much to our amazement to find that it was true that we were related on Graduation Day, our grandmothers were sisters on my mother's side. We promised to stay in touch. It made the day extra special.

I have a chance to begin fresh, start a dream of my own, and make this world a better place. I can see what I can do to become a confident, capable, responsible nurse. I had already learned to be a defensive driver and how to drive on the superhighways going very fast. I was learning how to drink alcohol carefully so as not to become drunk. Too many in my family have trouble with alcohol, and I did not want to become an alcoholic. Freedom and responsibility made me feel all grown up. I had a co-worker who was killed in a car accident on New Year's Eve from a drunk driver, it was so sad. I also had a male friend drafted into the service, entering the Vietnam War. It is a difficult time to be eighteen years old. The year 1972 was critical for me. Is that you, God? Will you help me stay on track for my goals?

Hello, New Self

I hope someday I wake up and say, "Hello, self, long time no understand." I am at this stage of becoming me. Touch me, I am real! I begin to feel who I am becoming—recognizing myself as my own person and not my mother. I am writing my own story, putting the pieces together. It is the process of being and becoming. Becoming a woman and looking to be accepted. Sometimes I feel grown up and sometimes like a crazy little girl, I do not know which one I enjoy more. People treat me differently now that I am not just a little girl, I am a young lady. I like that title; it makes me feel important, I often feel unsure, frightened, and alone. The future seems like a blank and it scares me. In discovering and accepting myself, I knew I had to forgive the man I never knew. He left me with deep scars, anger, and hatred that was not me. I had to trash it and replace it with forgiveness. I hope he has replaced his guilt, or he must be a very wretched older man. Someday, I will fit the pieces of my life together and say, "Hey! This is me, Rose Marie Page!" I am now an important person. I have graduated now to a "young lady."

Insecure Princess No More…Love Is a Decision to Live Happily Ever After

My fairy-tale life as a princess became insecure when I heard my father was alive. I remember feeling shock, grief, and being unloved. I saw my mother's tears as my own started to flow. They tasted salty in my mouth as I cried out loud. I smelled the alcohol on my aunt's breath. I felt sick to my stomach as it turned into a knot. As I learned the details of my mother's story, I found out what love is. Love is a decision! My mother chose to love me more than herself. She told me that God answered her prayer, and I am the answer. She told me she loves me very much and that God knew me before I was born. He rescued me from the illegal abortion my father had set up for me in New York City. Although I felt rejected by my biological father, I was reassured to have a stepfather who does love me. He came to the bathroom door to check on me. He said, "Aggie is my baby, okay?" We both answered yes. When I came out, he was waiting for me in the kitchen. He smiled at me and said, "He is no good. You are okay. Do not worry about anything!" I smelled the cherry tobacco burning in his pipe. That familiar smell reminded me that I am the princess here. I feel a little insecure, but I will be fine. Someday my prince will come, and I will live happily ever after. I will not let my deadbeat father destroy my dreams. I decided that day never to think of my father again and I did not, for a long time. Grief has stages, and denial is the first one. Like Scarlett O'Hara, I said, "I will think about this tomorrow, not today." Today I will be happy for my mother and my stepfather. I will forgive my drunk aunt and the father I never met. I hope I never grow up to hurt people like the people who used alcohol and has hurt so many people in my family. Not for me, I plan to live happily ever after.

Mother Teresa

"Let us not make a mistake—that the hunger is only for a piece of bread. The hunger of today is so much greater; for love, to be wanted, to be loved, to be cared for, to be somebody. We can do no great things, only small things with great love." by Mother Theresa (*The Joy in Loving*,[14] 1997, compiled by Jaya Chalika and Edward Le Joly).

Lord, teach me to become a young lady who loves much…

>Reflections of Joy in the Winter
>Psalm 46:10 Be Still…
>Jeremiah 1:5 I knew you before I formed you in your mother's womb.
>Can you remember when you first found faith for yourself?
>Have you ever felt the presence of God in your life? Did you recognize it?
>Have you ever heard a small quiet voice within your heart?
>Was it louder than the others around you?
>Have you ever felt grief and denial?
>Where do you find your security?
>
>Ending Part One
>Recognition is the first part of a Fairy Tale. Being Recognized and Loved.

---

[14] Jaya Chalika, Edward LeJoly, and Mother Teresa, *The Joy in Loving* (New York: Viking, 1997).

PART 2

SPRING

Seasons of a Woman's Life Journey
How to Overcome Selfishness, Fear,
Anger, and Postpartum Depression
Finding True Joy and Peace
Being a Woman Becoming a Wife

Recognition…Spring Begins

"Love is like a budding rose, carefully nurtured and soon unfolds. Two hearts as one growing Dear. Though one season has the roses, a heartfelt love grows and grows. Unlike the rose, a lasting love endures, blossoming throughout the seasons spent with every glance, every touch, every kiss well meant."[15] (UNKNOWN)

---

[15] Author unknown, *"Love is like a budding Rose,"* n.d.

Preparations for Spring, Knowing Who I Am

"A time for everything and a season for every activity under heaven. A time to be born, a time to die, a time to plant and a time to uproot" (Ecclesiastes 3:1–2). This verse was used in the song, "Turn! Turn! Turn!" by the rock group the Byrds,[16] in 1965.

Spring Begins

Spring fever is the restless feeling commonly associated with the beginning of spring. The theme of spring is rebirth as everything turns green again and comes back to life, as the buds burst forth suddenly. It refers to growth and hope, but that's not all, young love is also a theme. We see nature prepare for new life; birds, and rabbits creating nests. Suddenly flowers appear, pushing up through the warmed winter-cold ground, growing and reproducing. Thawing of the ground and a new awakening from the sun warms and welcomes everyone back outdoors again.

Mother Nature prepares, then surprises us, with new life and beauty all around us. As I prepare for spring cleaning and work on weeds in the flower bed, let me remember the important things in life and to remember those people who are most precious to me—my family, friends, and loved ones.

It will be a month of personal inventory of Step 4; to evaluate my growth and development in the stairway to life; to accept where I have been, let go of the past, and move forward in personal, spiritual and emotional growth and development. Time to continue the journey of spring.

Thought from the book, "Love Yourself,"[17] by Walter Trobisch. Understand that it is okay to be different. Jesus was different. He was an unexpected and unwanted child; his family was embarrassed by Him, then they realized that he was special. What I learned by studying the life of Jesus is that Jesus knew who He was, the Son of

---

[16] The Byrds, "*Turn! Turn! Turn!* (To Everything There Is a Season)" (Columbia Records, 1965).

[17] Walter Trobisch, *Love Yourself* (Illinois: Inter Varsity Press, 1976).

God and accepted Himself and His mission. I had to learn to accept myself, my situation, and learn to love myself so I could be gentle and kind and to love others. I learned to love and accept the girl in the mirror who is becoming a woman and a bride. April was a time of great growth in many ways and many seasons of springtime.

April is National Poetry Month. It is a month of growth and spiritual equilibrium moving forward in new and positive ways. It is time for spring cleaning; a time to get rid of the winter dust and put away warm winter clothes and make room for pastel colored, lighter clothing. The flower of April is the daisy or sweet peas which represent purity and innocence.

A Season of New Love

The name, April, is derived from the Latin word aperitif, which means it is considered the month of the growing season and when trees and flowers begin to "open." It is also believed that the month's name is named after the Greek goddess, Aphrodite (Aphros). Diamond is the birthstone of April.

CHAPTER 4

Being a Woman Becoming a Bride in Her Becoming

February 23, 1973

Today is this diary's one year anniversary. I am now nineteen years old and thought things would be simple at this point but I'm back where I started from one year ago. I am still confused, still wondering, still lonely, still me… I thought this diary would help me. I'm beginning to think I need psychiatric support! Maybe this is what it's all about. I can live with the fact that things will never be simple, I guess, but why do things have to be so complicated and confusing? I make things more confusing than they are, I think.

February 26, 1973

I discovered one of my problems in nursing school at the hospital. Why does it scare me so? Last week, I had a tiny eighty-three-year-old lady dependent on me, and I was terrified of her. There was no way I could do her any harm, and I know that it's just that it scared me having someone so totally dependent on my every action. I'm nothing. I'm so confused with my own problems and life. How am I supposed to help people? People (patients) in this hospital look up to me. Secretly I look up to them for one reason or another. Why do I lack confidence? I know it is my fault and wonder if I will ever change for the better, I hope. The way I need to change is to stop being so self-centered. I have to realize I also have to give and start giving love to those people; those people I may never see again, so I will never forget if I can give them part of my love. The real me—Jesus, help me let her shine through.

Learning to Trust—A Love Story

A Love Story that is real. A man hanging on a cross, a crown with vicious thorns, and that man with love enough for all. Jesus said, "Love one another as I have loved you." These are beautiful words emerging from a life that existed only to love and redeem. Can I doubt that we only exist to love one another? IS IT REALLY POSSIBLE?

To be torn between two forces, one that is good and one that is the face of evil. Which is most potent and appealing at the time? Who will be the one to overcome? Me. I need to listen to the one who loved me first. Love has touched my life. I need to trust the One who has given His all for me. Love makes all things new. Love does not pass, it is lost. Now that I have found my true love, I must hold on to it and let the Lord of Love bring us the happiness that love can bring. You enabled me to trust love and come alive. I look forward to the day we say I do. You are coming home, and we will begin where we left off in building a relationship that will last forever. With faith in us two, our dreams come true. The name of one of my favorite songs by Karen Carpenter is, "We've Only Just Begun," [18] and that is how I feel!

Young and in Love

I will never be too old to remember that I was once young and in love. It has been one of the most beautiful adventures of my life.

---

[18] Karen Carpenter, "We've Only Just Begun," *Close to You* (A&M Records, 1970).

We are innocent and impractical, radical, hardheaded, sensitive, unreasonable, naive, dreamers, but most of all, very happy.

A Bride in Her Becoming

The Second Book of the Corinthians 6:17 refers to the called-out ones, a gathering of those summoned. "Called out" translates to *ekklesia* in the Greek. "Like a bride," per Encyclopedia Britannica.

April 1973 is the month I got engaged to be married. And I got my diamond ring! It's such an exciting time for Bob and I. Our love was blossoming like the spring season around us. I was so happy when I came home to tell my mother the good news. "Mom, Bob asked me to marry him!" I said excitedly to her. She frowned and replied, "Oh no, just what we need!" What? "Not we, me!" I said. *Why can't she be happy for me?* I thought. She said, "You are too young to get married!" I reminded her that I turned nineteen this year, and I knew what I wanted. I love Bob and we will live happily ever after! She said, "You are too young, but you will not listen, so do what you want!" I started to cry. I will never hurt my daughter like this, I thought to myself. I will remember this day. But I choose to be happy today. I will not let her steal my joy! Help my mother understand me, Lord. Mom, please understand.

Fairy Godmother Dream Comes True

The day I first heard, "Will you marry me? I countered with, "No! I'm not ready yet." I planned to wait and travel across the United States. Six months later, it was like I was swept up by a whirlwind created by a fairy godmother. I saw the dress, the shoes, the handsome prince, and I was the bride. "You are too young," my mother protested. But I did not listen. I was on an emotional high, soaring on the wings of a dream come true! And the roller coaster ride began.

1970s Fun Facts About My Wedding Year and the Turbulent Seventies

Counterculture

Bob and I had a 1969 Red Volkswagen bug.

The price of gas was $0.36 a gallon.

There was a gas shortage, and we had to sit in long lines every other day.

Minimum wage was $2.90 per hour.

The 1960s Vietnam war protests were all over the country.

The Civil Rights Movement was in full swing.

The Equal Rights for Women Movement was keeping pace with it.

The Jesus Movement was a spiritual awakening happening in California moving across the US

Televised hippies protesting for social injustice were common

The evening news also featured women burning their bras.

Soldiers killed in action shipped home in body bags were also covered on newscasts every day.

The first Earth Day ever—April 22, 1970—President Nixon formed the Environmental Protection Agency. He also ended the Vietnam War. Watergate happened, and to avoid impeachment proceedings, Nixon resigned.

Music was disco and pop rock on eight-track tapes.

The Beatles broke up, and Elvis died on August 16, 1977.

Growing Pains

The Wedding Shoes

We had our first big fight. It was about a whole lot of nothing. I came home to tell my mother in no uncertain terms, "The wedding is off!" She said, "NO, it is not off! And you will pull yourself together, and you will be surprised tonight at your Bridal Shower!" I cried. Lord, help me forgive my future husband and continue to love through our first big argument. Remind me that it is small compared to the big picture of things. Forgive my immaturity. Please help me be kind and gentle and loving. Help me become a good wife to my future husband. Help me grow into my wedding shoes. I was surprised by friends and family with a shower. I got many, many beautiful gifts! It felt like Christmas came early. I loved it even though it felt funny. It was my first wedding shower ever and I hit the jackpot for the first time. Thank you, Lord! For all your Blessing to us from our friends and family.

November 1, 1973

Dear Jesus, it's hard to believe the time has gone so fast. I've dreamt of our day for so long, and now it's only two days away. God, I believe you are the person I have first to thank. For assisting me to learn, find, and enjoy "real" love. For the most beautiful man in the world. For helping the little things to come together, to make our wedding possible regarding money. I am getting excited. We are both tired out from trying to get things done. We'll need the vacation. Jesus, please help me decide soon about what I was talking to Bob about last night. —. I am mixed up as usual. Help us wait. BOB YERKA—DOES HE LOVE ME? DO I LOVE HIM? WILL WE BE TOGETHER FOREVER? IS MARRIAGE THE ANSWER? Yes! Love has its ups and downs, but love is beautiful.

November 2, 1973

Tonight was our wedding rehearsal. It was very funny. We had a good time even though I was so nervous. We went to the hall to decorate. It looks so lovely. We used paper rolls for the tables and paper ribbons on the end of each table, and paper wedding bells thumb tacked to the ceiling. The VFW Hall in Verga only cost $75.00. Then the food was another $100.00 and the drinks were $25.00 plus the rental of a punch bowl went for another $20.00 and the cake cost $20.00. On top of that, the band was $50.00, and my dress was also $50.00, and decorations and paper products added another $20.00 to the tally, and I did my own hair, grateful that my uncle drove me. We are to go away for the weekend for two nights in North Wildwood for about $20.00 per night for a Grand Total of $300.00. So we bought a new car as a wedding present to ourselves and moved to a new apartment for about $100 per month. With deposits, we spent about $500.00 for our wedding. A tight budget indeed. Thank You Lord!

So we went out with friends tonight after the get-together at my house. We went dancing and met girls from Gloucester Catholic High School. We were laughing and having fun until I fell off my heel and sprained my ankle. Then I was crying like a sad drunk. I was afraid I would not be able to walk down the aisle to be married the next day. We all laughed. My drunk state brought back some bad and good memories. I was talking to my friends Linda, Denise, and Pat and all the girls at my wedding. They all told me how lucky I was to have found a man like Bob. And I know that I am lucky. I am a sentimental person. I really enjoyed my bachelorette party. We all had a great time!

......I sat down and prayed that night and wrote my vows.

Keep Our Faith—Keep Us Strong

Dear Lord:

Be our Centerfold as the basis, strength, and power of our love. It is where it all began. It was a divine appointment for our meeting. Yes, I remember the beginning. It seems our love had always been there even before we met. Keep our love strong despite obstacles. Help us find our dream, somewhere, somehow, some way and some day. Our day has now come. We will be truly alive. Love is a beginning, show us the way, your way of a new life. I knew in loneliness that your love was satisfied. For life and love can be a lonely place, growing together in every way, every day. Together we shall become one. Openness, understanding, and communication, is a beautiful living thing that is a sign of love. The joy of love can't explain the very special closeness that only love can create.

Being willing to give up freedom for a life filled with you and our love.

We are experiencing and learning about each other and our life together.

One experience after another, building a story of our own unique life

Building a dream and to follow it step by step.

To be loved and to give myself completely to another. All things must pass, but love does not pass. It can only be lost. Now that we have found love, let us hold tight to one another. We have only just begun to fit the pieces together and discover the world that awaits us with faith in the two of us.

To be at home with the one we love. Marriage will be our home even if we are without a roof! Help us experience our legs and the strength we give each other to walk even through societal pressures without depending on a human crutch. Please make our legs strong. Help us stand on our own two feet and stand side by side and walk together, for we have experienced your strength, Lord. Help us have faith to experience our own strength. Show us the way and we shall walk in it. Love has no limits and no boundaries. For love understands love and needs no talk, it knows no time, it cannot be measured by the minute or the hour. Love is forever.

The Love Road

I've traveled many roads, met many obstacles and dead ends. Hopefully, I will travel many more miles on highways. I hope I always return home to where I started—back to the ones who love me. May he always be there. To be lost is a terrible experience but getting lost can teach a lesson in learning. You have to experience being lost to fully experience being found. I was lost but I found you. I was found and discovered. I realized my search had ended. I declared it my own holiday, our day. The end of the old year, an old life and the beginning of a new one. It started with a kiss, and we had only just begun. We still have many roads and miles to cover, only this time it is together. This time it will be one road, one direction, with one goal because we two will become one. This road will be constructed by our trust, paved by our strength and by our love never ending.

Bob, I am glad your love is a gift, for I could never deserve it. I am glad you love me as I am. For without your help, I could not change. I am glad you said you would never leave because I could never let you go. For my life could never be whole without you. I am glad a gift is something for free, for I could never pay the price. I am glad that He made you. For without you, there is no me. I am glad love has no limits and time cannot rule or keep records of wrongs. For our day has come and we will always have just begun! Lord Help us, I pray.

Our Day Has Come Nov 3, 1973.
The Awaited Day and Memories in My Mind's Eye

We all went to Uncle Jack's house to get ready. Mary Beth would not smile for the camera. But she looked so cute as my flower girl. And as usual I was running late. Bob and I called each other on the yellow phone with the long cord. It made for a good picture and memories of sweet nothings to say before our Big Day! My Uncle drove me in the back of his caddy with my long white velvet gown, I felt just like Cinderella going to the ball! It was dreamy! And I'm to live happily ever after. That is the plan. We made vows and planned to keep them. We also planned to have the best marriage ever in the history of our families because I really did not know of any really happy couples except for my neighbors, Sandy and Len. They seemed happy with three children. I used to babysit for them and wanted to be happy like them. I thought my cousin Dottie and Ray were happy too but found out later that was not the case. I knew they fought a lot. But we would be different. Jesus would help us to be different. We invited him to be a part of our special day. We asked him to help us to keep the vows we made to each other and help us to live happily ever after.

Our Wedding Day Prayers and Promises

I promise to be true to you in good times and in bad, in sickness and in health. I will love you and honor you all the days of my life.

The Prayer Father Powell Read at the Service

Lord, bless and consecrate Rose and Bob in their love for each other. May these rings be a symbol of trueness in each other, and always remind them of their love. Take this ring as a sign of love and fidelity. In the name of the Father, the Son, and the Holy Spirit. You gave man the constant help of woman so that man and woman should be no longer two – but one flesh – had you taught us that what you have united may never be divided. Look with love upon this woman, your daughter, now joined to her husband in marriage. She asks for your blessing. Give her the grace of love and peace. May her husband put his trust in her and recognize that she is his equal and the heir with him in the light of grace. May he always honor her and love her as Christ loves his bride – the Church. Bless them with children and help them to be good parents. May they live to see their children's children and after, a happy old age – grant them fullness of life and the saints in the kingdom of heaven.

Our Wedding Vows

To be a part of another's life. To have someone that is a special part of yours, mine, and ours. It must be that life was meant to be shared. For when a life is shared, we have the power to create a life by our love and life and love are what makes this world go round. They are what makes the world worthwhile. To love one another so much that he too becomes a part of myself but we two are made of one. I feel so full of joy. I could explode. You are a part of my fullness. For you, my love has made my person whole. You are a part of my joy for you as my love, my happiness, and any dream for the future. My husband, to have and to hold, to love and to cherish, to rejoice and stand by him in sickness and in health for better or for worse, my man from this day forward—November 3—I'm his forevermore.

November 25, 1973

The wedding was beautiful. Everything went smoothly enough, even though I was a nervous wreck! Married life is so beautiful. I love my Bob so very much. Washing dishes, clothes, making beds, cooking and making love, making love, making love, etc.... Just what every girl dreams of and asks for. Our cozy little bungalow that we both love is like a little love nest. We do not have much, but we have each other forever! Thank You for my Binky Bob! Thank You Jesus for answering our prayers.

November 28, 1973

This day was a very scary one. Our first big fight as a married couple. It was such a hurtful, difficult, and sad experience. It was my fault, but I do not know why. It was the first time I felt like running home to my mommy. I had to realize I was a married woman now. I have to stand on my own two feet and make my own decisions. I felt all alone, but I should not because I know you are with me, Jesus. Please keep our faith and keep it strong

The words "I am sorry" seems useless, and I felt helpless to show love. I wanted to say a lot of things, but they remained inside. I did not want to hurt him. But then all I could do was to feel the sorrow and the silence. That is when I felt alone. The mood was tense, and you, my Lord, seemed thousands of miles away. And we were the same distance apart. I knew he felt my tears on his chest that spoke louder than the words I needed to say. He took me by the hand and tucked me into bed. I felt like a loved child. Help me not to be so childish the next time. Help me learn to say I am sorry, sooner than later.

The beauty of the fight is the joy that comes in the morning. The joy when two hearts meet with a smile and the words "I love you" are finally released from within. I thought to myself, I should have said that last night. But it doesn't really matter now because we both know the words were there, only unsaid. Love the feeling, too big for the word.

CHAPTER 5

Being a Bride and Becoming a Mother

All My Dreams Were Coming True Very Quickly

It felt like a whirlwind. I graduated from Nursing School, got married, took Nursing Boards, started a new job and career. I became pregnant in January 1975 with my first child.

February 1, 1975
Becoming a Mother

Dear Jesus, it's already February 1975, and I'm two weeks late on my period. The possibility that I may be pregnant makes me very happy, especially after recently seeing Denise and Pat's babies. They are so beautiful. Life to birth is so wonderful. It's hard to picture a baby, a person who will look a little like me, and a little like Bob. It sounds beautiful!

February 5, 1975, 2:00 p.m.

Dear Jesus, I have good news! I've told my mother—I've called my husband and my girlfriends, but they were not home. I'm so excited, I could explode! Bob and I are going to have a baby! I was so nervous when I called to get the results and when the girl asked me if

I planned to follow the pregnancy or terminate it! Oh my God, what a question! Thank you, Jesus! I am so happy! It might be a little hard for a while, but we'll manage! I can't wait. Please don't make anything bad happen. The only thing that scares me—I really want this baby. Please let everything be all right.

February 6, 1975

Dear Jesus, I'm hurting deep inside—on the outside I am still very happy. The problem is my mother is not. She makes it very clear in her actions. She does not sound happy at all. Maybe that's the way all mothers are or at least my mother is. She wasn't happy when I told her I was going to get married either. She seems too selfish to me at times. Maybe someday I'll understand. I know she doesn't want to lose me. But she can't think that she is going to lose me. She is going to have a grandchild. I wish she would be happy. I think she tries to make me feel guilty, but I won't. I won't let anyone spoil my happiness at this point.

Please let her give in and smile for a change. I love her! I have to write about my phone experience. Your name—Rose Marie Yerka. Just a minute. Yerka. Yerka? YES! You are pregnant! *Zonk!* I think I knew all along but to hear that, it just shook me up a little, rather a lot. I guess I must have sounded that way too. It made me so nervous for some reason that I do not know. Just the thought of something, a life inside of me—how exciting. I think it does scare me. It makes me so happy. I was beginning to think something was the matter with me. Even though we were not trying. I thought there were so many times that we tried, and nothing happened. I guess when the right time comes, it comes. Thanks.

Bob took me out to celebrate last night at the Echelon Tavern. The piano man was there and he played, "We've Only Just Begun" for us. It was beautiful. I really enjoyed myself. Thank you for being such a wonderful husband.

Today I talked to Dottie, my second Mom. She made me feel so much better. I started to cry. Bob's mom was so nice to me too. She seems very happy. At least she smiled. I also talked to my mom later in the day. That also made me feel much better. I knew I could not be quiet and keep it all inside. It had me too upset, which I don't need right now. I wish I could understand my mother better. I realize that she has a lot on her mind, and she said that's why she acted that way. It felt good to talk to her the way I used to.

We went to look at the townhouses. Dot may be moving too. They are absolute Dream Houses! I fell in love with them. I would love to have one. I think Bob would too. Oh well, it may be just a dream.

March 3, 1975

Dear Jesus, tomorrow unofficially marks my third month. But I still don't feel any different, except my breasts are getting bigger. It makes me realize now how easy it would be for a young girl or anyone to have an abortion, if they had no medical or religious background.

I Am Pro-Life

The red rose is a symbol for pro-life. They use small rose lapel pins or stickers. Roses make me remember my mom's story of choosing life for me. In 1973, abortion became legal in America. As a nurse and a liberal woman, I considered myself Pro-Choice at the time when I got married, until I had the opportunity at the hospital to see the conception products, the body parts of a developing baby in the trash can. I was horrified as I saw arms and legs. This changed my mind completely. I thought it was just globs of cells. So then I became an activist, I marched outside the local hospitals with my children and went to Washington, DC, to the March for Life on January 22 many times. I am forever grateful that my mother was pro-life. I want to be the best mother ever.

April 1975

Dear Jesus, I'm beginning to look like a real pregnant lady. There are three other nurses on the floor in my condition. It is all we talk about. It gets me excited. I'm so happy. Thank you for this miracle in my life.

May 1975

This month I started wearing maternity clothes. They make me look so big. I got a little upset when my blue jeans didn't fit anymore. But I got over it when Bob bought me a pair of denim maternity pants. Now I wear them all the time instead of my jeans. One thing for sure, they are nice and comfortable.

The first time I felt the baby or what I thought was the baby— was so light. It felt like a flutter. Then it got so I would feel it at night. When I would lay quietly, just lightly at first, it was so nice having my hubby hold my tummy so we could feel life together. It's getting stranger to call our baby "it."

We have to start thinking of some names. Bob bought me a card and a bouquet of flowers for Mother's Day. It's beautiful!

May 28, 1975

Today at work for the first time while I was sitting at the nurse's desk writing notes, I felt my baby kicking up a storm! It's the first time I felt him/her in the daytime. It's a beautiful closeness between me and baby. I wanted to share it with someone. So even though, I felt a little dumb. But I told everyone anyway! Thank you, Dear Jesus. Please give us a healthy baby.

There was a little girl that was with my cousins last night who was handicapped. She had such a pretty face. I felt so bad and it kind of scared me, but I prayed for us to have a healthy, normal baby. I can't wait.

June 1, 1975

This month we got together one night and started thinking of names. What we came up with so far is: Christopher Michael, Kimberly Rose, Timothy Robert, Tara Marie. It was hard enough to narrow it down that far. You have to think of nicknames—origins and their meanings. It's really something.

June 20, 1975

This weekend we went down to Bob's aunt's bungalow in Brigantine for the weekend. I didn't realize how much I miss being alone. It was beautiful. I think it did us a world of good. I can't wait until we get our house on June 23, 1975. We agreed to buy it for $27,900. The sellers would sell it for $27,000 as a gift for the new baby. Thank you, Jesus. I know it must be You who is giving us these lucky breaks. I appreciate it.

June 26, 1975

Bob went fishing for a couple of days with his brother and friends. I really miss him, but I know he wanted to go, and I know he'll have a good time. He loves to fish. It's the first time since we were married that we were apart overnight. I don't know if I will be able to sleep. You don't realize how good it feels to have that person lying next to you until he's not there. All this month the baby seemed to be so quiet. After the quickening—stronger and more often, it's scary to be so quiet. Everyone tells me not to worry but I can't help but worry. I can't sleep until I feel the baby move and if I haven't felt it all day, or if it takes too long, I shake my body and then they might move a little. Please let everything be all right. I want a healthy baby.

July 3, 1975

Well, my hubby is twenty-five years old today. We're getting old. Old married people. It's a hot month and only three months to go and we'll be parents. It seems so far off and so unbelievable.

August 8, 1975

I feel like we've signed our lives away. So many papers. But now we are homeowners. I really love my little house. It looks better and better every day with each little thing that is put in it.

The Miracle of Birth and Question of Death—A Reason to Believe.

We bought a new dinette set and bedroom set. They are beautiful. We bought slipcovers for our living room furniture. Everything looks good. The only thing I can't decide on is baby furniture. It's the only room that is empty, except we have a baby shade and a shag rug.

I've dropped and I'm getting more and more uncomfortable and getting more and more tired at work. It seems the more you work the more they want out of you. Nursing is an exhausting career. (But I love it.)

We're working on the house little by little. It's nice to be able to take our time. Bob's father is in the hospital again for more radiation. He has numerous tumors across his shoulders, back, ribs, arms, and wrists. To say the least, he is in a lot of pain. Jesus, please help him to be relieved of such pain. It does not seem fair. There are so many bad people in the world. Why does such a good man have to suffer so much? He worked so hard all of his life and has been good to other people. He seems to be getting the short end again, like many other people. I hope you'll take care of him in the end. I hate watching the man suffer and see his wife and children suffer with him. It's just as hard on him. Bob's very close to Johnny. Help us all be strong. Please end his suffering and pain.

September 2, 1975

I started my maternity leave, none too soon. I was getting so tired and uncomfortable. It's funny not having to get up with the chickens. But it seems like I feel even worse not working. I went to the doctor. My blood pressure is up, and my weight is down. I guess that's why I can't wait until everything is over. I'm getting tired of being pregnant.

September 6, 1975

Well things are getting together at the house. We are painting and wallpapering. I can't wait to move in. Our bedroom set is coming on Tuesday, we'll probably be in shortly after Tuesday.

September 7, 1975

I washed windows, screens, hung curtains, and cleaned the bathroom. I'm so excited! Bob and Roby are wallpapering. I made dinner for them (hot dogs and beans) big deal! I was supposed to do Dottie's hair tonight. When I got there, Dottie had a shower for me. When they yelled, they scared me. It was really nice. I got some very nice things. We didn't get home until midnight. But I was so tired. For some reason I was feeling depressed, crying for no apparent reason. I knew I should be happy, but I was feeling really blue. I felt guilty for Bob because he and I wanted to make love, but I decided I had better not. Now I am glad that I didn't, because at 1 p.m., my water broke! I couldn't believe it! Bob didn't believe me, I said "Well either it's my water or I'm pissing myself!" I woke my mother. I thought it was weird because I had no pain… yet at two p.m., the contractions started two minutes apart every forty-five to fifty seconds. That was another thing I couldn't believe. To say the least, I was scared to death. Although I wanted to get it over with. It's September 8, 1975, but I am not due until September 30. My suitcase wasn't packed. I had no robe or slippers—no nothing. I kept saying, "This baby can't come now – the nursery isn't ready. So I called the doctor at 2:20 p.m. and he said to come to the hospital. I hoped to get Dr. Gotchel.

He seemed really nice though. I think Bob was nervous too. He said, "You mean we are going to the hospital tonight? How? You mean you are going to have the baby today?!" At 3 p.m., I have Bob reading "Preparation for Childbirth" from the doctor's office to me.

It's about time, huh? I kept putting it off. But I wanted him to know the breathing techniques because I know once the pain started coming hard, I would probably forget everything about my breathing. I got washed, shaved my legs, dressed, and made Bob shave at 3:30 a.m. I told him that Dr. Gotchel was not going to meet him looking like he did (after working on the house all day). He was so tired—me too. We got to the hospital around 4 a.m. They checked me and I was one centimeter from about 5–5:30 a.m. It was cold in the labor room. Next time, I am buying wool socks! I can remember shivering but feeling flushed. I knew Bob was tired and that I would probably be there all day, so I figured he might as well go home and get some sleep. I told him to go home, but he wanted to stay, and I was glad because I really didn't want him to leave. I guess it was between 6:30 -7 a.m. when I was six centimeters. I couldn't believe it in such a short period of time. They called Dr. Gotchel and he came in about fifteen minutes. Bob told me that it felt like hours, days, weeks! The pain was really getting strong, and I couldn't wait for my doctor. Dr. Gotchel came in, whistling. I was never so glad to hear anyone's whistle in my life! He said that we're too late for an epidural. I wanted to die! But instead, he gave me something of lower strength that really helped. He scrubbed and told Bob to get dressed. I was watching him. Bob looked so nervous. When they took me into delivery and set me up on that awful table in that typical awkward position, at one point I thought "Do I really want Bob in here and see me like this?" But then I was glad that he was there. He really helped and it was funny because the baby was breech, and we had a sneak preview.

I couldn't see what it was, so I asked the doctor "Let's ask the father," the doctor said and when Bob told me it was a girl, his face was beaming, because that's exactly what he wanted!

And when she was born, I heard her cry and saw that she was beautifully normal. I cried so hard, but I was so happy. Such a beautiful experience. I don't think I'll be afraid next time. I said a prayer to you, Jesus, in the recovery room because I knew what a long time I had in considering my first baby, and it was a breech delivery. Thank you. And Tara Marie is beautiful—4 pounds, 16 ½ inches long. She had to stay in the hospital after I was released. It was for a week. It gave me time to get ready. Everything was beautiful. I told Bob that we went in as a married couple and we will be leaving as a family. Now Tara is home, and we are all so happy. I like being a mommy. Tara Marie Yerka. She looks just like Bob. A real Yerka! Date of birth: September 8, 1975—7:41a.m., 4 pounds, 11 ounces, 16 ½ inches.

A Death

A week later, Johnny, Bob's Stepfather, got worse. He was on oxygen, and he looked terrible. The doctors didn't expect him to last the night. They told us there is nothing more they could do. The tumor is growing rapidly and blocking air passages. There is a lack of brain activity, causing involuntary motions. His breathing is very labored.

He looked so awful. I worried about this happening the whole time I carried Tara. You know what they say about a birth and a death. That's what I was worried about. It makes me feel terrible for some reason. He is dying. His body rejected the chemotherapy. Things don't look good. It just does not seem fair. There are so many rotten people in the world. So why do you take a good man like John? A young man with two young children, my sister-in-law, Judy and brother-in-law Michael. Lord, help them all. Especially my mother-in-law Betty.

I knew my husband was close to John, and Bob didn't realize how close. I've never seen Bob so upset. I wanted to help him so badly, but I knew that nothing I could say would help the deep hurt he was feeling inside. He went through the stages of death. He knew about the cancer and what that meant, but things happened so fast. It had only been less than six months. And the man had gone straight downhill. Bob pulled out the picture John painted for us. We must get a frame. The thing that really hurt Bob was that John had never seen our new home and will never see his granddaughter. It is sad and really depressing. Why John? So we took our baby to the hospital to see him.

Dear Jesus, please help John, his family, and Bob. I hope he can take it. Please help me help him. I love him. Bless John. Give him peace. Please don't let Bob lose his faith. Bless Bob. Give him comfort.

September 20, 1975

The funeral was long and sad. Bob was strong. And we are all glad that it is over. John isn't suffering anymore, and neither is his family. We hope John is enjoying forever with you Lord, although we all miss him.

December 19, 1975

Things are coming along pretty good. Christmas is coming and we do not have money. But at least we have a baby, a house, a tree, and each other. What else could we ask for when there is a birthday to celebrate? This is a very special birthday. My mother got a few Christmas lights to put on the house. Someone stole them. Someone robbed our friend up the street. There is still hatred, jealously, cheating, killing, and every other bad thing that takes away something from this beautiful time of year and it really makes me sad. Please make it a happy Christmas even though John is not here. I have to work, and we have no money for many gifts. I kept getting the feeling that this may be the happiest Christmas of all. This is our third and three is a lucky number! Thank you.

I'd like to thank my beautiful daughter. I think she's starting to look a little like me. It makes me feel so proud to have such a beautiful little one. She's getting so big. She doesn't look like that hospital picture anymore. She's up to 12 pounds, 2 ounces. She's had a little cold at this point, but otherwise, thank you for a healthy child, Lord. Remember, that's what this diary is for. It's for my daughter.

December 21, 1975

Today is John's birthday. He would have been only fifty-one years old. I have a feeling it's going to be a sad, sad Christmas, especially for my mother-in-law. It's going to be hard—her first Christmas without her husband. What a nightmare! I hate to think of Bob and I ever being separated! I love him so much! Please bless my mother-in-law. Give her strength.

February 6, 1976

My baby is growing, and she is so beautiful, Jesus. Thank you so much. It's a beautiful gift to be a mother. But today, something very sad happened. My girlfriend had her first gift of life inside of her body. Sure, she wasn't married, but he was. She has better things planned for her future, I guess. She made a selfish decision. She had an abortion. She took away her baby's chance and her baby's future. Help me not to judge my friend. I do not know how it feels to be her in that situation. But my mother did. However, I promised to keep this a secret.

Dear Jesus, I never thought that would be her decision, but even worse, I helped her a little. I knew she wouldn't go to her mother even though I suggested that she should. But she needed someone. I think I was more upset than she was. "Just like having a tooth removed," she said. This really offended my morals. Her morals used to be like mine. Please help her, Jesus. I hope she learned something from all this. Help her remain the person she used to be instead of being like everyone else. It seems like there aren't many people with morals. I'm sorry. I feel like I lost my friend after her abortion. She avoided me or was it my imagination.

I have been so emotional lately. I do not understand what is going on with me. But when I missed my period, I started to get alarmed. I cannot be pregnant again, Can I?

So I decided to go to my family doctor to get a test. He came out and said, "Well Rose, the rabbit died! (For reference, the doctor would inject urine into a rabbit and if it died you were pregnant!) Congratulations! I started to cry as he laughed. My head went into a spin. Can we afford another baby? Now I started to realize how my friend might have felt about being pregnant. At least I have a husband. We will make it somehow. Lord, help us and forgive me for crying. They are tears of joy. Babies are a blessing!

Bob was thrilled. He was hoping for a boy. That would give us the rich man's family. I hope the money finds us.

April 13, 1976

Tara is getting so fat, but I always wanted a fat, healthy baby. Being buried is a horrible thought. I can't imagine what heaven will be like—because sometimes I feel like I'm in heaven when I'm with the man I love. I'm afraid and dread the thought of him ever dying and leaving me or vice versa. Help me at this time, Lord, and season to focus only on the birth of our Savior And to prepare for my new baby. Help me be a good mother. I have been so busy working and being a good mom and wife. I have no time for my journal. I will wait till the baby comes. I cannot wait to have some time off. Help me, Lord.

December 16, 1976

I had a very busy day—a manager's meeting to start with, then picking up my order while going from shopping to packing orders to pick up to doing paperwork, etc. I am totally physically exhausted. Got to bed at 1 p.m., and at 1:20 a.m., my water broke! I couldn't believe it! Even though I was in false labor last week, the doctor and I thought I would go into labor around the twentieth. It was almost exactly like Tara. Even the time. Plus, another breech! I couldn't believe it. I did very, very good. I was so proud of myself. I was in total control. Reading that book really helped. But my doctor did not get there for my para-cervical. I don't know whether it was because of the breech or what, but it was pretty bad toward the end. I could not believe how bad. Dear God, I often wonder why you make it so hard—the Bible says it's a punishment to all women because of Eve's sin in the Garden of Eden. Please help me through this!

My doctor didn't get there until twenty minutes before I delivered. I was so upset. I thought it was so unfair. I had done so well and then to have that added emotional stress. My poor husband. I was crying, asking him to please help me.

I had to be knocked out at the end and after all that work; then I got into a crying jag from the gas. December 17, 1976, we had a beautiful 6-pound, 14-ounce, blond-haired, blue-eyed boy… perfectly healthy. He's beautiful! I saw him in a dream the night before. And he is what made it all worthwhile. Thank you, Jesus!

I'm so happy and my husband is thrilled. He will be named John Robert after Johnny. We were both secretly wishing for a boy so he could be Johnny's namesake. He looks like Tara did, except he has a lighter complexion. He's really cute.

I couldn't believe how tiny a newborn is—how delicate, whether male or female. Plus, the beauty of looking at that little person and realizing that he was what was inside of me for nine months. It's just a MIRACLE.

Spiritual Forces and the Name of Jesus

I worked at the hospital where I delivered my baby. A month before there was a suicide on the seventh floor. That is the psychiatric floor. A man jumped through the window at the end of the hall. I had nightmares about it. *How could he have enough force to get through that glass,* I thought.

I was crying after my husband left me in the hospital. I felt lonely and scared. I do not like hospitals, only to work in and not to be the patient. I decided to go and watch him leave from the window facing the parking lot. As I walked down the hall, all of a sudden, I felt a force pushing my body down the hall. I was shocked! Then I kept seeing myself crashing through the window and falling to the ground, dead. I started to cry out the name of Jesus, Help Me! And immediately it stopped. I was shaken with fear. Lord what was that? Please protect me. I prayed. I decided not to tell anyone. It was too crazy and scary to even talk about.

Too Busy to Journal

There are not many entries in my journal for my second pregnancy. I was too busy and in shock. How can it be, pregnant again so soon? It was like I. How could it seem almost the same? I could not even remember my last period. I said to the doctor, I do not know, you tell me how this happened. But it did and only six short months after my last baby was born.

The blessing was that it was a little boy. We named him after his grandfather and mine, John with Robert as his middle name. He came early as a Christmas present and tax deduction on December 17, 1976. I had a dream the night before about delivering a blonde-haired blue-eyed boy and I did, within an hour of his sister. He was big enough to come home two days before Christmas. He looked so precious under our tree. What a gift from the Lord to us.

We brought him home and placed him under the Christmas tree. He is my best gift ever! Thank You, Jesus. My friend had an abortion. She would hold him and become very emotional. It was shortly after that; she would not answer my calls. I think my son reminded her of her baby. I lost a good friend to abortion. It made me very sad. Please help her Lord.

December 30, 1976

John is getting big already. I can see his face filling out. He's s' cute! It's so much fun to have a little one around again, except at 4 a.m.! Our family was getting bigger. All we needed was money to go with our ever-growing family. Lots of good stress in my life. I would have to return to work at least part time.

December 31, 1976

Bob and I had a wonderful New Year's Eve. Even though we couldn't afford to go out, Kathy had volunteered to babysit for us. It was very depressing at first. I guess that is one of the things that I have to contend with, being the mother of two.

We had a candlelight dinner with champagne! It was very romantic. It was nice and relaxing. I got all sexy in a negligee. It didn't matter anyway because my husband is horny as it is! That's all the good stuff. The other thing that happened that was good but scary was that we made love, very softly and gently so it would not hurt, but what we didn't think of is that we had nothing to use for birth control, which ruined the beauty of the moment because I had been worried ever since.

I've been praying a million times since then—please Lord, we can't afford another baby and I'm not sure I want to go through that again so soon. It makes me want to cry every time I thin' of it. I'm embarrassed to tell anyone about the other night. I had a dream that I was in labor. I woke up crying. I'm afraid of going through that again. When I think of how I wanted to die. Anything to stop the pain. I'm glad my husband was with me. I really needed him.

Growing Pains

January 1, 1977
New Beginnings

This morning I woke up with a lot of cramping which scared me. Dear Jesus, please don't let me be pregnant again.

Baby Blues

Crying when you should be smiling.

Feeling blue when you should be happy.

Feeling confined and helpless to a situation you can't control.

Feeling inadequate to perform the routine chores—bored to death having no one to talk to or with.

Wishing there was someone who could take my place for just a couple days. I hope these feelings go away soon. It makes me feel so guilty. The grass is always greener on the other side.

That someone was here all the time. I just wouldn't listen to what he had to say. My husband, my comforter, my friend. I love him so much. To hear that familiar voice brings back so many memories. Sometimes I feel guilty even thinking about it.

Just a voice can heal the hurt, put aside the distance and time and make you remember the good that we shared. I never realized this, I would still feel this way, until I heard his voice once again. But unfortunately, a voice and good memories are not what keeps us happy throughout life. They make a smile and a warm feeling inside of beauty.

They're not enough when you've had a hard day and you're feeling blue or you're so happy you could burst. *Are you there, God?* Do you see me?

Learning to Let my Husband Understand

For it is all through life that we need someone to share with, the good things and the bad things. Through sickness and in health, for richer or for poorer, till death do us part. Some loved ones will be there and some will not. It's the ones who will be there that deserve all my love, without an ounce to share. For he has made me happy forever.

Bob took me out to dinner. I really enjoyed it. It was nice just to get away and talk. Then we were home. It's so funny; we had fun.

I found myself telling Bob how much he means to me. Especially after seeing the lips of someone I loved and thought I could kiss them, and I know that's not the kind of happiness I want. It made me realize what I want, and it is GROWING STRONGER IN LOVE. It has grown to a family—which is our instrument of love that can bring more happiness. And thank you for the lover, my beautiful husband, a beautiful daughter, a beautiful son, a beautiful marriage, a beautiful family and happiness, I never thought possible. We have each other. We are one and our love is growing deeper, faster and stronger. Our dreams will come true.

The Joy of Being Changed/Remembering my Childhood Wish—A New Beginning

Ecclesiastes 3:1: "There is a time for everything, and a season for every activity under the heavens" (NIV) Winter is my favorite season. It is where all the other seasons start and end. It shows the Circle of Life. One of my favorite books is by Jim Rohn, called "Seasons of Life." He tells of the importance of knowing what season you are in to create priorities for your everyday life. He said, "For things to change, you have to change." Rohn, Jim (*Seasons of Life*,[19] 1981). Change was always hard for me.

In winter, I saw a new beginning and fresh start. I can celebrate the wins of the last year and free myself from the regrets and resentments. By starting fresh and letting them all go, I could forgive myself and others for last year's past mistakes, I was free to start over again to change and become a better me.

Being is easy, the fact of existing, a living person. To become means to change or grow to be fitted or suited. To become is what happens to you. Experiences helped me to become more understanding and merciful to others. I always considered myself to be an "Optimist." I had hoped that things would turn out well, to look forward with reasonable confidence, to believe and trust. The word hope in the Hebrew means knitted. I felt the events of my childhood shaped me to be able to love myself, my God and others. The past, present and future are woven together like a braid of my mother's story, my story and my family's story, they have created a wonderful life. I always wondered, "Where do I fit in?" I felt different from other children. I was an only child, probably spoiled, shy and curious. I was quiet and happy most of the time. I loved creative play and watching people. I had a beautiful smile and talked with my hands. I had blondish light brown hair shoulder length with hazel eyes and golden flecks that changed colors with the clothes I wore.

My mother had dark hair that she wore in a ponytail or pulled back and up, unless she had a permanent. She was obese, about five feet tall and always wore old worn-out house dresses. She smoked cigarettes and had nicotine on her fingers and smelled like smoke. She was sedentary although she loved to cook and bake and make grape jelly. She did not look like the other mothers. But she was mine and I loved her and my stepfather very much. And I know they loved me.

This winter season holds both Christmas, New Year, my physical birthday and my spiritual birthday. These were special red-letter

---

[19] Jim Rohn, *The Seasons of Life Dallas* (Texas: Jim Rohn International, 1971).

days for me. I grew up poor, even though most times I did not know it. Only at the end of the month when the refrigerator was empty, and we had ketchup and mayonnaise sandwiches because the peanut butter and jelly and bologna and cheese were all gone. And I enjoyed pancakes for dinner too!

On Christmas, it was like magic. Everything I asked for would appear under the tree even though I was poor. My mother would start getting ready months ahead of time. She would remind me to be a good girl and keep my room clean and take care of the toys I already had and Santa would bring me more. So I would actually give all my dolls a bath, wash their hair and braid it and wash their clothes. Then they would be lined up in my room ready to meet Santa Claus. I always wanted to stay up and see him too. But as soon as I heard his bells I went to bed and closed my eyes in fear that he would not leave my heart's desire. My favorite Christmas was the year Barbie came out. I not only wanted the dolls, but the case and a wardrobe. I can still see the tree with six little hangers on the tree with Barbie's clothes and the black truck style case under the tree with a beautiful blonde-haired Barbie in it.

It felt like magic! I found out as an adult that those clothes were not Barbie clothes. My friend had hand-made them for me because Barbie clothes were more expensive than children's clothes back then. But I did not know the difference and was thrilled. I used boxes to make the camper and play for hours traveling around the United States in my imagination! I have always loved Christmas. The best thing about winter is to end the year and begin another in a day. It always reminded me of how fast time is moving. It helps me to create new perspectives, priorities and goals.

Epiphany is an awakening to new ideas and the serendipity and special surprises that new beginnings bring. Epiphany represents when the wise men came to see Jesus and brought him gifts. As a child we would go to church to celebrate that on the Sunday after New Year's Day, after being in church on New Year's Eve too. I was Catholic and it seemed I was always in church. But I looked forward to it, learning about all the celebrations. So Epiphany… my mother would sometimes save a special surprise gift for me leftover from Christmas. It was called, "Little Christmas" by my Italian friends. I still love the idea of Epiphany. My mother told me to seek Jesus like the wise men. And that became my quest. I wanted to know and love Jesus like my mother.

Winter is where I found wisdom, it was the thread I was looking for my whole life. It would bring true success and it comes from God in the person of Jesus. A lifetime journey of searching led me home to wisdom where it would all begin to come together to teach me what I would need to know to live a good life. To be able to pass on to others a legacy of love like my mother had passed to me.

CHAPTER 6

Being a Wife and Mother and Becoming a Superwoman

Hello, New Self Again (A Wallflower Has Bloomed)

I found a good babysitter for a couple of days a week. It feels so good to be back to work as a nurse. To get away from the routine for just a couple of hours. I really enjoy it—and I really enjoy coming home! I am much happier, which makes me a better wife and mother, when I am working. I want to be someone besides Rose Yerka, wife and mother. I am now Rose Yerka, nurse and Fashion 220[20] consultant and manager. Fashion 220 is the trailblazer in water-based skin technology; also selling fragrances and hair products of the highest quality. It is nice to be someone. It helps to round things out. Your life cannot be completed by other people's lives. It's got to be yours. I feel like a woman now—a whole woman.

Married Life

I was happy, but I felt fragile. Why? I was four years younger than my husband and unprepared for the stress of marriage, and

---

[20] Fashion 220 Cosmetics, https:/www.fashion220.net (Aurora, Ohio, 1962).

a new nursing career. Then within the two years of becoming the mother of two children, fifteen months apart, I felt overwhelmed. I saw the disappointment on my husband's face when he saw the piles of laundry. He hugged me when I cried for no apparent reason. I felt so unhappy, tasting my salty tears and smelling his English Leather, mixed with my Wind Song and it did not comfort me. I thought I should be happy; we are good together. This is my dream. Why am I so unhappy? Is this all there is? I felt nervous and overwhelmed when I heard the baby cry and saw the piles of dirty diapers in the pail. I had so much work to do before I went to work.

The nights were the worst. I could not sleep and was up all hours of the night with the baby. I felt so tired. I was working part time at Cherry Hill Hospital and Underwood Hospital as a nurse with the pool. My mother watched the kids while I got some sleep before going to work. Many days I could not sleep, so I would go to the liquor store to buy a six pack of beer to help me sleep. I would pick up beer nuts or roasted nuts to go with it. I loved the salty flavor of the peanuts to cover the nasty taste of the beer. I never liked beer before. I remember putting on baby powder to cover the smell of the alcohol so my mother would not know that I had been drinking. I loved that smell and it made me feel less guilty. Why am I so sad? I should be happy. Is this all there is? I would fight with my prince because I was not happy.

After all, I thought it was his job to make me happy. He said," I got you everything you wanted. A house, a car and kids! What else do you need to be happy?" I do not know. Maybe they would all be better off without me. Something must be wrong with me. I am mentally ill like my aunts. It must run in my family.

The Plan

Bob said, "You are sick. You need a doctor." *Maybe he is right*, I thought. I will get an appointment and get the medicine and just go to sleep. I cannot handle this emotional pain anymore. Lord, forgive me. I know I am wrong to think this way. I do not want to hurt my husband and children. Lord, help me. At work, I saw two unusual cases. One lady had a heart attack and was screaming out, "Lord, forgive me. I am sorry. Don't send me back there!" She was stiff as a board like she had rigor mortis. I tried to calm her down to no avail. She kept saying the same things over and over and crying out. Then I felt goosebumps. I asked myself, *Is there really a place called hell? What did she do to go there? She looks like a nice lady.* Please don't send me there, Lord. I know suicide is wrong, but you already know how I am feeling and what I am thinking. Please forgive me now.

Then at another hospital I had a male patient who was in a coma. I was giving him a bed bath behind the curtain. He opened his eyes and started to talk to Jesus. He said," Lord Jesus, I need one more day." Nurse, please call my wife to come in to see me." I got goosebumps again. I dropped the washcloth in the basin and ran out of the room. I thought, "Is he really seeing you, Lord or hallucinating?" His wife came and he told her everything she needed to know about the household business. The next day, he was gone.

I found out he died on the bridge as they were transferring him to a Philadelphia hospital. The time of death was exactly the same time I had charted his wake from the coma. I got goosebumps again. I guess it is real. Is there really an exact time to die? Can I go sooner? Lord, forgive me for what I am thinking of doing, but you already know. My family will be better off without me.

The Voice
January 17, 1977

One morning as I laid on my couch, trying to get to sleep and planning what doctor to go to see for the medicine, I was flicking the television channels and drinking my beer. I heard a voice that sounded strong and commanding like a drill sergeant. "There is someone in the TV audience contemplating suicide. Don't do it. Jesus loves you and has a plan for your life!" My jaw dropped and I fell to my knees. And cried. "Is that you God? Are you real? Do you see me here? Do you really have a plan for me?" I prayed with the man to receive the gift of New Life from Jesus, and forgiveness of my sins from his death on the cross for me. I remember feeling fresh spring air in my living room with no windows open. It was like breathing fresh air from heaven. I felt warm, like someone was hugging me. Tears of joy streamed down my face. I was laughing and crying at the same time. The peace I felt in my heart felt like a security blanket on me, the Insecure Princess.

I learned that Jesus was the Real Prince I was looking for, I was his daughter and that made me a Royal Princess. He was the one who knew me since before I was born. He sees me and has a plan for my life. He meets all my needs. He saw me crying for help and rescued me from myself. He filled me with the Joy of His Presence.

The Second Epistle to the Corinthians 5:17 says, "Therefore if anyone is in Christ, he or she is a New Creation. The old is gone and the New has come."

"Joy is Prayer. Joy is Strength. Joy is Love. Joy is the part of Love by which you can catch–someone"—Mother Teresa on Joy (*The Joy of Loving*, 1997, Viking Penguin).

After so many changes, new roles and raging hormones in my short twenty-three years, I experienced real changes from the inside out. My face had changed when I looked in the mirror to wash my face from my tears. I looked peaceful and joyful, and I had a sparkle in my eyes. I had a 360-degree turnaround. I was joyful and excited to share about My Coming to Jesus Experience!

My search ended in the winter of 1977. I had a baby boy and he was the best Christmas gift ever. My second child was born on December 17, 1976. I now had a rich man's family, a girl who was sixteen months old and a new baby boy! He would be our tax deduction and was born in the bicentennial year of America. I knew I should be happy. I was happily married with a good husband, a home, a nursing career, a part time business as a beauty consultant with a company car. I was blessed and I knew it. Then why did I feel overwhelmed, sad, depressed and suicidal? My hormones were roaring out of control. It felt like postpartum depression. I was drinking about a six pack of beer a day, which only made things worse. My husband was at a loss. He asked me "What more do you want to be happy?" He did not understand, and I did not know what was wrong at that time. I decided to go to a psychiatrist and get medication to take and just go to sleep forever. As a Catholic, I knew it was wrong, but I knew God already knew and He would have to forgive me for being stupid and out of control. I just could not go on. I asked for forgiveness ahead of time.

I had to go back to work and the pool seemed to be the best idea. Night work would be best. My husband would be on the night shift and my mother would watch the kids in the morning while I could get some sleep. It was working, but one morning I almost fell asleep at the wheel and found myself on the median strip in the middle of Route 295 on my way home from Cherry Hill Medical Center. I saw the bumper sticker on the car in front of me. It said, "Do not be caught dead without Jesus." Tears fell from my eyes while my heart raced with fear. I was almost killed today anyway.

It was just another day except I could not sleep. I kept thinking about how else I could kill myself, but I was scared. I just wanted this pain to end. My kids were with my mom. I turned on the TV to take my mind off my feelings.

For the first time after twelve years of Catholic school and weekly church attendance, I felt God's presence. And for the first time, I heard the Good News and read it in red letters in my Catholic Bible. It said, "You must be born again of the spirit." I felt the life changing power of God come into my heart as I opened it to Him. I had a Spiritual Birthday. It was the best day of my life, even to this day. I since then celebrate my Spiritual Birthday every year and I am ever so grateful to my Lord and Savior who sees me and hears my prayers.

Now I realize there was not a day that the Lord was not with me. He was walking by my side all my life. Jeremiah 1:4 says, "Before I formed you in the womb I knew you, before you were born, I set you apart." I waited for that day when I would come to the end of myself and invite Him to be the Lord of my life.

The First Red-Letter Day

This was the *first red-letter day* that I experienced. That means I wrote in red in my journal so as not to forget the details of this special day. Now I need to learn to listen. Psalm 46:10 says, "Be still and know that I am God" (NIV). Proverbs 16:3 says, "Commit to the Lord whatever you do and he will establish your plans" (NIV). My life now had a new purpose and meaning. He would give me the wisdom I need to be a good wife, mother, nurse and businesswoman.

Winter is where I found wisdom, it was the thread I was looking for my whole life. It would bring true success and it comes from God in the person of Jesus. A lifetime journey of searching led me home to wisdom where it would all begin to come together to teach me what I would need to know to live a good life. To be able to pass on to others a legacy of love like my mother had passed to me.

I learned much later in life that step 12 is to spread the message and pass it on and to practice in all of my affairs. And know that more would be revealed in God's time as you grew to be and become more. Wisdom in the seasons is where it all begins. Learning who I am and who I want to be. Step 1 is knowing that when everything is out of control, I can trust in God, my higher power to take control. Knowing that I John says, "God is Love." Winter is my season of love, my favorite season. My life has come full circle on my forty-fifth spiritual birthday. It is a joy to be and become the person He wants me to be. This is my story that started in the season of winter. I learned about love as a gift from God. Galatians 5:22 says, "The fruit of the spirit is love, joy, peace…"

The Devil Comes to Steal, Kill, and Destroy

So the first person I called was my mother. To my surprise I heard her Irish temper kick in. "What are you doing? You are Catholic. You know those TV ministers are very rich men and cannot be trusted, especially Billy Graham. Maybe you do need a doctor to help you. You do not need a TV church. You have a church!" I was devastated. Maybe she is right? Bob said," You did what? Prayed with the TV?

You do need help! Make an appointment with a doctor." So as fast as it came that day, it was stolen away. My sadness returned. But I did start reading the Book of John from the Bible. I got to chapter three, verse three: "No one can see the kingdom of God unless he is born again." Verse five, Born of the Spirit and verse sixteen, I remember. John 3:16 says, "For God so loved the world that he gave His only Son so that whosoever believes in him should not perish but have everlasting life." That stayed in my mind.

I asked God to show me if it was true. The changes I noticed was that I was no longer afraid of death. I was more patient and kind with my husband and children.

Being Changed by the Word of God to Become a Christian

I met a Christian lady named Diane. She had a Bible on her coffee table. She opened it and showed me John:3. I told her I was Catholic. She said that is fine, Jesus loves us all. She invited me to a Billy Graham movie that night. The movie was called, "Never Alone,"[21] it was about a woman who tried to commit suicide by putting her head into her oven. Her phone kept ringing, and someone invited her to a Billy Graham Crusade. I was sobbing. I signed up to get a Bible Study, called Peace with God[22]. My mother said, "We Catholics never study the Bible. Be careful, they will be asking you for money. You wait and see." I thought, not yet.

IT IS YOU AFTER ALL GOD! YOU SEE ME!

The Gift of Another Chance

Just as a new season gives a second chance to finish well for your year's goals, this "newborn again spring season" would bring a new maturity for a secure princess growing into a Christian woman.

---

[21] Billy Graham, *Never Alone* (Minneapolis, MN: World Wide Pictures, 1976).
[22] Billy Graham, *Peace with God* (Tennessee: Nelsen, 1953).

Growing Pains

February 18, 1977

I am getting old—twenty-three years old. My diary is now six years old. I really enjoy going back and rereading things. It is like portions of my life flashing before me once again. It makes me feel old, yet good. And good feeling loved. It helps me realize where my head was and helps me understand myself then and now by how I was then. Everyday seems like a new beginning—Life goes through cycles. And I learn something from each experience. I hope someday Tara will get to know me through my diary and help her through trying times in her life. And realize I was through the same things. I love to think and write things down that mean much to me then at this time because I find they mean even more to me and remind me of the person I am and what makes me tick.

Survival and Then Some "Superwoman"[23]

Life's meaning can become blurred when we view it through dirty windows. What are my expectations of life? Do they measure up to the reality that I see? No wonder I feel disillusioned. My American Dream has turned into a nightmare! I wish I could wake up!

"Dirt out the door and under the rug!" How to be a wife, mom and all-around superwoman? Gotta learn shortcuts! Of course!

- TV dinners from the freezer to the oven to the table helps very much. And fast food in a pinch
- Permanent press from the washer to the dryer to the hanger in the closet
- Pampers and Sesame Street babysitters and convenience stores

---

[23] Shirley Conran, *Superwoman* (New York: Crown Publishing,1978).

This is just to name a few. What would a modern woman do without such things? Housework is another necessity of sorts. But superwomen, like me, cannot afford to be fanatical or even efficient, just smart! At least that is what I thought.

After all, what difference does it make to sweep the dirt under the rug? None. Except when my clumsy company trips over the uphill rug. That is when my acting skills come in handy. "Oh my, where in the world did that come from?" I asked with dismay! For the most part I thought if dirt was out of sight, it was out of mind, until rude awakenings like this one. It can be swept out the door for months but even steps get dirt buildup and eventually even that dirt needs to be swept down the driveway and into the flower bed until spring. Before I got the dishwasher to hide the dirty dishes, I had to make do. I found the oven to be suitable, especially for dirty pots and pans. You will know when it is time to get busy washing when there is nothing to cook with or a foul odor in the kitchen. You will know where to look first! Of course, there are things that a woman like me keeps a secret for years and never would admit to without a lot of guilt. Well, the secrets in my closet, under the bed, the rugs, in the oven and out my door finally caught up with me after many years. It was the same with my spiritual condition. Everything looked fine on the outside. But on the inside, what a mess!

March 1977

Kids are able to keep each other occupied. Tara loves John and John's legs and arms start flying just at the sight of Tara, no matter what she does to him! She's getting to be such a good "Little Person." Sometimes she drives me bananas! She is so much like me and we go around! VERY STUBBORN like her father!

April 1977

Easter month—thank goodness holidays don't come too often. Trying to get both kids ready and getting them dressed is a job.

I had started to go to church for lent and did go until it was over. I enjoyed it. It helped me to be a stronger person. We got some pictures of the kids. They make holidays memorable for me too! Bless John. We miss him. He always enjoyed the holidays.

May 1977

Mother's Day was nice. Being a mother is nice. It's only once in a while that I truly enjoy it. Mainly the little things like, "I love you, Mom" or "Hi, Mom, what are you doing?" or "Mommy's baby." And when we get a bath together, Tara washes my back! I love it! I always wanted a daughter to love so much and help me be a good mother and still let her love me through it all.

My son, when he smiles and needs me, falls asleep in my arms; it all makes being a mother an experience I'd never want to forget. There are other times when I'd like to hang from the chandelier (if I had one) just to get away! But I love them all—even my BIG ONE bought me a watch!

I concluded my four-month qualification for my company car! I couldn't get it too soon. My car is dying before my eyes. I hope it lasts six months. It makes me so proud that I will have earned it. It's a real achievement. Bob is so proud of me.

May 28, 1977
Special Birthday and a Lesson to Remember

One birthday, my friend Kathy gave me a ticket to see Elvis in concert in Philadelphia at the Spectrum. We were both fans. The concert would not be until May 28, 1977.

With excitement, we went to the show. It was high energy and exciting and packed. As I was enjoying the show, I started to notice things about Elvis. He had blown up like a balloon. Even his neck was huge. He seemed to be winded and was sweating profusely. I said to my friend after the show, "I am worried about Elvis. I think he has heart trouble." My friend laughed at me and told me it was just my imagination and that he had put on a wonderful, high-energy show. Anyone would be sweating after that performance.

On August 16, 1977, Elvis died of a heart attack. I was sad, but not surprised. Observation is one of the things about being a nurse. It made me happy that I had seen one of his last shows. It would be one of his final bows. Life is uncertain, even for the rich and famous. Lesson: Live one day at a time as if it is to be your last. Learning to relax and enjoy life. Spend extra time with the Lord, getting to know him better.

The Great Escape, 1977

Something new and different I could not see except into my mind, and there I found only darkness, but I could not stop now. I followed my mind until my whole being was enclosed in the contentment of inner peace. All I had searched for throughout my whole life and never found, was with me all the time. All I had to do was take a look inside myself. If you could read my mind, you would be as confused as I am! My mind is my most precious possession. It seems my whole being is controlled by the fine piece of infinity created by someone far greater than I. For sometimes this device called my mind runs away with me and I race through time and space at the speed greater than light or sound. Sometimes it takes me a couple of minutes to return to the rat race of everyday reality. How do I love to fly? My mind has taken me places no jet plane, boat or rocket can compare. For no one but me can travel through the mirror maze of channels in this land of enchantment, this place called my mind.

Reflections on Brokenness

Is that you GOD? Do you know me?
Psalm 46:10…and know…(NIV)
Psalm 13:5 Take Questions to God…Trust in his unfailing love…
Jeremiah 1:5, "Before I formed you in the womb I knew you" (NIV).

Things to Remember… Jesus Changes Everything

"The most exhausting thing in life is being insecure," by Anne Morrow Lindberg, (Elliot, Debbie, "Long Lasting 'Gift,'" February 26, 2006, heard on *All Things Considered*.) Before I had religion and after I had a relationship. Memories of becoming born again. Before I was struggling, looking for happily ever after. I was insecure, afraid and felt unloved. I had guilt and shame about my feelings. I felt sad, angry and depressed. I was tormented in my mind with suicidal thoughts.

Hearing God's Voice

After I experienced emotional healing and joy, I felt love like a security blanket wrapped around me. I felt joy in the presence of my God who saw my tears. Have you ever felt insecure? Can a person be insecure or only our environment? Have you ever asked who am I? Did you wear a mask to hide the real you? Did you know that God loves you and has a plan and purpose for your life? I did not.

Springtime is time for training and working hard. It can be a whirlwind of activities and plans. What seeds are you planting?

Finding Joy in the Spring…a time to plant.

My favorite song to describe the Springtime of my life is "Love Grows Where my Rosemary Goes"[24] by Edison Lighthouse (1971).

Love is growing.

End of Part 2

---

[24] Edison Lighthouse, "*Love Grows*" (England: Universal Publishing Group, 1970).

PART 3

SUMMER

**Twelve-Step Journey to a Fruitful Life
How to take two steps forward
and one step backward
Bargaining/ Depression/ Finding a better Way
July, August, and September 1978–2015
Finding (Love) Patience, Kindness, Goodness**

In summer, be careful of the pesky weeds that will try to take over the garden of your life. It is time to work hard so you can also have some time to rest and enjoy the warm weather. Being outside in nature can teach many good things even from God's creatures.

Look at the birds of the air, they do not worry. Even a dragonfly takes time to rest. The hummingbirds and butterflies delight us with their beauty and grace. They work hard in the summer season to prepare for his return flight back to South America along with the Monarchs.

Summer is a season of great growth and preparation. Seeing the fruit of your labor from the Spring season and preparation for the harvest. Learning to find rest and be still in God's presence.

The Gift of Another Season, A New Season of Growth

Just as a new season gives a second chance to finish well for your year's goals, this "new born-again summer season" would bring a new maturity for a secure princess growing into a Christian woman.

Maturity

The greatest inheritance I can leave my children and their children is a Christian foundation and legacy and Christ Centered Education. I was not sure what that would look like, as I was still attending my Catholic Church. And now I am there every Sunday, thirsty to learn the Bible. I went to twelve years of Catholic School, so I felt I had a good education even though I did not know the Bible. In 1963, Bible reading, and prayer was taken out of the public school by judicial fiat. Humanism was the replacement at the Junior High School level. So I wanted to learn everything I could to be ready to teach my children. I had been restored back to a life of purpose, everything seemed to be falling into place. The joy I had was proof like the glass slipper that validated Cinderella's identity. I have been with the Prince of Peace, Jesus, and He has changed my life.

CHAPTER 7

Being a Superwoman and Becoming a Successful Businesswoman

I started my career with Fashion 220 at a seminar. I was just curious but became intrigued with what I saw and heard. These were regular people succeeding in their own business. This is what I wanted. I think what impressed me the most was all the people, about two thousand in one room and the excitement of all of them was contagious!

All I needed was the desire to succeed and the strength and determination to keep striving for the better things in life. I came home and booked twenty-five shows, held seven in one week, and fifty-one in seven weeks and became a manager! Wow! Seventy-six in all!

My next seminar was with Bob. We went to Hartford, Connecticut. It was fun. It was nice to get away even though I was looking very pregnant by now. The city and hotel were beautiful. We took pictures. I got excited and did another forty-niner. We were invited to a filet barbecue. I love my job! I can make so much more money, make my own hours and work around my family. Everyone thought it was anything but simple to leave Underwood Hospital, but I was happy to quit. My life is so much better than before, and I love what I do!

See You at the Top/Dreams Do Come True—the Company Car

Completed my next forty-niner to start qualifying for my company car. It won't be too soon as my car is starting to die. I will miss it because it is the first car I purchased on time for myself. I hope it lasts for six months while I finish my qualification. Six months later I got the papers in the mail to go pick up my car. I was so excited! Bob kept reading the papers over and over. "Are you sure this is legal?" As we were given the keys to drive it home, I said" Guess so!" I was so PROUD of myself. I did it! I really needed to do something that was my own thing. I was working for myself and it was fun! I tried to accomplish each challenge and was rewarded for each accomplishment. I wore a huge silver charm bracelet, lots of jewelry, beautiful clothes, and drove a company car. Now I am a successful businesswoman!

Not Mediocre Anymore

I was on my way to the top now! Except for one major distraction. I was so, so busy with my business and Tara I had no idea that I had missed several periods and was now expecting another baby again! How could I do it all and have it all?

The Good, The Bad, and the Uncertain Cost of Success
Look back to look ahead

When I think I am twenty-three years old. I have been married for three years have lived in four different places have been pregnant for eighteen of the thirty-six months, have two children, a house, a dog, a cat, two cars have had four different jobs, *I feel old*! Sometimes I feel confined, but most of the time happy and lucky to have a wonderful husband and two beautiful children.

The Grass Is Always Greener

My friends' lives look so tempting. They have freedom, good jobs, nice cars and clothes. But what else do they have? It is not what you have in life that makes you happy but who you have to share what you have with that keeps you happy. Profound thought!

Stinking Thinking, Feeling Ugly

Everyone loves a winner; that's why no one likes me. Maybe this time I'll be lucky. Maybe this time I'll win. There are many contradicting thoughts quarreling in my head. It seems to be a war between the good, the bad and the uncertain. There will only be one loser, me.

Some people can die before death. For these people lose their spirit before it leaves their body. And their minds close themselves to the outside world. That person becomes alone with herself. Without other people, different ideas, new experiences, without change and without giving the world a fair chance. All growth for her will stop. Without thought and change there is no life.

Choose Life

The first step for me is to return to where life exists. On my own will, then and there, I will begin to choose between life and death.

Surviving an Emotional Divorce "A house is not a home."

What a Joke! Marriage means no time for love. It means hard work and aggravation. Unfortunately, it also means loneliness at times. I found myself turning to a familiar friend, alcohol. It took my worries away! I love my house and I love my kids and my security. But most of all I love my husband. And I miss him very much since we have had children. We are so busy there seems to be no time for romance. It is coming up on our 4th anniversary and it is starting to get to me. Love is slow growing, and I can tell because sometimes it hurts like a growing pain in my heart.

Lord, help us rekindle our love. THEN CAME MARRIAGE ENCOUNTER. IS THAT YOU GOD? I saw the notice on a bulletin board at the Catholic school where I was taking a speed-reading course. It said, "Take a Fresh Look at Your Marriage." I grabbed it and put it in my purse. I thought, "We need this." I put the coupon in the mail. Two days later a woman called. She said she is calling from Marriage Encounter. I thought, *No way. That is for old people, not us.* My friend's parents went there. So I started to offer excuses. "We cannot afford it. It is too soon. I do not know if I can get a babysitter. We are having problems in our marriage." She said that was the reason I should have planned to come this weekend. It can change your lives. "So after not talking to Bob all week, I invited him to pay for a weekend away. I said, "Isn't our marriage worth it?" He reluctantly agreed to go.

Growing Together
Marriage Encounter—Love Is a Decision and Hard Work
May 1978

Dear Jesus, thank you for helping us find marriage encounter. It put new life and happiness into our relationship. We were nervous, had a fight on the way and right after we got there, Bob had brought beer with him and planned on watching the football game. They kept us so busy we could not even go to the car. Sometimes we even fought about how to do what they were teaching us! But it was worth it. We are growing again! Love is growing again. "Search and you shall find." Thank you for giving me the wisdom to know it was time to start looking for you again. You know I love you. But I easily stray by getting caught up in all the worldly things. Thank you for leading me to the right people in my search. I finally feel adored by my husband. We learned that love is a decision not a feeling.

November 3, 1978
Finding Me, the Beauty

Dear Bob, thank you for four wonderful years! I can't imagine my life without you. It was you who helped me find me and now we are us. We make a good team, brains and beauty, a good combination. Please remind me how much I love you when the going gets rough. Let us become closer and never drift apart. We have many years together and I hope they will be just as wonderful as the first four years. You make my life worthwhile, show me the way, make me feel loved and are the lights of my life. You are my better half. I love you always. Happy anniversary, Rose. Lord, help me try to like myself as much as I love Bob.

October/November 1978
The Call
Is That You, God?

Dear Jesus, I had several things happen to make me realize that it was you I was searching for, not all the things I ran after.

Reaching Up and Out
Learning to Pray

You lead me to a prayer meeting I never thought I would be interested in. I was scared the first time, but I found nice people to support and help me there. As my mother and husband made me doubt what was happening to me. My enemy tried to steal what you had planted in my heart. You were speaking to me. I just never listened!

January 11, 1979
Bob's Conversion

The night before I had read the Bible about you Lord, knocking at my door. All I had to do was to invite you into my life. Tonight, at about 8:30 p.m., three Billy Graham evangelists knocked on my door. They were following up about a movie I had gone to and the Bible study they sent to me. They prayed with Bob and I to receive you as our Lord and Savior. It felt so good. It is like a relief of tension, I felt so happy! Now, Bob understood what I was talking about.

Getting Ready for the Next Season

Thank you for a beautiful Christmas. It was so nice having you as our guest. Help me keep preparing my heart and my house for your return. Teach me to pray about everything and to do so your will.

January 15, 1979
Faithful to Pray the List

Dear Jesus,

1. Please help me with our meeting (FTT Rosebuds). Help our girls do well.
2. Please help me have enough money for sales tax for our car.
3. For Kathy to get better physically and draw her to Yourself.
4. Help Mike to feel better. He looks frail. I love him.
5. My mother draws close to you and stops cursing, it's not like her.
6. Aunt Fran and family grow close through rebirth, new baby.
7. Jim (atheist) starts seeing You everywhere and Joan. They had a fire, and their cat saved their lives Praise the Lord!
8. Mary Jane guide and heals her marriage with Jack.
9. Betty Yerka to be herself, we love her. Lead her to You.
10. Roby's father can be healed through You.

Please help me help others and do Your will.

Love,
Rose

A Gentle, Quiet Spirit

Help me develop a quiet spirit. Sometimes I feel like screaming. If you want me to be quiet. Why did you give me a big mouth?

January 17, 1979

Dear Jesus, thank you for being with me during a trying day yesterday. Please take my impatience and temper away. Help me speak soft and kind like a Christian should. Help me change into the person you want me to be. I feel tired today. Give the strength to get up and go to get started right. I pray for those who cannot get up physically like Mike. Please take charge of his life and give him something to look forward to. Please use me today wherever you may and give me the strength to do your will.

I love you,
Rose

January 18, 1979
An Instrument for Your Hand

Dear Jesus, I could never thank you enough for dying for my sins, so help me love you more and more. That is why I write to you every day to make me love you more and to grow. It is so easy when I just take time to look around at the beauty you have made. The snow was beautiful yesterday. Please make my soul white as snow and point me in your direction because that is where I want to be. Please mold me into the person you want me to be. Use me as an instrument for your hand. I love you, Rose

January 19, 1979
Lead My Life

Dear Jesus, help me grow steadfast in my faith and be like an apostle for the Good News. Please lead my life. I feel incapable. Help me get through this busy day and let the training go well. Heal my family and friends, and the friends I have not met yet and give the whole world your peace. I love you. Thank you for another day.

January 29, 1979

Dear Jesus, I want to do what You want me to do. I want to be what You want me to be. Please change me. I am disgusted with myself. Please make me become reborn so I can be" just any old ass," to do your work. Let myself decrease and Yourself increase.

February 25, 1979

To be surrounded by your love so powerful and strong that you collapse me into the arms of the lover. Thank you, Lord Jesus, for filling me with your spirit. A tingling warm rushing feeling from my head to my toes and an overwhelming dizziness until I could no longer stand. I give you my life, mold me, shape me.

February 26, 1979

Dear Jesus, For the first time ever, I truly feel the love of Your Father. It feels warm like the sunshine and soft like satin. I felt full and heavy, so much that You brought me to my knees and back. I felt surrounded with Your love and just so much so that I collapsed into Your arms. I don't know what it was or why, but thank You, Lord, for making Your presence of Yourself and your spirit known. I know You're in my heart, and I love You oh so much! Please give me the strength to set time aside for You every day. You are all that truly matters in my life, because You are the only one that cannot be taken away.

March 2, 1979
Break the Curse

Dear Jesus, today I like to lift up those getting baptized tonight, especially Bob and Kathy. Please draw them close to You Lord. Remove all doubts from their minds. Help me die to myself every day, and to stop cursing or screaming. Help me show Your love. I love You.

March 5, 1979
The Journey Begins

Dear Jesus, Thank you for this seminar. Let me feel comfortable with the tongue thing. Help those who expected an emotional experience and were let down. Jesus let them know through your spirit you are with them. I love you and am ready for our journey.

March 2, 1979

Dear Jesus, please forgive me for the numerous sins I committed against You this week. I'm truly sorry and ashamed that You gave me many opportunities to be a Christian and I blew them all! Give me the strength and determination to try harder and die to myself, Lord.

April Fool's

April started with a snowstorm and a spiritual storm. Mother Nature said, "April Fools!" The Lord taught me not to be fooled by appearances and not to believe every spirit and things are not always as they seem. I was learning spiritual discernment. A lesson I would need for a lifetime of Victory in Christ. The Spirit world is just as real as the physical world. The Bible says, we do not fight against flesh and blood but against principalities and powers in high spiritual places. Bring every thought into captivity to the Lord Jesus. Faith is like a blossom that buds from within. Our faith, as a newly married couple, had carried us forward about five years in our relationship. Then we said, "OK God, we can take it from here." We had each other and a rich man's family, so it seemed like that. "All was well."

April 1, 1979
Spiritual Warfare

Bob is a jokester. He woke me up today saying, "Hurry up, the kids are late for school!" After I rushed out of bed, I looked at the calendar and realized it was Saturday. "April Fool's," he shouted. I was so mad at him. But he had made breakfast of pancakes and sausage and dressed the kids. So I forgave him quickly.

He did have to work and help a friend. I had a Fashion Two Twenty Show, so the kids would be dropped by my mothers. We would not see each other till dinner time. The weather forecast is crazy today. It says possible snow for today. But no worries, they are wrong at least 50 percent of the time. It is spring and looks beautiful outside. I wore my normal attire of suit and heels carrying the purple cases filled with makeup supplies and placed them in the back of my own silver Pacer. That was my favorite car. Mainly because it was my first car with payments. It kind of looked like a space capsule with a big hatch back window. It has been acting a little strange lately. Sometimes it would not start. But it was not the starter or the alternator. I would stay home all day. When Bob got home it would start right up. Much to my surprise. But I was happy that nothing was wrong.

My show was in Stratford off of the White Horse Pike about forty minutes from my home in Westville. While I was at the show it started to snow. By the time I was done, it looked like a blizzard outside. The roads were icy, and the visibility was poor. I called Bob to tell him I was on my way home and that I would pick up the kids. A short distance along the pike, my car acted like it was going to stall out and started to sputter. I pulled into an automotive store just in case we needed a part. I asked to use the phone to call home for help. When Bob got there the store was closing. The car started right up again like before. So Bob said, "I will take your car the back way home through Deptford. You take my car on Route 295. The roads seem a little better that way." That sounded like a good plan. We kissed goodbye and said, "See you soon."

Within about ten minutes as I got onto Route 295, I felt the feeling of *dread*. I heard this loud voice in my mind, "Your husband will be killed in a car accident tonight and you will be a widow like your mother-in-law." I felt cold chills all over my body that went down my spine. I cried out, "No, Lord! Do Something! Send Your angels! Surround the car and protect my husband! I am not strong like my mother-in-law. I cannot take care of two children by myself! Please intervene and stop this accident!" I cried and sobbed and prayed all the way home. What I noticed was that I did not know what words to pray. I just opened my mouth and words that I did not understand were flowing out of my mouth. I thought, is this really happening? Is this you God? Are you praying for me? I felt peaceful knowing that God was in control of whatever was happening to my husband. I Corinthians 14:2 says, "For anyone who speaks in a tongue does not speak to people but to God. Indeed, no one understands them; they utter mysteries by the Spirit" (NIV).

I had seen other people speak in different tongues at prayer meetings at the Catholic Charismatic meetings, and I thought it was fake. Bob and I decided we didn't want anything to do with such things. Now in my desperation I find that the Spirit of God is making intercession for me and my husband because I do not know how to pray. I was overwhelmed with the presence of God in my car all the way down Route 295 to West Deptford.

When I arrived at my mother's house to pick up the kids, I called Bob. He was already home, safe and sound. So I felt foolish to say anything. I decided it was my imagination and let it go. Did not even mention it to my mother. When I got home after we put the kids to bed, Bob said, " I want to tell you something. Your car is crazy and something is wrong with it. It is an electrical problem. When I was driving along Almonesson Road in Deptford, your car shut down completely; there were no lights, no brakes, and the doors and windows were locked and there was no power! I was going into the other lane and ready to hit a car head on. I thought I had to break the window and jump out. But I kept trying to start it over and over and needed to decide within seconds. I never prayed so hard in my life! All of a sudden it turned on, I was able to regain control back into my lane and missed the head-on collision within seconds. I thought my number was up! It was the scariest thing that had ever happened to me." I asked Bob if it had been about the time I was getting onto Route 295. He said, "Probably. Why?" I told him I knew it. And I shared the story with him. I asked, "Isn't that the road your father and uncle were killed on in a car accident?" Bob said, "Yes, I thought of that! Very strange." I replied, "Yes, and they were both thirty-three years old when they died like you are now. It is like a curse. I prayed against it in the Spirit. Bob said, "What do you mean?" I told him, "I knew I was praying all the way home to mom's house without understanding one word of what was coming out of my mouth." We looked at each other and both got goosebumps on our skin. Then we kneeled down and prayed. We thanked God for his intervention to save Bob from the accident. Bob rededicated his life to Christ that night.

Learning the Power of a Prayer Chain

I was attending the Catholic charismatic prayer group. My daughter Tara was sick, very sick. She had a very high fever, 106 degrees. Took her to Dr. Gekas for a shot and medication. He said if she got worse to call.

Later that day, instead of getting better, she was getting worst. The fever would not break. She was now also projectile vomiting. It was the scariest thing. She was reminding me of the Exorcist Movie. I called the doctor. He said, "Take her to Cooper Hospital. It may be meningitis!" I froze with fear!. Oh no! Lord help us.

I called our prayer chain and asked them to pray. Her fever was 106 degrees. I wrapped her in a blanket and we headed out.

When she got there in about fifteen minutes, they took her temperature. The nurse said it was 98.6. I said there must be something wrong with your thermometer! Take it again, please. Same result. I must have looked dumbfounded. She asked me, "Are you sure you know how to take a temperature?" Yes, I am a nurse too. I guess the Lord heard the prayers of all those on my prayer chain for my daughter.

Tara looked at me and said, "Can I have some juice?" They gave it to her, and she drained the cup. She smiled and said, "I guess Jesus fixed me, Mommy." Yes, he did. Thank You, Jesus!

Growing Pains

Learning the Business of Life
How to Hear from the Lord and Listen and Obey

After my second nursing job (after my second child), I decided to go into business for myself instead of nursing. It would be less stressful, and I could make my own hours. I was invited to a Fashion Two Twenty Cosmetic Show. It was fun and I became intrigued after hearing that the consultants make an average of $25.00 per hour. When I came home to tell my husband of my new adventure in careers, he was not too excited. He said, "You are too shy to do that kind of thing! You can't do it." My angered response was, "Wait! I will show you, I can!" And I did. I studied the products and the script, went to the training and was on my way. My best friend, Kathy, was at my first show.

Afterward, she laughed at me. She said, "You even told the same jokes!" I was doing show and tell and following the leader. But it was working. I was making more than double my full-time nursing job which only paid about $12.00 at that time.

My confidence grew and so did my clientele. I had formed a group called the Rosebuds. We were working together, and I became a branch manager. I had a new self-esteem. I felt good about what I was doing. I had to dress up and wear heels and make up every day.

I attracted business everywhere I went. My script was, "I have been so busy with my business… and people would ask what is your business? I would set up appointments every day. I had seven per week for seven weeks in a row. This was called a 49er. They had a silver charm bracelet, and I was winning so many charms, you could hear me coming anywhere. Everyone wanted to know what I was doing. Within six months, I won a company car! When we went to drive it off the lot, my husband went with me. He asked," Are you sure this is legal?" He read the papers all the way home. I was so proud that I had shown him what I could do.

We got invited to parties with new people and the Royal Road to Riches. This was a big national event. We went to Atlanta, Orlando and Las Vegas. The company would give out awards. My husband and I got to walk the purple carpet. We would be all dolled up for pictures. It was surreal. Made me feel like a famous person. When I would go for gas in my new company car, men would ask for my number and of course I would say, "Sorry I am married." I felt beautiful! It was very different from a real job. I was able to hire my neighbor to watch my kids during the day and clean my house. And my husband would watch them at night. I was very busy. As a branch manager I had an office with a closet filled with inventory. I did my own training and had parties for people who could not go to the big events. I loved my new life! But I did realize that beauty is only skin deep. Underneath my make-up I still had a sense of insecurity. I felt like Cinderella waiting for her shoe to drop!

From the Frying Pan into the Fire

When the Saudis buy a company, what does that mean? Especially when it was not announced! We found out via Wall Street. What a shock after years of dedication not to mention blood sweat, tears, smudged mascara, no shows and many overlooked insults, undigested meals and two speeding tickets to boot and many growing pains! "Is this all there is? Is this company the same?"

The Lord gave me the answer to that question. So I know the time has come to resign. I felt like I was getting a divorce. Many relationships are over five-years-old, and it hurt to give them up, but I did.

So when I heard that a Saudi Arabian businessman had purchased the company in early December, 1979, I actually felt sick to my stomach. I heard the Lord speak to me. He said, "It is no longer the same company. It is time to get out." I left the meeting in tears and excused myself, saying that I did not feel well.

My up line, Janet called me to check on me. When I told her that I would be leaving by December 31, 1979, she said I was just spooked. I tried to explain about hearing from the Lord, but she thought I was crazy.

So I started to sell all my inventory by doing Out of Business Sales. I gave back the company car and on January 1, 1980, I was done. That same day, the new company had put the products on the shelf and tripled the price of the product. They told their consultants that they could no longer sell at shows. All my branch manager friends lost all of the money they had invested into inventory. Some said to me, "Why didn't you tell me?" I told them I tried, but everyone thought I was crazy. "How did you know?" I told them, "The Lord told me!" He saved my husband and I from financial ruin. Thank you, Lord!

A Second Chance to Learn How to Do Business

Then I met a doctor who was excited about selling soap. That was just too much! However, curiosity does get the cat and me! I vowed that I would not go from the frying pan into the fire. The name of the company was Amway[25]. It's awesome to find a vehicle to make your dreams come true. It is like someone who gave you the key to open a door that had been locked for years and contained all of your hidden desires and hopes for the future.

---

[25] Charles Paul Conn, *The Possible Dream* (Old Tappan, New Jersey: Fleming H Revell Co., 1977).

No, I didn't go into the fire. We had struck the match to get the fire going. Our enthusiasm had been ignited for a chain reaction. Praise the Lord!

Life without dreams is empty. I believe we have not only been given dreams but also have been gifted with the ability to make them happen. With the Lord's help that is what we plan to do.

Broken dreams mean broken hearts, broken spirits and broken relationships. I never knew that until now. When you expect to be relaxing, soaking in the sun on the sandy beaches of Jamaica, enjoying the blue waters, white coconuts etc. and instead you are washing dishes, rinsing dirty diapers, cleansing toilets and making beds, it makes for a broken dream and broken spirit I will never take a chance on something in business again! It was not the business, it was me.

Never say never to the Lord. When He gives a dream, He is always reminding you of the dream. He will also tell you when the right company arrives in your life.

Unrealistic Expectations

Survival and then some. Life's meaning can become blurred when we view it through dirty windows. What are my expectations of life? Do they measure up to the reality that I see? No wonder I feel disillusioned. My American Dream has turned into a nightmare! I wish I could wake up! I am a mess!

May 20, 1979
A Major Mistake—Story of Spiritual
Discernment—Dying to Self

Dear Jesus, give me your strength to face myself and realize I am dead! I am nothing but everything I think I am not. I am a *mess*! Thank You for letting me learn to *hate* myself enough to want You to change me. Please, Lord, change *me*, not Bob, *change me*! Take away my stubbornness and bitterness. Turn it all into love and peace with me. Let me pour it out to those who hurt me. Lord, heal my pride.

I hate myself for being so small and weak. I am nothing without You. Help me always to give whatever glory there is Lord to You and not me. I am into the *pit*! I ask Your help to *demand* the enemy to let go of me. I am Yours, Lord. I am Yours. Help me save me from my enemies. I feel like I have been eaten up and vomited up again. I am at the lowest point of my life, Lord. I ask You; I give You myself completely today!

Spiritual Warfare and Hearing God's Voice…Learning Discernment
Learning to Hear the Voice of My Heavenly Father

Everyone has a story to tell. I knew Mrs. D. from my Catholic high school. I was happy to meet her at a marriage encounter meeting. She shared how marriage encounter had saved her marriage. I felt hopeful. She had three children. She hired a private detective to follow her husband, who she thought was having an affair, to find out he was a gambler. They were working on their communication with marriage encounter. They invited us to visit their home. So we went with our kids to play cards. The kids were sent to the basement to play. They were serving red wine and also offered grass (marijuana), much to my surprise. I had never tried it before, nor did I plan to. But they acted like it was no big deal. So I thought, why not? It would be nice to have new friends that were working on their marriage too. Many of my friends had already divorced.

After just one drag of the drug, I felt sick as a dog, the room was spinning, and I had to go lay down. The living room was red and black. When I closed my eyes, I saw things like a black shadow leaning over me, I heard laughing and taunting. "You are guilty. You are not holy! I got you now! You are a hypocrite, a fake! Where is your Jesus now?" Hecklers were laughing at me! I felt an evil, cold sensation on my body and I felt nauseous. I saw the dark shadow standing over me. I felt a heaviness on my chest like I could not breathe. My heart was racing with fear! I said, "We have got to get out of here and go home! I pulled myself up off the sofa and stood on my unsteady feet and walked, holding onto the wall so I would not fall. I held the railing to go to the basement to get to the bottom of the stairs and I saw the five children. I was descending the stairs and I smelled feces like a cesspool. My children looked like they saw a ghost, scared to death. The other two little girls were laughing and pointing to their naked little brother. He was covered in feces and had written on the wall with the feces. I could not make out what it said. What is going on? I asked sternly. The laughing stopped. I felt cold goosebumps on my skin again and felt an evil presence in that room too. I grabbed my kids by the hands and dragged them behind me up the stairs. I told my husband, "We are leaving!"

The parents both were also laughing and making light of the situation. They told me not to be mad, that I would feel better tomorrow. "Sorry you had a bad trip. Sometimes that happens the first time," they said. I assured them that "There would not be another time. This is my last time. I will never do that again."

The next day was Sunday. I went to my Catholic church as usual. Bob did not feel like going. He stayed home with the kids. He does not like my church. He was a Lutheran. He said," I go to church to pray. But every time I close my eyes to pray, I hear the people shuffling up and down, standing and kneeling. I can't pray or keep up with all that moving around. Might as well stay home. I don't understand all the rules of the Catholic Church. I had to sign my kids over just to marry you. And I cannot receive Communion with you because I am not Catholic." I knew what he meant. I do not agree with all those rules either, but I still have to go to church. Afterward, I stopped by my old school in Verga and parked all the way in the back where no one could see me. I was crying out to God to forgive me for last night. I cannot believe what I have done. What a fool I am! I confess my sin of going along with something I knew was wrong for me. I had betrayed myself. My own measure of rule, I could no longer trust myself to make the right decisions. I had believed a lie. It is a big deal for me. I realized these new people were not my friends. I don't even know them. I had scrambled my views to impress them. And much like scrambled eggs, you cannot unscramble them, sin has consequences. I started to cry uncontrollably. I surrendered my life to Jesus once again. My life had become unmanageable and out-of-control step 1 again! Step 2, I believe in a God to bring me back to sanity. I turned it over to Him. Step 3.

My fairy tale life had become a nightmare and my enemy was laughing at my fear and failure, I was broken and lost again. I feel depressed and disappointed with myself. I asked my Lord and my God to forgive me. Recognition that He hears my voice and sees my tears and knows my heart. I heard a small gentle kind voice of the Holy Spirit[26] speak to me. "My daughter, do not be afraid. You are of Me!" I felt love like a blanket over me. Lord, is that you? Do you see me? My Father God still loves me and adores me like His daughter. He offered me true unconditional love.

Adoration Is the Second Part of a Fairy Tale

I am amazed by His gentle yet powerful love like a hurricane over me. I felt goosebumps like warm healing over my whole body. The power of love and peace overshadowed the fear. Faith, hope and love replaced it. Lord, is that you? Do you see me?

When he called me daughter, I felt like a princess and daughter of the King. He recognized me as His own. I do not need to impress anyone anymore! He loves me. I can trust the God of history who promises that one day, "All will be Well."—Today it is well with my soul. I am living my own fairy-tale real-life story. My story is not done yet… It has only just begun!

My Mother's Conversion

My mom prayed with the TV too! She is also reading her Bible. She finally understands what I am talking about and now she is pray-

---

[26] Pat Robertson, *The Power of the Holy Spirit* (Washington, DC: Salem Books, 2022).

ing for her sisters. She is going to church with Aunt Franny. I am so happy. Thank you for letting me share the good news.

Now we are praying for my stepfather and her brother, my Uncle Jack. I have a long list of prayer requests because we have a big family.

Loss Of My Stepfather and a Supernatural Visitation February 17, 1981

My stepfather Marko, (whom I called Mike), was Slavic and stood about six feet tall. He was always smoking a pipe and I loved the smell of his cherry tobacco. He had one arm and one eye. He was in an accident at work on the tugboat. He looked like my grandfather, as he was ten years older than my mother. He always wore overall jeans and flannel shirts. We had a garden and pear trees and grapevines and chickens in the backyard. He worked hard outside most of the time. But then he got prostate cancer, and everything changed. I never saw him as handicapped. He was stronger than most men. It was hard seeing him go downhill. Lord, please help my stepfather. My mother brought my stepfather home from the hospital. There is nothing else they can do for him.

I am worried about him. He never went to church with us. He always waved his hand and shook his head no when I tried to talk to him about God. Now what is next for him? He has had a stroke. He cannot speak or move his right side. But as a nurse, I know he can hear me.

So I started to read him the Bible in the book of John. When I got to chapter three about being born again, I explained to him about salvation, that Jesus is preparing a place for him. I asked him if he wanted to invite Jesus in his life and to ask him to forgive his sins.

It seemed impossible. He looked like a zombie. So I asked him, "Mike, can you hear me? Do you want to receive Jesus?" He started to move his stub arm up and down. I could not believe my eyes. I started to cry. Then I prayed with him. Jesus, you answered my prayer for my stepfather. Thank You.

The next day my mother called crying. She said, "I think Mike is dying. Maybe I should take him back to the hospital?" I told her I would come right over. I got my son, John, now three, to come with me. My mother was in the living room crying. I went to comfort her. My son went right into Mike's room. He came back out and said," Don't cry grandma. Jesus is here. He will make Pop Pop better." My mother and I looked at each other. I asked, where is Jesus, John? He pointed to the bed. "He is on Pop Pop's bed." I looked and saw no one. As I entered the room, I felt peace. My stepfather looks peaceful. I took his pulse and watched for respiration. None. He is gone. Jesus had taken him home.

Red-Letter Days of the Joys of Being and Becoming
Life is a Full Circle

The joy of being and becoming a human being not a human doing is the goal. Making time for the important things. Learning not to waste energy on minor things. The Lord has shown me how to create balance and contentment. Taking time to be in His Presence and to hear His voice in the quiet. He has relaxed my mind from the anxiety of a full life. He has taught me to save time by spending time in prayer with Him. He has made all things beautiful in His time in my life. He has kept me beautiful, healthy, physically, mentally and spiritually. He has taught me how to create red-letter days, days that are special because I have heard from my Lord, and He shows me His plan for that day. He gives me wisdom and shows me unsearchable things. Life is a full circle.

The New Home
August 1982

We need a bigger house because we would like to plan another baby. And my mom cannot take care of her small house. So she said, "How about we find a big house for all of us?" It was a good idea. We found a mother-in-law apartment house in Deptford. I really like that one. I thought I wanted my mother to have her own living space. On my way to a Bible Study called Women's World at the Baptist Church, I heard the Lord speak to me again. I was praying about the house. "You will have the house in Woodbury Heights and go to the Baptist Church." No, no I thought. Not that house, I want the other one! And I already told the ladies from St. Margaret's Catholic Church that I will be attending there.

Later that night, I saw a Christian TV Show. They were talking about the small quiet voice of the Holy Spirit. "Was that you God?" And so we moved into the house in Woodbury Heights. Thanks to the owners who took back a second mortgage for us to be able to afford and my mom paid the down payment.

When my daughter, Tara saw the house, she was so excited. She ran from room to room. In the kitchen she opened every drawer. She exclaimed, "This house has everything, even a bread drawer! Thank you, Jesus for my new house. And we planned to live happily ever after in this home big enough for all of us.

September 8, 1982
Tara Comes of Her Own

Tara finally had her own bedroom. We painted it pink. On her seventh birthday, we had a Cinderella party. It included a canopy bed and a princess cake.

The night before the party, I fell asleep and left the cake in the oven and it burnt. I cried with exhaustion! So I decided to decorate it anyway and make cupcakes the next day.

The night of the party, Tara called me to her room, she was crying. I asked what was wrong with her. She said, "I feel bad that I have so much and the kids on TV are starving."

I said, "Let's pray for them." And we also prayed to show she was thankful for her birthday blessings.

I was going on a business trip for my job at the birthing center to learn to use a new computer called a graphic stress telemetry, a breast screening technique. I was going to La Jolla, California.

When I was tucking her into bed, she was crying again. She said, I am afraid I will never see you again. That you will get killed!" I tried to reassure her but she was inconsolable. I said, "Even if I die, you will see me in heaven." She said, "No, I won't."

I did not know what to say to her. When I spoke to my spiritual mother Joan from my church. She said, "I think Tara is ready to receive Jesus. Ask her if she wants to receive Jesus' into her heart and receive his gift of eternal life.

So I had the privilege to pray with my daughter. I told her that now she had a spiritual birthday too. And we planned to celebrate.

She cried out for me. "Mom, I am scared! My lamp is talking to me!" It was a second-hand doll lamp. She told me it was talking and motioning with her hand to come to her.

I said, "That is it. She is out of here in Jesus's name! You belong to Jesus now. She has no place here!"

The next day, she came to me and said, "Mom, I feel different. I feel Jesus in my heart!" She smiled. Within a couple of weeks, she led two of her friends, Joanny and Janice to the Lord. The Lord has great plans for my Tara.

October 24, 1982
New House, New Baby

I Planned my third child, Amber Rose Renee, while working at the Birthing Center. She was hiding in the beginning from the ultrasound. I heard Your voice that day. You said," Do not trust the machine, Trust Me!" That night I went to a healing service with Aunt Jeanette. She has really bad arthritis, will you help her Lord? That night I got called out for healing. The minister said, "There is a woman with a female problem, yes, you," he pointed to me. The Lord is healing you tonight."

My Amber was born naturally at the birthing center on her due date. She is a Sunday child. We almost did not make it in time. We arrived at 2:00 p.m. and she was born at 2:12 p.m. Bob delivered her! It was what we obstetrical nurses call fast and furious! I was there for four hours, celebrated with cake and champagne. Then we brought her home in a decorated basket. My best birthing experience! Thank you, Lord. Amber Rose Renee is a blessing!

Growing Pains

Your journal will be a book! *The Joys of Being and Becoming*

Up with my new baby and laughing in the middle of the night while reading the book, *Motherhood: The Second Oldest Profession,*[27] by Emma Bomback. My friend Kathy had given it to me as a gift. I was crying at the same time. I am so tired. So I decide to write in my journal to stay awake. As I read over it, I am thankful for the Lord's presence in my life since high school. Praying about it, I hear the Lord's voice tell me that "the journal will be a book." He gave the title and the twelve chapters. I am amazed by *The Joys of Being and Becoming* myself. Thank you, Lord.

December 14, 1982
Lord's Message to Me

Matthew 7:7: "And it shall be given unto you." "Seek and you shall find. Knock and the door will be opened to you" (NIV). Matthew 6:19–21: "Do not store up for yourselves treasures on earth, where moths and vermin destroy, and where thieves break in and steal. But store up for yourselves treasures in heaven, where moths and vermin do not destroy, and where thieves do not break in and steal. For where your treasure is, there your heart will be also" (NIV).

Déjà vu!

September 1983

I thought, *I am getting fat. I have to get to the gym.* Nothing is fitting. As I laid on the couch thinking about what to do, I felt life! I know how it feels. It is a flutter inside like a butterfly or gas moving quickly. I froze. "It cannot be! Not again! I told Bob I have to go get a pregnancy test. He looked puzzled, and asked why? "Well, what do you think?" I said sarcastically. He said, "It is probably just gas." The doctor came out with the test results and said, "Rose, the rab-

---

[27] Erma Bombeck, *Motherhood: The Second Oldest Profession* (MacDonald, 1983).

bit died!" Then he started to laugh and I started to cry. I could not believe that I am pregnant again. You are due the beginning of March 1984. It was hard to get used to, but I had everything I needed. My baby is only going to be a year-old next month. I am still nursing her. Well at least I know why I am gaining weight. Please Lord, help me.

September 24, 1983
His Stubborn Love by Joyce Landorf Heatherley[28]

The women's conference was at St. John's Methodist Church. The second day I was in the ladies' room in the last stall next to a stained-glass window. I thought, "This is a strange place with a beautiful window." But when I was sitting and looking through the beautiful window, the Lord spoke to me. "Just as this mosaic window has all the pieces fit together, so it is with my plan for your life." A time for all things. The petals unfold.

What a Way to Start a New Year? 1984

Bob and I celebrated New Year's Eve with the body of Christ, enjoying food, fellowship and worship together. Hands held in prayer at the moment, 1984 brought in a joyous feeling and a happy beginning. When we got home, Bob and I had fun watching our unborn baby celebrating too. Very active and a contracting uterus will make it hard to sleep again! A slow start but we are off to the races to get ready for Sunday School. At breakfast, I noticed that my uterus is still contracting. Well, no time to waste, I'll worry about the later. It is probably nothing. "I feel like I might be having the baby, but I can't because it is too soon! Let my class know in case. It caused a nice laugh. However, I become more and more uncomfortable, and I can't even stand up. Lay down! I am counting the contractions at home an hour and half later at two to three minutes apart. Should I call

---

[28] Joyce Landorf Heatherley, *His Stubborn Love* (Michigan: Zondervan Publishing, 1971).

the doctor? Bob says "Yes!" I knew that meant a trip to the hospital to be checked. Oh well. PTLA! (Praise the Lord Anyway). I have not been in the hospital for over seven years since I delivered John. What a strange feeling. I felt so vulnerable and weak and broken. Especially when I heard I would have to stay for a couple of days. What a shock! I hoped they were wrong and that these contractions would stop. SOS prayers from Bob and I go up. Then the alternative choice, a shot of Vistaril and 45 minutes resting on my side. If they stop, I can go home. Try to relax Rose. I feel stiff as a board. Help me, Lord to relax. Four o'clock and all is well; the OK to go home! I slept for 14 hours. We celebrated our New Year on January 2nd with our new year tradition. I placed three pieces of corn on each plate. We will share two things we are thankful for from this last year and one thing we look forward to this new year, 1984.After that ordeal, that tradition had much more meaning for me. It was hard to number the blessings, my family, a faithful husband, loving children, get well cards from my church family, my health, how I take it for granted and how quick it can change (I am sorry Lord). 1984, I am looking forward to a new baby! Forgive me for doubting the blessings in my life. Sometimes I do not realize what I have until I come close to losing it. The thought of delivering a nine-week preemie scared me to death! Also, I was scared to be away from my kids and husband. Oh, how much I appreciate all these things! Help me to make each minute count this year. Help me savor life, even the little things. Yes, what a way to start a New Year! Sometimes I only learn things the hard way! Thank you, Lord.

Timing for Everything under Heaven
Valerie Ann—February 14, 1984—
Best Valentine's Day Ever

I am the room mother with the cupcakes and paper products for the party for my daughter's class for Valentine's Day. That morning, I started to have contractions. I told Tara that I may not be able to make the party because I have to go to the doctor to get checked out. My theatrical daughter started to cry, "Oh no, the baby is going to spoil the party!" I said maybe it is a false alarm, it is not supposed to come till March. But I will bring everything to school just in case. And so that was that or so I thought. I had a love basket planned for my husband for that night with wine, cheese and chocolate. I told him to put it in the car just in case. He laughed. Hours later, I asked for the basket. I sat in the rocking chair laboring and sneaking snacks with my Valentine in between contractions. She was born early in the evening. We called home to notify my mother and children. My son cried and locked himself in the bathroom. He said, "Doesn't God know that I needed a brother?!" I replied, "Maybe next time?" Then I thought, "What am I, crazy? There will be no next time!" Because she was born on Valentine's Day, we were looking for a special name. She was to be Michelle or David. Neither seemed to work for this special delivery. The Lord told me, "Her name is Valerie Ann. She is my gift of love to you!" And she is! She has taught me so much about love, I am blessed.

June 24, 1984
I Am Life

"I am not interested in what you have been or who you are now, but what I will make you become. You are important to my plan. Allow me to be the Lord of your life. I am life and hope to a hopeless world, to you and your family. Why do you struggle so much with Me? Let Me have My way with you and you will see clearly the way of the Spirit in your life."

A quick blur, and a New Year again!

Déjà vu again!

October 1984

I am still nursing my sweet Valentine baby. Feeling a little over-whelmed with two babies, but they say that the Lord will not give me more than I can handle. As I was feeling morning sickness hoping it was just my imagination, I went to my family doctor for a pregnancy test, just in case.

He came back from doing the test and said, "Mrs. Yerka, the rabbit died! Congratulations!" he laughed. Then I cried. Oh lord help me! How will I do this? How can we afford another baby? What will Bob say?

Please forgive me for doubting your plan and your blessing. I can now understand many of the women I meet at my office as a nurse. Abortion seems like a option but it is not for me. Me the child who was saved from my mother's womb. I am blessed and evidently fertile Myrtle! Lord be with this new baby! And help me be a good mother to five children.

Growing Pains Again

May 12, 1985

Pregnant again. Lord, I feel guilty. So many women are trying to have children at my work. Why are you giving me all the babies? Please help me. The Lord told me "This baby will be a girl and her name is Charity Joy." I thought to myself, "Is that even a name?" I looked it up and it means 'loving delight.' He said, "She will be a blessing to you in your older years." And she is! Lord, I trust you! She looks like me and is a sweetheart. Thank You Lord.

1985 and 1986, A Blur of Activity

Charity asked, "Mom, where are my baby photos?"

"Who had time to take pictures? Not Me! Sorry, Cheech!" My pet name for my youngest. The only one I remember is giving her the first bath in the kitchen sink, with the other two little girls helping. A favorite memory!

April 14, 1987
Maturity, You Are Ready "What
can I do for you today, Lord?"

"My daughter, you are of Me. I have anointed you by My Spirit for the job I have for you. The time has come for maturity. I am the vine you are the branch in bloom to bear fruit. You have been in my classroom under My teaching. You have had hands-on experience and good teaching. It is time to go forth as an arrow into the battle. You are My disciple. I send you forth in My name with the power of the Holy Spirit. You shall heal the sick, cast out demons, reach the lost, in My name and by My Spirit. Be not afraid for I am with you always. My hands are your hands. They have been anointed for My service. They will touch others for Me. Prepare for battle, arm yourself and your family. You have all you need. Just as nature is maturing your daughter into a woman: I will mature you in Me. It will feel awkward at times, and you will have to walk by faith. Trust me that the time is right. Just as you did with your marriage and first child. You felt that you were not ready, but you were. You acted the part and succeeded. I have healed your mind. I have given you a new vision of yourself. Just as you saw the difference in education, you were a step above. So I am moving you to college level material. You are ready for practice what you have learned and put into your life the principles of my Secret Kingdom. You have been ripening like a fruit ready for plucking. You will enjoy your maturity process and progress."

Fruitfulness

From the Lord to me: "I am the vine and my Father is the Gardner. He lops off every branch that does not produce. He prunes every branch that bears fruit for even larger crops. He has already tended you by pruning you back for greater strength and usefulness by means of His commands I gave you. Take care to live in me and let me live in You. For a branch cannot produce fruit when severed from the vine. Nor can you be fruitful apart from me. For apart from me you can't do a thing. Live within my love."

Reflections from the Lord

May 13, 1987—Beautiful Rose

"My daughter, your time has come. You are blooming into my beautiful rose. I will make your life a beautiful story for others to read. They will want the joy you have in me. You will see yourself as my chosen one, holy and dedicated to me, a special treasure unto me." I heard the Lord speak to my heart.

June 23, 1987—Love Disciplines

"My daughter, do not be discouraged. Whom I love, I chasten." The Lord spoke to my heart.

September 9, 1987—Test of Fire

"In all this you greatly rejoice, though now for a little while you may have had to suffer grief in all kinds of trials. These have come so that the proven genuineness of your faith—of greater worth than gold, which perishes even though refined by fire—may result in praise, glory and honor when Jesus Christ is revealed" (1 Peter 1:6–7 NIV).

October 28, 1987—Discipleship

"I want you to be a student of My Word." I heard the Lord speak to my heart. Delight in doing everything God wants me to do and meditate on His word, day and night and think about ways to follow Him more closely. Do not be a puddle duck, only eating what you find on the surface. Be a diving duck. Dive deep for the hidden treasure. Give thought to each line, each clear precept and then practice it with godly fear. To really know God, you must grow in your knowledge of His word. *Time to grow in my knowledge of the Word.*

Chapter 8

Being a Personal Failure
Becoming Ready for Change

Growing Pains at Home

It is not so easy. Why do I wait to wash my windows until I can hardly see out of them? At that point, it takes twice as much time, cleaner, paper towels, and patience. The bi-yearly event that I hate is cleaning the oven. A major task that requires armpit length gloves, a monkey suit and 100 percent horse powered elbow grease! A bathtub ring so great that I can see the headlines now—"Yerka children carried down the drain by some unknown super germ!" The floors are so dirty that even the dog will not eat everything on it! When company is coming, I am faster than a speeding tornado with Mr. Clean in hand. I make them believe my sparkling floor is an everyday occasion. However, only my family knows my secret. As a matter of fact, when they see me cleaning, they ask the following logical question," Mom, who is coming to our house?"

Spiritual House Cleaning

I thought this morning as I struggled with my oven, that this represents my Christian life. As for Bible reading, a verse a day keeps the devil away! As for study, John 3:16 is my favorite memory verse. As for confession, I wait until I need a cleaning like my oven does—desperately! And the Lord uses His elbow grease to help make my light shine like new. If my oven could speak it would probably cry out from being so sore from scrubbing. Sometimes I wait so long that my reconciliation actually hurts me. Lord, help me not to be a lazy housewife but more importantly no to be a lazy Christian. You have already done the completed work. All I must do is submit to your will. Jesus you are my invited royal guest in my home and my heart. I should keep my heart and life clean and free from sin by confessing it quickly and avoiding it completely. It is the spiritual house cleaning that must be to keep this temple fit for my Lord and King Jesus Christ. Lord, thank you for the lesson from this black, filthy oven. A sparkling clean oven is a beautiful sight. I definitely have to make opportunities for this enjoyment more often.

Situation Comedy

Lord, help me see the funny side of the things that plague me each day. Like the spilled milk, messy diapers, dirty faces, boogie noses, smelly socks, burnt toast and Cheerios in my shoes just to name a few off the top of my head. These are blessings in disguise. This is a test to prove my love for my family. Help me love and laugh, so my children and my husband will have fond memories of a home filled with warmth and love. And may they remember many funny memories of the mishaps of growing up years together. Help me enjoy the time as it will be few compared to my lifetime I have been given. Help me respond with laughter of the beautiful comedy of each passing day. Let me find the good things in my life, like squeals of delight, cheeseburger smiles and slobbery kisses! There is situational comedy in everyday life with kids. Thank you for a house filled with them!

Self-Talk

Is this all there is? All dreams coming true! Not what I thought. Hard work. So many changes. Friends are still young and having fun! The grass is greener on the other side!

I am now a mother of two small children, and three babies 15 months apart and married twelve short years. I am working the night shift as a nurse. I also worked a part time business as a beauty consultant. I had my second home, five children, a boy and four girls. I am living the American Dream!

The Honeymoon is Over

A relationship is a story between two people. A story sometimes left untold; for love has no beginning or end. God does not have to show His face to let us know He is there. No explanation needed from God. There are two sides to every story. Each side harbors a heart with a story of its own. As time passes by the story must grow. Growing is putting things together. Sometimes puzzles and troubles arise and the plot thickens into perspective. Memories come and go, but love stays forever clear. Moments to cherish love are defined with no explanations needed. What the heart has once owned, it shall never lose, I only have my side of the love story to share. And I had a lot of growing up to do to stay lovable and needed to learn to be kind to my husband. Neither of us knew exactly what to expect from this perfect love, least of all, imperfection. Rose had to learn to eat humble pie and to say I am sorry. Even though the movie, ``Love Story" with Ali McGraw and Ryan O'Neill said, "Love means never having to say you are sorry." Bob had to learn that he had married a young woman who was his bride, but she planned to grow into a mature woman who had a strong will and a mind of her own.

Babies

Add positive stress to the marriage. Our Love had grown and so did our family. Being a mother was the hardest job I ever had, but the joy was great. The hours were long and tiring but Bob was always a big help. And sometimes he was not there. My mother pitched in to help me; she could see my stress.

I was happy to go to work and be around adults sometimes. But I began to feel overwhelmed with it all. Up at night, bottles, dirty diapers and dishes, in and out and then start all over again the next day; I would cry at the drop of a hat or one more thing. I felt sad when I should be happy.

A Dysfunctional Wedding Dance

As we learned to do the "Dysfunctional Dance" we had learned from our families of origin, we struggled not to step on each other's toes. As one of us changed and grew stronger in our role, the other sought to find balance and adjustment. This worked for five years until nothing was working any more. It seemed that our love had grown cold and distant like we were strangers again. I thought divorce was the answer. But where would I go? And how would I cope with five children?

From the Journal of the Journey

Years of seminars, including "Resets: Becoming More Like My New Self" and Realizing the Lord's Hand on My Life." Early recovery from 1992, I had to learn to become more like myself. What to do, what to avoid, how to trust myself and others. I learned the disciplines of a beautiful woman[29] and a Christian family and learning to be still and listen to God's instructions for my life.

---

[29] Anne Ortlund, *Disciplines of a Beautiful Woman* (Word Books: Waco, Texas, 1981).

1993
Becoming Patient with Myself and Others

The most important workshop was called "How Are Things at Home?"[30] with Orv Owens. He shared how we needed to have a structure of responsibility for our children. So now my five children were given the responsibility to look after each other and the baby looked after the cat. We apologized for not being the best parents to them and promised to do better. I still remember the looks on their faces. We had much fun together as a family during that time. We learned to play restaurant. We all dressed up. Bob was the chef, I was the waitress, and the kids were our special guests. We made menus for them to choose from the various leftovers. That night there were no complaints! Smiles and laughs were all around! Special memories of fun times.

Learning about Change

I found Herbalife[31] from an ad in my new church bulletin. I had spent a week trying to lose weight for my anniversary vacation. I had gained 20 pounds in four months. My extremely unhealthy dieting plan was not working. So I said a prayer after a week asking God to help me. The very next day I saw the ad. It said, "Lose weight now, ask me how?" I got started and lost twenty pounds in just four weeks and had twenty customers in two months. I had a new business and a new body. But I found out I also needed to change my mind. Our philosopher, Jim Rohn at the Herbalife Extravaganza said, "For things to change you have to change." It almost sounded like the same things I was hearing at church. I became a student of change.

---

[30] Orv Owens, "How Are Things at Home?" (1993).
[31] Mark Hughes, Herbalife International Inc. (Los Angeles, California, 1980).

May 1993
Mother of the Bride, a New Role

I feel old. I cried when she told me. And I cried for six months. My daughter Tara and Mike are getting married. I told my daughter the same thing my mother told me. "You are too young to get married." She did not listen because I was so young too. Bob did not cry till the day of the wedding. We stuck him in the powder room so we could all get dressed. When he came out and saw Tara's dress hanging from the fan over our bed. He started to cry. I said, "It is too late to cry. We don't have time." We hugged and prayed for them. We pray they invite you in their marriage and have the joy we have. Lord, bless them. In your name, Amen.

October 1996
Becoming a Mom-Mom (Not Me, My Mother-in-Law)

We planned a baby shower for Tara at my house. It was very exciting to be adding a new baby to our family. It required much prayers, as the seizures had returned with the pregnancy for my daughter Tara. She had many falls and a broken bone. It was a very stressful time for us. I was a homeschool mom with my married daughter staying with us to care for her. But it was almost time for the baby to come. As my son carried the packages in from his girlfriend Christy, I saw the tag on one little one. It said, "To Grandmom Yerka." I asked, "Why the present for Grandmom?" My son looked at me and laughed. "Mom, get with the program. That is you!" I let his words sink in, and then I said, "That is not me. That is my mother-in-law!" I will be called Mom-Mom! Lord, help me grow into my new role again. Aliceea Tiffani was born on October 12, 1996. A beautiful healthy baby girl. Thank you, Lord, for answering our prayers. Help me be a good Mom-Mom. I feel so blessed because the Lord would send me many more grandchildren through the love of Tara and Michael: Bethani, Caylee, Emma, Jacob, Addison and Caleb. And now Aliceea's children, my great grandchildren, Aurelia and Adam.

May 16, 1997
Emotional Healing of a Deep Wound—My Father's Funeral
Time for Closure with the Unknown Man; Fast Forward…

My mother told me my father died. I called my counselor, Mary in a frantic state and felt both fear and anger. She said, "You know what this means. You will finally find closure if you attend the funeral. You need to go for yourself. It is very important!"

I told my mother and she was furious! "You don't owe him anything! He did not even buy you a shoelace!" I answered. "I am going for me, not him. I need this." Just like Mary had said to me. But I was scared to death. I feel sick to my stomach, I could not eat or sleep the night before. I thought, "Why am I scared to see him face to face? After all he is dead."

My best friend Kathy offered to go with me for support. My hands were sweating as I signed in, I wrote, Rose Marie Page (Yerka) my maiden and married name. The funeral home was empty. Only a few women sat on the side and in front. They were all much older than me and my friend. We were the youngest in the room. As I surveyed the faces in the room, I saw a very familiar face. "Joan!" I gasped. Who is Joan? My friend asked, what is the matter? I have known her for years from the doctor's office where I work. My heart started to race and I felt like running out of the room.

Kathy said, "Stay calm. Do you think she will recognize you? Do you want to talk to her? If not just do what you came here to do." No, I am not here to see anyone but my father.

I only have words for him alone. I need to do this even though I am scared to death.

"Okay let's go together," Kathy said. We marched stately like all the old women on the side with our eyes straight ahead. We went up to the coffin. I knelt and Kathy stood by my side. I saw the priest out of the corner of my eye. I thought he would just have to wait… I prayed, please help me remember what I need to say. He never did answer my letter. Help me really forgive him, Lord." Amen.

I kept my eyes open and just stared at him. He looked old, small and frail. He seemed to have a scared look on his face, not like some of those I saw die who looked so peaceful and relaxed. His face was tense and wrinkled. So here I am with this Unknown Man. I have dreamed about this day for 25 years. Please help me remember what I need to say. He never did answer my letter.

"I want you to know that you made a big mistake, but God did not. He provided everything for me that you did not. I learned to be a good worker and goal oriented to have not only what I needed but also what I wanted. My life has been blessed in spite of your absence.

I was angry at you for years. I was embarrassed at my lack of a family tree because of you. When I had my own children, I often wondered how you could just walk away. I told myself I was better off not knowing you. My uncles said you were a nice guy and told me they would arrange a meeting. But by then you were in Florida. I went looking for you but could not find you. But I did visit with my cousin Mary Pat and found a photograph of my grandmother. So not all was lost and of course we went to Disney World.

I felt sorry for you for being so selfish and shallow. It took me years of counseling to come to the point of forgiveness. I realized that hurting people hurts people and cannot give or receive love. Only the Love of God can heal deep seated wounds.

I hope you came to know my Jesus for the forgiveness of sins and that you are with him now. If not, I know I will never see you again. You are in a place or torment that is worse than all the pain of my lifetime. And this priest cannot help you now. It is too late. May the Lord himself be merciful on you and heal me of my disenfranchised grief I have hidden for 25 years. My secret has made me sick. So as a ghost comes out of the closet, may my pain in my heart be gone. I forgive you. It looks like by the looks of this funeral that you led an empty life. May the Lord forgive you and you be with him in paradise. I hope so for your sake and for your daughters." Amen.

As I opened my eyes and turned to walk away, all eyes were on me. I had prayed too long. Not the normal Catholic prayer. Instead, a long talk with my Lord and my unknown father. I felt like a weight had been lifted off of my chest. My counselor was right. I needed this for me. Not to offend my mom, who I have been meshed with for most of my life, but just for me and closure for me.

This chapter is over until my half-sisters decide to find me. I would hope to have a relationship with them, if possible. Can you work that out someday, Lord? I hope so. If not, I understand.

The next time I saw Joan, she did not say a word about it. I was amazed that she did not recognize me. You made me Invisible. In your time, Lord—will you reveal me to her? We'll see! Maybe someday?

Growing Pains

May 26, 1999
Red Letter Day
Be Still and Know You Are God

Here I am at the park, "He says, "Be still, and know that I am God…" (Psalm 46:10 NIV) and You meet me here and have fellowship with me. You sat with me, comforted me, and You told me You are my friend and that I am Your own. As soon as I saw the fountain and heard the water and felt the fresh air on my face, I heard Your voice.

"My daughter, I am the Fountain of Life. I give the Living Water. I remove the stench and foulness of the stagnation of sin in your life. You are like a tree planted by the water. Your life is in Me. My Spirit will refresh you like the wind. It will be fresh air to renew your soul. Your innermost being that is only known to Me; I will reveal it to you so you will be made whole. I shall wipe away your tears and set your spirit free!"

June 26, 1999
The Song in My Heart

At 3:00 a.m., the Lord woke me with a Christmas song in my head and on my lips. "Up in the Attic, Down on My Knees."[32] My

---

[32] Amy Grant, *Heirlooms: A Christmas Album* (Capitol Cmg Genesis Universal Music, 1983).

precious family is more than an heirloom to me. The memory of the moment His love first pierced through me, all that I have come from and all that I have been through and all that I am hoping to be, my precious Jesus has made something beautiful of my life." I thought this song would be perfect for Tara to sing at the Ladies Tea.

August 7, 1999
The Blessing

To be early and on time is perfect. This has always been a trouble spot for me. Imagine me being a day early, all prepared everyone planned around me and my day. As I sit in the empty parking lot, I feel more confused than angry with myself. But then I remember the sovereignty of God—He will use even my mistakes for His purposes. With this reasoning. I think He let me use my time to go shopping, catch the Secret Sale and look for a mother-of-the-groom dress. The wedding is only five weeks away. The first dress I tried, felt perfect, looked beautiful! Three new suits plus two bags of clothes for less than the original price of the dress tag. I was blessed!

Mother of the Groom

Have you gotten your dress yet? Yes, it is a miracle! The very first dress I looked at fit perfectly and was on sale for half price, and it was just what I wanted! It was a long wine-colored dress with a jacket and I already had shoes to match!

I cannot believe my little boy has grown into a man and is getting married so soon. Where has the time gone? I will dance at his wedding and rejoice with him. Thank You, Lord, for preparing me and for the beautiful new daughter in law, Christy, that will be added to our family. Hold them close to you and bless their marriage. Amen.

August 8, 1999
Celebrate Shelly

As I listen to the oldies on the radio, I feel good from memories of people, friends, and family. Rocking with the oldies all night long, singing and dancing! All of a sudden, I realize where many of these songs are familiar from, the most unique funeral I had ever attended. My cousin Shelly, the disc jockey! We celebrated her life with the music she loved. I cherished the memories I have of her in my heart tonight. My prayer is to celebrate Shelly.

I remember the story of Melody's pajamas. On the night of the funeral looking for Melody's pajamas, Margie found the same dress they had bought for the funeral in a bag with tags and receipt for three days before her death. A confirmation that the Lord was with Shelly and comforting us!

Another Red-Letter Miracle!
Reflections

Learning to forgive myself and others. To be honest with myself, others and God. Have you ever felt insecure? Did you have to work hard to hide it? Family Secrets can make you sick. Who helped you through your struggle? Who did you have to forgive? How has forgiveness changed your life?

CHAPTER 9

Being a Personal Failure and Becoming Free to Change

April 7, 2000
Ocean City Retreat
The verses that spoke to my heart.
"God is making all things new" John 20:1–18.
"Freedom in Christ I felt God's presence
on the beach" (Galatians 5:1).

The beach is windy and the surf is rough. But the peace within my soul as the sounds of the ocean speaks to my spirit, I heard the Lord call my name again! He is calling me to a closer walk with Him. He wants to give me life abundantly as He sets me free from the bondage of sin, past hurts and ancestral influences.

I am feeling free to change and fear is leaving me. I feel grateful. Working hard as a homeschool mom. I am learning so much in home school. Learning to listen to my teenagers. They can teach me much about myself that needs to change.

Our favorite homeschool memory is the famous question when you tell someone that you homeschool. They all ask, "Home school? Where is that?!" We put that quote in our first yearbook!

Time is flying by until fear returns.

A Very Tragic Day to Remember
September 11, 2001—Fear Returns

I was at church with my girls at our ladies' Bible study. As a homeschool mom, I included this day into my kid's curriculum. They provided child care for the moms.

When we arrived, our pastor came to tell us the church was going to close. He told us to pray together before we leave for our country. We may be under attack. My mind went into a spin.

We prayed and listened to the radio all the way home. At home we saw the planes go into the trade center in New York and watched in horror as the first tower came crumbling to the ground. We were all in shock and crying. They kept showing it over and over again like Groundhog Day, and then the second tower came down. I tried to comfort my children and told them lets pray and turn off the tv for now. We prayed for the Lord to be with all those people.

In May 2001, we had gone to the towers and the United Nations for a field trip. I stayed down at the mall under the tower instead of going to the top with the other teens who did not like heights. I remember sitting on a bench and feeling the building move. I had a frightened look on my face. The man next to me said, "Lady, you hear the trains underneath us. There is train station down there." I kept thinking of all those people under the buildings. I had nightmares about them. That day was the first day I took a bottle of wine into my bedroom. Fear had taken root in my heart again.

The evil sight of a plane hitting both the World Trade Center and the flames and then the collapse of the buildings was overwhelming to watch over and over again on the TV news. I had nightmares of the thousands of people buried alive and the smell of burning flesh was in my mind. I was there at the end of May. I could picture it all exactly. The underground mall and the train station and all the hundreds of thousands of people there on an average day.

I was drinking sherry alone in my room. My addiction was coming full circle. I was no help to anyone not even myself. It was a downward spiral.

Lord, Help me!

October 1, 2001
Letting Go of Agnes

Back to the lighthouse in Cape May. My friend Mary Lou and I drove down on a Sunday afternoon. I just found out that my mother is dying. Her dialysis is not working any more. I need to take some time off from work and prepare myself emotionally to lose my best friend. As I prayed on the beach, I heard the Lord remind me that he had given me four more years with my mother. That it is time to let her go. I felt the warm tears flow down my face. I told him that I did not know how I would make it without her. He told me that I am now the matriarch of our family. He has made me stronger and would be with me. Be prepared to say what needs to be said to your mother. She is ready to come home.

My mother had met with her priest Father Curren. He told her God would let her know when it is time. My mother said I am tired of dialysis. I want to go home with Jesus.

As I focused on the Cape May Lighthouse, I heard the Lord speak to my heart. "I am the way and the light. I will be with you and carry you through this time. You will become stronger for your children. Keep your eyes fixed on me. Do not be afraid."

We had our last Christmas together. Her brother Jack died on December 21, 2001. I took her to the funeral in a wheelchair. They had lunch afterward at O' Donnell's in Gloucester City.

My mother got to see her nieces Linda and Gerry and Ann and nephews Michael Page and Michael Robinson and Jack's sons Bobby and Tommy. She was sad but happy to see all of them. It would be the last time she sees her family on earth.

The Christmas Shoe and Healing Tears

The best Christmas ever was 1976 when my son was born. "The Best Gift of All" was the song from Sandy Patti that touched my heart that year. The worst and saddest Christmas was 2001 and 2002. After September 11, 2001, knowing all the families who had lost loved ones was tear-jerking. We had an angel ornament holding an American flag at the top of the tree. And knowing that it was my mother's last Christmas was bittersweet. She was growing sicker and sicker and weaker and weaker and weaker after dialysis. There was so much to do. My friend Mary Lou had recommended a video of my mom.

We made a video of my mother to get some of her story. I asked her to tell her story. She said, "I am too old now. You tell my story." But she told me what the secret to a good life? She said, "Love, lots of love!" Love is a treasure in our family, her legacy that she would leave behind.

So we were shopping for her needs and some wants. She always got a new robe and slippers, nightgowns, and some clothes. But she wanted ribbon candy, chocolate cherries and a real wreath with a bright big red bow on her nursing home door along with her ceramic mother of pearl lighted Christmas tree. all the kids came to carol with bells and dressed up. My mother's face lite up with Christmas joy when she saw the grandchildren.

My Mom's Funeral

It was not until she was thirty-five that she met my father, the love of her life, or so she thought. He had lied to her. He was married with three children. When she became pregnant with me, he offered to pay for an illegal abortion in New York City. My mother said a prayer that day, asking God for a sign to know what to do. She felt a new life that day. It was Rosemarie. She felt God's answer in her heart. He said, "I will take care of you and be the father to this child." My mother decided to love despite the cost to herself. It was not a popular choice in 1953. She had chosen to love just like her mother had loved her and her mother, even at the expense and her own life. My mother had to give much of herself to become my mother.

My mother sacrificed her life for mine in many ways. She was happy to be able to come and live with me after the death of my stepfather. We decided to buy a house big enough for all of us. The house had a mother-in-law suite. It was perfect. She was a big help to me with all my children as they came along.

My Aunt Jeanette even came to live with us. That was after my cousin had thrown her out. She too was an alcoholic. It was a rescue, but what could my codependent self do? I loved her and we always had room for one more in this big house. It turned out to be a blessing, we were a family of nine! And she stopped drinking.

My mother had outlived all my aunts but one. She spent four and a half years on dialysis. She had to move to a nursing home. During that time, she did get a life of her own. She called herself the Angel of the Manor. These people are not in their right minds, someone has to watch after them. And she was happy to do so, even though she would complain.

She went to dialysis three days a week. She would be wiped out afterward. So it seemed she only had one or two good days. I could see she was getting tired. And I was feeling sad.

The doctor told me the dialysis is no longer working. He said, "You might want to spend more time with your mother as it is limited." I took a leave of absence from Dr. Chandra's office. I went to see her every day and interviewed her. I found the list recently. One of the questions was, "Do you have a photo of my father?" I do not remember asking her. She was always upset talking about him. I do not think she ever did forgive him. I hope she did for her own sake.

When she was dying, I stayed in the room overnight. The doctor said she could last weeks. "She will blow up and smell bad and it will not be a pretty death," the doctor said. I prayed to the Lord to please just take her home.

She only lasted one day. Her sister came to see her. When Gerry came in, my mother opened her eyes. She said, "I must be dying if you are here." It was sad but true. The Pages only came to funerals and did not visit one another no matter how closely they lived. But she brought her a beautiful crystal angel in a white satin box. I still have it to remind me of both of them, my mother and my aunt.

We asked if she wanted anything? She said, "I want a Coke." The nurse said she can have whatever she wants now. She enjoyed every cold sip. Then she pointed to the corner of the room and said, "I want to go with my sister." I told her that Gerry had left. She said, "No, it is Ann." I got goosebumps. Aunt Ann had been dead for years. She was the first sister to die. I hope that meant she was ready to go home to heaven. The doctor said that she could last two weeks. He said she would blow up like a balloon and smell very bad. I prayed that would not have to happen. She had been through so much.

When she had decided she was done and did not want to do this anymore, I got very angry. I guess I did not want her to give up. But she assured me that it was time to be done.

That night my friend Mary Lou came to be with me. We washed my mom and made her comfortable. I heard the death rattle, but I denied it. I went to get her more pain medicine. When I came back Mary Lou told me she was ready to go. I got in bed with her and hugged her and cried. I felt her take her last breath. Then I felt this warmth and peace that entered the room. I knew Jesus was here.

The nurses for the next shift came into the room within a minute. They said, "She is gone, isn't she?" We feel the peace of God in the room. "Yes, He came to take her home."

Thank You, Lord, for not making her suffer. My mother died January 12, 2003 in the season of winter. I have come full circle.

Her funeral was in the Catholic Church. My pastor Bruce and her priest did the service. My daughter Tara would sing "Amazing Grace" and my son would read the Scriptures. We had a boom box playing praise and worship music. I was to do the eulogy. I hoped I could get through it without tears.

I brought her bag from the nursing home with some of her favorite things to tell the story. It included her back scratcher, her rosary beads and Bible and prayer book and photos of her grandchildren. I really do not remember what I said except that I hope to be like her someday. She was a woman who loved and was loved.

There were about 100 people there at the church. My pastor picked up on the fact that she was 90 and only had one sister surviving and that I was an only child; yet this church is filled with people remembering her life. She lived well and left a living legacy to her family. It is a legacy of love.

About 75 people came back to my house. All of my friends helped to make food, clean the house and serve the food and clean up. I was surrounded by the love of my friends and the loving memory of my mother. I hope to continue the circle of love in the next generation to come.

Lord, I know You want me to become a woman for all seasons. A Proverbs 31 woman is what I hope to become a matriarch for my family to leave a legacy of love for my children and grandchildren and great grandchildren too.

The Healing of the Christmas Shoes
A Labor of Love

The timing of the *Christmas Shoes*[33] movie came at my saddest Christmas, 2002. It was our first Christmas without my mother. Also the funeral home had sent a snowflake in the mail to put on our tree. I cried until my eyes burned. Then the movie had tears flowing freely for all of us. Me and my girls. We listened to the song over and over and sang along with tears in our eyes remembering my mother this first year without her. I would still have six more years with my second mom, Aunt Jeanette and eleven with my cousin Dottie. All these women taught me how to live well. All made mistakes and had some regrets but the Love had covered the multitude of sins by God's Grace.

2003—Missing My Mom

Lord, You sent me to the retreat. You gave me my own room, and I slept in Your presence and laid my head at Your chest. I cried and cried. I know You were catching each tear in Your bottle. You told me I am now the matriarch. You will strengthen me for my children. Heal me, Lord. Thank You for Your comfort. Amen.

---

[33] Michael Mahoney (producer), *The Christmas Shoes* (CBS Television, 2002).

Growing Pains

Through the Years, Time Flew By, 2003 Was a Blur
Being and Becoming Changed to the
Matriarch of My Family?
June 1, 2004

I read the book, *Boundaries*[34] by Cloud and Townsend. Learning how to identify manipulation and to develop a healthy relationships. Things will get worse before they get better.

June 7, 2004
Spiritual Warfare

Recognizing the horrid voice of the enemy and the fear it puts into my heart. What do you want me to do, Lord?

"I did my part already. Is it possible you are doing a New Thing? Do you want me to help my enemy?"

June 8, 2004
Rest, Restored and Refreshed

The star show wowed me! Dazzling and twinkling to delight my heavy heart. I begin to sing of my "Awesome God" at Sea Pines. "How Great Thou Art!"

July 2, 2004
The Potter's Hands

Isaiah 64:7–8: "No one calls on your name or strives to lay hold of you; for you have hidden your face from us and have given us over to our sins. Yet you, Lord, are our Father. We are the clay, you are the potter; we are all the work of your hand" (NIV).

---

[34] Henry Cloud and John Townsend, *Boundaries* (Michigan: Zondervan, 1992).

The Process of Becoming Beautiful,
Exchange Beauty for Ashes[35]

"Become more intimate with me. Remember your purpose. To become the woman I have designed you to be. I have taken the ashes of the past and exchanged for beauty and grace. I will restore the flaws and add the testing in the fire that makes you strong and unbreakable."

July 18, 2004
Spiritual Eyeglasses

Pastor Bruce preaching on Genesis 22 reminded us to "Revisit the place where I first met my Lord, my journals and red-letter days! I need to remember when your Holy Spirit spoke to me. Then look at how the devil came to rob, steal and destroy.

I have been blinded by my mind, will and emotions and flesh. I need my spiritual glasses to see what is already done in the spirit world. And to clearly see the path marked out before me. You promised to break down the walls of hostility between Bob and I. Help me not to rebuild them. Do not let pain and fear paralysis me. I have work to do. Help me, Jesus!"

July 21, 2004
The Abscess

"I am the Great Physician that performs the spiritual surgery necessary to make quick radical changes for emotional and spiritual healing to move you forward. An emotional infection is dangerous, it goes unattended. It effects your heart and mind. You need to allow Me to remove the memory by bringing it up, dealing with it and then removing every bit of infection. A daily dose of My Word, my spiritual armor and the people I bring into your life will bring the healing process. The process is unseen by others but the emotional relief of

---

[35] Joyce Meyers, *Beauty for Ashes* (New York: Warner Books, 1994).

pain and removal of the spiritual abscess will reveal a more Beautiful You. Being and becoming all that I have created you to be. Trust in Me." I heard the Lord speak to my heart.

The business of life made 2005 and 2006 a whirlwind. Taking One day at a time learning to trust the Lord.

December 27, 2006
Where the Battle Is Won

Jeremiah 4:1: "If you, Israel, will return, then return to me," declares the Lord. "If you put your detestable idols out of my sight and no longer go astray" (NIV).

A great crossroad in my life, a major turning point. I have been driven to this place to make a decision of my will. I have been working hard every day these past seven months (May 26, 2006, to December 25, 2006) Learning to make choices that are good for me. I have been tested and retested on what I have learned.

In the sacred place of the soul alone with my God the battle is won. Nothing has any power over me anymore! I can go and move ahead knowing the battles have been won. I will continually get alone and return to the Lord and settle any issues between myself and the Lord.

December 27, 2006
A Year of Change and Lessons in Godliness

Crossroad. The Lord spoke to me from Jeremiah 4:1 "If you return to me…" (NIV)

January 2, 2007

Boundaries with myself and my family. Change and Integrity. Time to take my life back.

2007 time moved quickly AS A BLUR…… But this is what I learned.

Trust Even in the Pain

My Tara is expecting here first baby boy. She has four beautiful girls, Aliceea, Bethani, Caylee, and Emma. Mike is so excited. But something was wrong. Tara was calling me for prayer when I was visiting my daughter Amber in Virginia, who had just had her first baby girl, Abigail Rose. We were staying together at a hotel on the beach. I remember calling all the strong women prayer warriors I knew as I walked and prayed with them. My heart was breaking for my daughter. Lord, please take this pain away from my child.

When I returned to New Jersey, I went to her in the hospital where she was to deliver Joshua. As I experienced this pain of a still birth with my daughter, I felt your comfort and presence. But I still wonder why this beautiful baby was taken home to heaven before he had a life to live.

The funeral with the little box was the saddest funeral I had ever attended. My daughter was devastated. Lord, please carry her through this pain. I pray.

So Joshua is always counted as my first grandson. And I will meet him in heaven someday.

June 25, 2007

I learned an important lesson about holiness. Holiness is an integrated personality. It is not doing things. It is who you are when no one is looking. The Lord was giving my life back as a gift. I had fewer and fewer lost days.

December 20, 2007

My life was delivered from destruction. It had been a year of completion in many ways. My healing was being worked out deep within my heart. The pain was no longer controlling my life. The ghost was out of the closet. Praise the Lord!

Reflections
In the Valley I Learned Who Jesus Really Was

Galatians 6:3: "If anyone thinks they are something when they are not, they deceive themselves" (NIV)

Armed and Dangerous

I have seen the Glory of the Lord in the middle of the emergency and operating rooms, mental hospitals, nursing homes, counseling rooms, conference rooms, bathrooms, bedrooms, row homes, custom homes, municipal buildings, Supreme Court steps, the street of the cities, in the line of a grocery store, the welfare office, in the tears of a child, and the anger of a teenager. My Lord has always shown up when I needed him the most. He always made His Presence known.

In many ways: Kindness of a stranger, prayer of a friend, visit from a pastor, and encouraging note in the mail, the sight of a hummingbird in my hand, a lady bug at the beach, a red fox at the river, and old man at the lake, a green and beige Mercedes, a blue camper, a brown motor home that takes regular gas and is classified as a car, just our size! The sound of a person reciting the salvation prayer, a song on the radio, the beautiful blue eyes of a street person, free tickets to the boardwalk, winning a fifty-fifty ticket when money was tight, a sparrow at my window of my car or at the window of the Orlando Convention Center, a graceful fall on marble steps, and the still small voice at the Cape May Dunes comforting me when my mother was dying. The Lord's presence and favor surrounds me every day. My list is endless. I am blessed, armed and dangerous with His word and His presence and angels watching over me!

Reflections
In the Valley, I Learned Who Jesus Really Was

Galatians 6:3: "If anyone thinks they are something when they are not, they deceive themselves" (NIV). Stoop down…to those who are oppressed. I see my patterns. Enlarge my vision before the test. I see why Satan wants to sabotage me. Help me Lord with this thorn in my side! Help me see what I need and substitute healthy rituals. You told me who and how to reach out? Help me know the enemy's strategy to have Victory!

CHAPTER 10

Being a Crushed Woman, Dying to Self, Becoming a Vessel Alive to Christ

Lessons from my journal to allow the crushing to let my light shine and become unbreakable.

January 25, 2008
A Gift from the Lord
"Time to celebrate your wholeness"
January 29, 2008
Restoration

Isaiah 49:1: "Listen to me, you islands; hear this, you distant nations: Before I was born the Lord called me; from my mother's womb he has spoken my name" (NIV).

Isaiah 49:15–16: "Can a mother forget the baby at her breast and have no compassion on the child she has borne? Though she may forget, I will not forget you! See, I have engraved you on the palms of my hands; your walls are ever before me" (NIV).

January 30, 2008
Breakthrough Day
Restoration

Isaiah 49:15–16: "Before I was born the Lord called me...He restored me..." "See I have you engraved on the palm of My hand."

Breakthrough Day
Celebrate Recovery

Isaiah 50:1–2: "Where is your mother's certificate of divorce with which I sent her away? Or to which of my creditors did I sell you? Because of your sins you were sold; because of your transgressions your mother was sent away. When I came, why was there no one? When I called, why was there no one to answer? Was my arm too short to deliver you? Do I lack the strength to rescue you? By a mere rebuke I dry up the sea, I turn rivers into a desert; their fish rot for lack of water and die of thirst" (NIV).

Isaiah 51:12: "I, even I, am he who comforts you. Who are you that you fear mere mortals, human beings who are but grass" (NIV).

Isaiah 51:21: "Therefore hear this, you afflicted one, made drunk, but not with wine" (NIV).

Isaiah 52:12: "But you will not leave in haste or go in flight; for the Lord will go before you, the God of Israel will be your rear guard" (NIV).

Isaiah 54:2a: "Enlarge the place of your tent and stretch your curtains wide! Do not hold back!" (NIV)

Do not be afraid. I will make you Fearless! I heard the Lord encourage my heart.

February 18, 2008

I am another year older and I realize my mind is on the battlefield. I needed to let my faith settle any questions in my mind. The Lord of Love was ministering to me who was much afraid. Just like the book called, "The Dream Giver,[36] by David Wilkerson." I was learning to become fearless.

March 3, 2008

Discovery of self from Ephesians 1:11: "In him we were also chosen, having been predestined according to the plan of him who works out everything in conformity with the purpose of his will" (NIV). From Ephesians 6, I put on the armor of God every day. I was armed and dangerous with Bible verses that would cover my mind with peace and courage. I became unbreakable! My life had purpose and design by God.

March, 2008
Mirror of Brokenness

Ephesians 1:11: "In him we were also chosen, having been predestined according to the plan of him who works out everything in conformity with the purpose of his will" (NIV).

It Is in Christ That We Find Who We Are
Discovery of Real Self

Who is this puffed up, black and blue woman in the mirror? The self that is battled and worn. His Word is a mirror to see my real self, broken but not beaten. I walk in purpose and destiny with my spiritual eyes open, to hold the sword of the Spirit. I am the home of the Spirit of God ready to soar! I have seen the glory of the Lord. Satan knows my name.

---

[36] David Wilkerson, *The Dream Giver* (Colorado: Mulnomah Books, 2003).

March 11, 2008
Poison down the Drain

Proverbs 20:1 NIV "Wine is a mocker, strong drink is a brawler; whoever is led astray by them is not wise." Thank you, Lord, for the victory today.

Psalm 146:7–8: "He upholds the cause of the oppressed and gives food to the hungry. The Lord sets prisoners free, the Lord gives sight to the blind, the Lord lifts up those who are bowed down, the Lord loves the righteous" (NIV).

March 13, 2008
"Move Forward, Do Not Park"

What is God telling me to do NOW? Move forward, do not park. Go to the next level. Stir myself out of complacency. Promotion comes from the Lord. He is working behind the scenes.

"Are you ready to Get Well?"

Stop making Excuses! Desire to Change. God said to remove myself from the path of blame. Accept responsibility. Make changes without excuses or it will have power to stay in my life! Do not be double minded.

"Make room for new things in your life."

"Live with passion. Prepare your mind for Action. All your days are written in My Book. Be my witness. I will give you Supernatural strength and serendipity every day of my intervention in your life!" The above are what I heard in my heart from the Lord.

May 20, 2008
Winds of Change

The First Epistle of Peter 1:13–16: "Therefore, with minds that are alert and fully sober, set your hope on the grace to be brought to you when Jesus Christ is revealed at his coming. As obedient children, do not conform to the evil desires you had when you lived in ignorance. But just as he who called you is holy, so be holy in all you do; for it is written: 'Be holy, because I am holy.'"

Proverbs 29:23: "Pride brings a person low, but the lowly in spirit gain honor" (NIV).

Ponder Holiness and Godliness

Step 6: I am entirely ready to have God remove all defects of my character. "Holy" means having a fully integrated personality. Being whole, nothing missing or lacking. A heart set apart for the Lord.

Luke 12:48: "But the one who does not know and does things deserving punishment will be beaten with few blows. From everyone who has been given much, much will be demanded; and from the one who has been entrusted with much, much more will be asked (NIV).

"Responsibility is the ability to respond appropriately. Revelation gives the possibility of change, its conception and perception. It cannot be taught only when caught." I heard the Lord teach me about responsibility.

"Stop the Clutter"

"Go back and listen to what I want to do in your future. A picture I have given you on the inside of your mind. See the vision before you."

"Productivity is a result of focused effort. You need to remember the intention and the discipline. I will provide the Koinonia, the covenant fellowship with Me and other believers to sanctify you in your body, soul, mind and Spirit."

June 5, 2008
Pentecost Dynamos

"A day of God's favor is worth more than a year of labor." I heard Paula White speak these words on the television. I realize the Lord has granted me his favor in many ways.

A New More Powerful Me!

The First Letter to the Corinthians 10:3–5: "They all ate the same spiritual food 4 and drank the same spiritual drink; for they drank from the spiritual rock that accompanied them, and that rock was Christ. 5 Nevertheless, God was not pleased with most of them; their bodies were scattered in the wilderness" (NIV).

"I hear when you call Me. I answer all of your questions, like yesterday with the car. will you trust Me to care for you, to keep you safe? It is I who rescued you from your mother's womb. I have a plan for your life. It is Time to Walk in it. Do Not be afraid. Do Not Look back!" Pray for Big…the story of Donald Trump Apprenticeship Program with Paula White testifying to Jesus to Him. Eight years later, He becomes the United States President. WOW! I trust you, Lord.

June 12, 2008
Communing with God

Jeremiah 29:11–13: A conversation. "'For I know the plans I have for you,' declares the Lord, 'plans to prosper you and not to harm you, plans to give you hope and a future. Then you will call on me and come and pray to me, and I will listen to you. You will seek me and find me when you seek me with all your heart'" (NIV).

Jeremiah 30:17: "I will restore You" (NIV).

Jeremiah 31:34: "'No longer will they teach their neighbor, or say to one another, "Know the Lord," because they will all know me, from the least of them to the greatest,' declares the Lord. 'For I will forgive their wickedness and will remember their sins no more'" (NIV).

June 16, 2008
The Gift of Recovery
A Student of Self

The Lord has shown me patterns of destruction that are in my life. Patterns of ADHD, I become overly stimulated, responsible and concerned. To then become…irresponsible, stressed out, overly relaxed, lackadaisical. I want to forget my problems. I reach out for the addictive agent or behavior. When all I needed was healthy boundaries, a day off the merry go round of life to slow down and take my hands off of the problem.

"…Be still and know that you are my God" (Psalm 46:10 NIV).

"Pay Attention"

Proverbs 4:20: "My son, pay attention to what I say; turn your ear to my words" (NIV).

Reflections of Yom Kippur
October 9, 2008

Catalina Island with Bob for our thirty-fifth anniversary. Your presence and the big picture you have shown me fifteen years ago amazes me. The smog of the California shoreline lifted. The beautiful blue clear sky with the heavenly clouds over the mountaintops revealed the beauty of this island. Lord, I want to be of use to you.

Galatians 6:5: "For each one should carry their own load" (NIV).

2009
New Vision "Promises to Come This Year to
Experience Change, Time to Advance"

Matthew 6:33: "But seek first his kingdom and his righteousness, and all these things will be given to you as well" (NIV).

Deuteronomy 8:18: "But remember the Lord your God, for it is he who gives you the ability to produce wealth, and so confirms his covenant, which he swore to your ancestors, as it is today" (NIV).

February 6, 2009

"Remember the White Stone shaped as a heart. It will remind you of your innocence as you were justified by My Word. Trust in Me. Be willing to endure and be consistent. Lean not to your own understanding. I will help you take back what Satan has robbed from you. Satan is a terrorist. You need to just stand in the battle. Put on your spiritual armor I have provided. My word is the sword in your hand. Learn to use it. Let My words come out of your mouth and stand firm. Your enemy will flee."

"You are in transition to where I want you to be. Depend on Me and not your own ability. You have been tested well. Pick up a tambourine and Praise My name for such a time as this! Cast your trouble on Me and trust in My promises for your life. Desire Only One thing, My Presence. Dwell, continue and endure. I will establish your success. Behold I am doing a New Thing! Listen for My Instructions."

"It is Time for you to enter into a more intimate relationship with Me. It is Time to sanctify yourself in My Presence and allow Me to use you for My Glory."

Ezekiel 44:4 "I saw the Glory of the Lord fill the Temple and I fell Facedown" 5 "Listen Closely and give attention to everything I tell you concerning all regulations...vs 23...No Wine in the inner Court." Lord the Battle is yours. Please help me.

February 16, 2009
Divine Completion

Two thousand nine is a year of the Spirit. "Get ready for predetermined destiny. You are pregnant. It is time to deliver and give birth and become everything I have told you. You will finally see the results of years of your life with Me. Look forward to something you have never seen before. I am doing a new thing in your life."

February 18, 2009
Happy Birthday Memorial Stones

"Be happy to be Rose. Remember the many things I have done in your life. Be ready to celebrate and tell the stories. Your red-letter days when you listened to My voice. The divine appointments that helped you to recognize My hand in your life. The many times I have spared your life. The interruption of the demon of alcohol to rob, steal and destroy your life. The race car driver told you, 'You must be living right.' To convict you to see my mercy and grace in your life. I have given you much to be grateful for. Remember too much is given, much is required. Look at the stones and shells that are memorial stones of the things that have made up the red-letter days of your life.

"Happy Birthday, Rose. This is an appointed moment. I will begin to show you how your life is coming together with My plan. I am in the process of restoring what has been lost. I will restore you to wholeness. See the big picture of your whole life. It is a circle. The past, present, future, the fulfillment and your eternal life with Me. I am giving you a heavenly perspective so you will be patient with yourself. Do whatever I tell you to do. I will direct your path. Open the eyes of your heart so you can see me work in every area of your life. Walk into the great adventure of your new life with Me and become what I created you to be—a godly woman by My design. Trust in Me."

March 29, 2009
Be Glorified in My Life

"My daughter, you are of Me. You are Being and Becoming all that I have designed you to be. You will be Free to live the life you have dreamed for you, your husband and your children. Your life will be filled to overflowing. You will bring My Life to many I have destined you to touch in My Name. In your life, I will be glorified and you will experience true freedom."

May 7–8, 2009
Day of Fasting and Prayer
National Day of Prayer
The Lord Spoke to Me

My Daughter,

"I revealed the big picture of the plan I have for your life many years ago. You thought at that time, it was all about Herbalife. Over time I have shown you the vehicle that has been to give you a pulpit and to build leadership skills within you.

Now is the time for the assigned work to be done. For the many souls you will touch for My glory. I have your angel assigned for the work. Follow My Voice and lead. The angel is before you. Fear not, I am with you. every place your foot walks, I will have the angel push back the darkness in the way.

You will experience Psalm 91 in your life. Do not be afraid of the lion roar or the tricks of the serpent. They are under your feet. You will take back the territory the enemy has stolen.

Allow Me to be glorified in your life. Lift up My Name. I will draw all those you touch unto Me. The spirit of python will not stop you. Be Bold and Courageous. I am with you and the angel is before you to complete every assignment! Be about My business. I will take care of yours!"

June 10, 2009
Life after Dirty Politics

Cleanse me, Lord. Free me from the anxiety. I walked humbly before. Forgive my sins and make me whole. Make me free from the thorn in my flesh.

"Be not afraid of the future. I hold it in my hands. You will see with your eyes my plan unfolds. Do not look to the right or to the left. Keep your eyes straight on the narrow path and you will see Me there. Come on in! I await to show you great and mighty things you do not know. Do not be afraid of the clamor around you. Find your freedom in Me! My angel is before you every step is marked out for you. Follow me. I will make you a Fisher of Men."

June 11, 2009
The Bird Serenade: A Day to Remember

Along with the sound of barking dogs, a large industrial lawn mower, I heard an unusual sound of air swishing and flapping among the trees. I looked and saw the graceful landing of a Beautiful Blue Heron at Glen Lake in Woodbury Heights for the first time. I quietly walked along and followed her peeking through the trees. Our eyes met on several occasions. Then she begins to wade into the water at the lakes edge. She turns her head and watches me once more. Then she spreads her large, majestic wigs and flies to the other side. Once she has settled her eyes upon me again. I am in awe of her beauty and grace. She reminded me of why we have a lake association.

As I sat back into my car. I enjoyed the sounds of many birds each singing their own song enjoying the day. I absorbed the wetland smell of the lake and the paramount view of my green surroundings. See the robin come sit on the fence by my car. All the others I did not recognize. I listen to all the unique calls blending together like an orchestra each waiting their turn to come in on time. It is a beautiful bird serenade.

They invited me to be still and to know their creator for whom they sing. My heart sings with them in praise for My Creator and Lord Jesus! Thank You for this day to remember.

I found a bench on the other side of the lake to sit and Meditate on these things. It gave me a new vantage point to observe the beauty that surrounds me. Your Word to me today comes from

Mark 6:31 "Then, because so many people were coming and going that they did not even have a chance to eat, he said to them, "Come with me by yourselves to a quiet place and get some rest" (NIV).

Saying Goodbye to Spiritual Sisters and Family Members Linda and Carol

"I have anointed you. You have the oil that has been given to you. Now go and I will anoint and put my healing on Linda. Do not be afraid." Carol said, "No, do not go. Today is not a good day for my sister." I replied, I must go when the Lord says go. He knows what is going on with your sister. I came to the door. She was so happy to see me. After about an hour of her telling me her story of the dramatic events in her health, I asked if she would like to invite Jesus in her heart and life to help her. She said yes, so I anointed her with oil and we prayed. I felt the Spirit of God enter her home and life. She said, "Thank you, I feel better. The fear is gone!" Thank You, Jesus!

She went through all the treatments and we celebrated her cancer-free day! She came for dinner. We had Steak, champagne (only one glass) and cheesecake.

Then at here celebration of Life, June 24, 2009, the song, "I Can Only Imagine"[37] by MercyMe, explained what Linda was now experiencing! Thank You for giving me the courage to go! Bless her daughter Missy and grandson Adrian, I pray.

It will be what seemed like a short time that I had to say good bye to Carol her sister, my daughter in laws mother. It was a sad time for our family. She told me, "Take care of my girls, Christy, Sarah,

---

[37] MercyMe, "I Can Only Imagine" (The Worship Project, 1999).

and Missy." It has become my goal to be available and keep a mother's eye on each one. And also our mutual grandchildren, Carolyn Rosemary (she is named after all of us including Nanny Mary), and John Robert "Jack" Jr., named after my son John and my husband.

They are all a blessing in my life.

Yom Kippur
September 28, 2009

At the river, my place of rest, I heard your voice again. "Be Still and know I am God. seek first My Kingdom and all these things will be added to you. Feel the fresh air upon your face, the sun rays on your back. Let the burden roll off! You can do all things through Me and My strength and nothing on your own. Breathe in a refill of My Spirit. A New Wind of Revival is coming. Allow my power to work through you. You are not alone. Find the secret place every day and hear my voice. See the butterflies. They are free and so are you!" Praise you, Lord!

Freedom Is My Word

The eagle is soaring today! I saw it at the park by the river. I heard the Lord speak to my heart. "Walk in freedom from this day forward with a strong ankle. Follow Me. You are a fisher of men. Allow me to prepare you for my best. Be at one with Me. Do not look to the left or the right. Do not listen to the noise and babbling each day. Listen to me!" Yes, Lord!

Proverbs 24:6: "Surely you need guidance to wage war, and victory is won through many advisers" (NIV). Safety in a multitude of counselors.

The Second Letter to the Corinthians 3:17: "Now the Lord is the Spirit, and where the Spirit of the Lord is, there is freedom" (NIV).

The First Letter to the Corinthians 7:21: "Were you a slave when you were called? Don't let it trouble you—although if you can gain your freedom, do so" (NIV).

Romans 8:21: "That the creation itself will be liberated from its bondage to decay and brought into the freedom and glory of the children of God" (NIV).

Galatians 5:1: "It is for freedom that Christ has set us free. Stand firm, then, and do not let yourselves be burdened again by a yoke of slavery" (NIV).

Galatians 5:8: "That kind of persuasion does not come from the one who calls you" (NIV)

These are my favorite quotes from the monument wall at Fort Mercer in National Park, New Jersey. My favorite park! The Lord reminded me that blood had been shed for my freedom right here at this park.

"The harder the conflict, more glorious the triumph" (Thomas Paine)

"Liberty must be gained by inches" (Thomas Jefferson).

Reflections of Success
October 16, 2009
Butterfly at My Window

As I sat with my new Herbalife friends in our Atlanta high rise hotel room on the 28th floor, I felt the presence of your Holy Spirit. At that moment, my roommates saw a butterfly at the window just watching us. It was a WOW Kairos moment in time, a time that God had orchestrated to reveal His presence to all of us in the room. I know you will reach my agnostic friend.

I Heard Your Voice Speak to Me

"I want you to know what I have already taught you. I want you to follow the instructions I have already given. It is a new day. allow the dark clouds of night to lift away from your life. A new dawn is here and you are a part of the landscape. Pay attention and look for the signs I will give you. In the past you have only seen reflections of success. You did not see your name written up there upon the hall of fame. A woman of faith leading and teaching and inspiring others to search for Me and find true success in every area of their lives. You have been on side roads in the past. You have searched for a back road to success. Do not be afraid to get on the highway. I am the navigator. I will take you places you never dreamed possible. If only you will trust in Me to discipline your life. You will be a beautiful woman by My design. You are unique. You need not follow someone else. Follow me and you reflections of success will become an everyday reality, and you will live the life of your dreams. Come into My light. It is a new day. The hour is late. You do not know how many days left to fulfill your destiny."

October 20, 2009
Water the Seed

"Water the seeds of faith in the people who need nurturing around you in your life."

December 1, 2009
Day of Destiny

My first Christmas visitor was Mariella Van Gurp. Another Kairos moment. "Today is the day of her salvation" Praise the Lord! The angels in heaven rejoice with me! Blessed Marielle and her family here and in Holland.

Spiritual Battlefield
The Lord Spoke to My Heart from Ephesians 6:10–17(NIV)

"Your fight is not with people. A new level of spiritual growth requires you to put on the full armor that I have provided. The Divine Closet of Spiritual clothes will make you strong in my power. The helmet of my salvation will protect your mind where the battlefield takes place. The breastplate protects you heart and vital organs. My shoes of peace make you steady. The belt of truth is where everything is placed for the battle. The shield of faith holds back and extinguishes the fiery dart of your enemy. The sword of My Word drives back the darkness. Hide my Word in your heart that you might not sin against Me. Be strong in the power of My Might. It is not by power but by My Spirit. The Battle is not yours. It was won at Calvary by the Blood of My Son Jesus. Apply the Blood to every situation where you see the enemy at work and say the Name of Jesus. Stand Firm and the devil your enemy will flee. You will be overcome by the blood of the Lamb and the word of your testimony."

January 4, 2010
New Year Thoughts
Facing the Giants on the Boulevard of Dreams

A new year, new friends and old friends from Herbalife join for a fellowship time. The plan: movie *Facing the Giants*[38] and Dream Boards. As we sit crowded together with magazines and scissors around the little TV. I felt Your Spirit speak to me. "You prayed for this. For a group of leaders to build Herbalife in this area." This is a Kairos moment! I thought like the movie says, "With God, all things are possible! Thank You, Lord."

April 10, 2010
Stop, Yield, Caution!

"Learn to know My voice. Learn to hear it above the noise of the world. Unclutter your life and do only what I call you to do. Discern the sounds of the different bird calls around you. You do not know them, but I do. Do you remember the distinct call of the nightingale in Orlando outside of your window? I spoke to you that night as she sang her song to you all night. You do not understand the information you have been given but I do. Be not afraid of what you think. You cannot possibly understand the bigger picture. But I

---

[38] Alex and Stephen Kendrick (directors), *Facing the Giants* (Sherwood Pictures, 2006).

am the Alpha and the Omega. My plan is from the beginning to this time and into a brilliant future. Consider this insight landscape to motivate your work in my plan. For your life, your town and your church and your country. I will accomplish that which I will at this time. Become a vessel I can use for My glory. If I am lifted up, I will draw all men who hear my voice unto myself. You will be fearless because My perfect love cast out all fear. Walk in love."

June 21, 2010
Heavenly Vision

Acts 1:8: "But you will receive power when the Holy Spirit comes on you; and you will be my witnesses in Jerusalem, and in all Judea and Samaria, and to the ends of the earth" (NIV).

Acts 26:19: "So then, King Agrippa, I was not disobedient to the vision from heaven" (NIV).

"Get up and go see the beginning of the new season." Yes, Lord. I go to investigate at 5:35 a.m. and this is what I saw, a red ball of fire thru the trees with light rays thru the silver lined clouds. Praise the Lord! For seeing the first sun rays of a new season, and experience to celebrate!

Thoughts for 2011 and the Empty Nest
Eliminate and Concentrate

Jeremiah 33:3: "Therefore the showers have been withheld, and no spring rains have fallen. Yet you have the brazen look of a prostitute; you refuse to blush with shame" (NIV).

Jeremiah 33:6: "During the reign of King Josiah, the Lord said to me, "Have you seen what faithless Israel has done? She has gone up on every high hill and under every spreading tree and has committed adultery there" (NIV).

Jeremiah 35:13–15: "This is what the Lord Almighty, the God of Israel, says: Go and tell the people of Judah and those living in Jerusalem, 'Will you not learn a lesson and obey my words?' declares the Lord. 'Jehonadab son of Rebab ordered his descendants not to drink wine and this command has been kept. To this day they do not drink wine, because they obey their forefather's command. But I have spoken to you again and again, yet you have not obeyed me. Again and again I sent all my servants the prophets to you. They said, "Each of you must turn from your wicked ways and reform your actions; do not follow other gods to serve them. Then you will live in the land I have given to you and your ancestors. But you have not paid attention or listened to me.

Learn the lesson. Obey the word. Do not drink be…turn…reform…action…then…the Promise. Know who I am and Your purpose. Get serious. Listen to the unsearchable things of God. Thin your possessions and get ready to move.'" Our plan was to move downstairs into the mother-in-law suite in our large bilevel home. It was my mother's room. My son and his family was coming to live upstairs. Our empty nest will be filled again.

June 15, 2011
"Be a Hero"

When I ponder being pushed down and falling down and losing elections and running again and again.

Second Corinthians 4:9: "Persecuted, but not abandoned; struck down, but not destroyed" (NIV).

Even with the broken ankle growing stronger through change. Strength to keep talking to the next person. Opening my mind to use the talents you have given me and the courage to start over. God's will for me is customized.

Philippians 1:3: "I thank my God every time I remember you" (NIV).

Job 23:14: "He carries out his decree against me, and many such plans he still has in store" (NIV).

I hear the voices of others telling me that "You are an inspiration to all of us. We are watching you."

Lord, let me ponder your words to me on the beach in Brigantine Day Spa. "Do not be afraid of the process. Do My will My way. Stay in balance."

Romans 13:14: "Rather, clothe yourselves with the Lord Jesus Christ, and do not think about how to gratify the desires of the flesh" (NIV).

Hebrews 12:1–3: "Therefore, since we are surrounded by such a great cloud of witnesses, let us throw off everything that hinders and the sin that so easily entangles. And let us run with perseverance the race marked out for us, fixing our eyes on Jesus, the pioneer and perfecter of faith. For the joy set before him he endured the cross, scorning its shame, and sat down at the right hand of the throne of God. Consider him who endured such opposition from sinners, so that you will not grow weary and lose heart" (NIV).

Isaiah 41:10–13: "Fear not I am with you. Do not look around in terror or be afraid. "I am your God. I will strengthen you and harden you in difficulty. I am with you who says to you, Fear Not I will Help You."

July 22, 2011
Live Above the Pressures of Life

"Walk in the Spirit so you do not fulfill the lust of the flesh. Walk in love. Be a Hero to those who are watching you. I, the Lord, will get you the results. Be steady and persistent."

August 5, 2011
Times of Testing

Our female pastor was fired. I felt shaken. What is going on, Lord? I trust you are giving my pastor wisdom.

Then I went to the counselor, he says "Take it to the judge!" Before the council, educate and prepare before the vote and opt out of The Agenda! As I stood before the council, I could feel my hand shaking at my side. They said no. So now I have to take it to the judge. I would have to sue my town to get the question onto the ballot for the people to decide.

Bob's Antidote

"Rose you are barking up a big tree and your dog is too small!" Is he saying that I am a toy poodle? No, I am a Golden Retriever; the best dog! God has called me to bark loud up this tree until Dobermans and Shepherds and Pit Bulls come to see what is up there! Praise the Lord! Help me to be persistent.

Help me be a Hero!

Help me to act like a princess, a daughter of my king. Like all dressed up for a wedding playing the part of the bride. I need to realize that others are watching me. You told me, "I am of you! You bring Me delight when you do My will!"

Bob was right. You cannot always fight city hall and win. But I did what the Lord told me to do. That is good enough for me.

New Priorities

January 6, 2012
What Is Important

"Thin your possessions and get ready to move. I will show you what is really important. You are moving downstairs so now you have a reason and a deadline. This is the trial run for what I have shown you years ago."

March 4, 2012
Remember your Pastor

As I was praying for Pastor Bruce today, you spoke to my heart. "Today is a special day for your pastor. Do not take him for granted. Bless him today. Today is his birthday."

Lord, forgive me for taking your man of god for granted. Thank you for the blessing he has been to me. You have used him to teach, mentor, challenge and love me. I remember my pastor today and count him as my blessing from above. Bless him on his birthday and his new book. Amen.

May 5, 2012
Recognize His Voice—Voices and Choices
Pastor Bruce

The Second Book of Timothy 1:7: "For the Spirit God gave us does not make us timid, but gives us power, love and self-discipline" (NIV).

We default to our past and listen to the wrong voices.

Six to ten young people leave church by age fifteen.

How to listen and respond to God's voice is through the process of sanctification

Romans 12:2: "Do not conform to the pattern of this world, but be transformed by the renewing of your mind. Then you will be able to test and approve what God's will is—his good, pleasing and perfect will" (NIV).

Then testing produces discernment to hear His voice.

The Second Epistle to the Corinthians 5:17: "Therefore, if anyone is in Christ, the new creation has come: The old has gone, the new is here" (NIV)!

Psalm 81:11–12 "But my people would not listen to me; Israel would not submit to me.

So I gave them over to their stubborn hearts to follow their own devices" (NIV).

God's voice sounds like your own conscience. Asking us to do things we do not want to do and I would not think to do it.

Matthew 4:5–7: "Then the devil took him to the holy city and had him stand on the highest point of the temple. 'If you are the Son of God,' he said, 'throw yourself down. For it is written:

'He will command his angels concerning you,
and they will lift you up in their hands,
so that you will not strike your foot against a stone.'

Jesus answered him, 'It is also written: 'Do not put the Lord your God to the test'" (NIV).

161

What is it that is taking me away from what God has called me to be and become? Taking my time…what stops me? What is the next step…? Reveal it to me Lord. Then commit it to you. Lord, forgive me for the busy life and busy ears listening to other people. Help me to hear from You. You have set me aside on a shelf for this season. You are preparing me for a new place in the Body of Christ. Help me find my place? In the boiler room as a prayer warrior? And a witness to my own family and children by the power of my own testimony. Let me be an encouragement for those hurt and broken, like the girls at the doctors' office. A discerner for those who are confused. An evangelist for those like Marielle. To be a leader in my church and community. Help me to stand in the places You call me to go. To be firmly planted and grow in Christ.

Empty Nest
March 5, 2012
A New Season

We are moving downstairs. What a blessing this home has been to our family. Help us create clear boundaries and be a blessing to my son John and his family. As I sift through my treasury. I am like a fisherman with a dragnet, finding everything. But I must sort it out and gather the good things you want me to keep and what can bless others. I need your wisdom to only keep what you want me to keep. My library is a dream. Let me pass on the legacy of love from my treasury of books, photos and journal in this new Season.

November 11, 2012
Citizen of Faith

Ephesian 4:1–5: "As a prisoner for the Lord, then, I urge you to live a life worthy of the calling you have received. Be completely humble and gentle; be patient, bearing with one another in love. Make every effort to keep the unity of the Spirit through the bond of peace. There is one body and one Spirit, just as you were called to

one hope when you were called; one Lord, one faith, one baptism"
(NIV).

November 27, 2012

"I will give you wisdom and discernment as you seek to do
My Will. Do not trust yourself, only trust Me. I will show you how
to be faithful in the little things and to be focused on the goal. Get
organized and stay organized and I will add hours to your day to
accomplish the work."

New Year of Reshaping: 2013

"I am doing a new thing. This is a new season. Be ready…
Repay old debts. Let go of old relationships. Learn to see things in
a new way. Do not worry where you fit in. I am reshaping you for a
new place in the Body of Christ. Do not look back. Just feel the wind
and the sun at your back and step forward. I will guide you in a new
direction. You will know where you fit in when you arrive. For such a
time as this, you will be like Esther walking into your destiny."

"Just like getting to the beach is a safe and familiar place, but
it is the end of New Jersey. You cannot go any further. You need to
accept the seascape as it is with broken shells and all. The beach has
survived the storm. It is still here and so are you! Learn to dance in
the rain and in the moment. Be still and know that I am God. There
is a specific walk for you to do. I have designed you and your life to
fit together with My plan. The tapestry has been carefully woven by
My hands for your life to make a beautiful design. You're a woman
who is by my design. A woman for all seasons, who will walk with me
to accomplish and finish the works planned for your hands. Trust me
to speak to you at this retreat, 'A Woman for All Seasons.'"

February 10, 2013
Highly Esteemed

"Pray and Praise. Listen to my Word, and obey My Word. Be bold and courageous, confront sin and you will become a woman for all seasons just like Daniel was a man for all Seasons. He was highly esteemed and dearly loved by Me. He had political wisdom for the place where I put him. Stop praying and asking and begin to give thanks. Trust me to choose the best way to answer your prayers. He was humbled and I used him greatly. He made disciples not just converts. Learn from Daniel to trust in Me to give you My advice about all these matters of concern. I am with you. You are my daughter, highly esteemed and loved."

February 22, 2013
My Last Sermon

"Keep Jesus first in every area of life. Follow Him, and if you cannot see the hem of His robe, you are lost!" That would be my last sermon today.

March 2, 2013
New from the Inside Out

"Everything will be brought into the light for my examination. Do Not hide yourself from me. I will peel away every ugly layer of useless things that hinder your growth, physical, emotional and spiritual. Allow Me to cut away all the dead things that drain your life and threaten your health. Just like a wound that is cleaned. I will bring forth new skin, so shall you become new from the inside out. Your beauty will be evident and you will look like Me."

March 22, 2013
Come Follow Me

The closest point between two destinations is a straight line. There may be other adjacent lines and points that will make a longer path to the desired destination, but only one narrow and direct path.

When Jesus called me to follow Him, I was excited to follow him closely. I had a "Anything spirit." Anything the Lord called me to do, I was excited and ready to do.

When I learned more about following Jesus, I became more aware of my own weakness. I felt humbled to be a Christ follower but willing to learn to do *anything* for Him.

Then I learned how to do more things for Jesus. I became more confident in His ability to use me. I now wanted to do *everything* for Jesus.

When I learned how to do everything for Jesus. I became weary of doing good. I needed to learn to let go and let God do everything. I heard Him say, "Pray more, do less."

When I learned to "pray more, do less" for Jesus, I now wanted to be more like Jesus and let Him do His work for me.

As I followed the crooked path, I could see the straight path ahead of me. I saw the hem of His garment and I heard His voice.

"Come follow Me. My way is easy. My path is straight. Do not become weary or sidetracked. Keep your eyes on Me, and I will direct your path. Come follow me."

May 5, 2013
Recognize My Voice

Romans 12:2: "Be transformed by the renewing of your mind then to the heart to transform you. The testing produces discernment to hear My voice. Seek Me with your whole heart. My voice sounds like your own consciousness. Asking you to do things you do not want to do or would not think of doing. Do not test Me. Spend time in My presence and ask me what your next step is to do my will. I will reveal it to you. Then I ask you to commit to doing it."

Lord, forgive me for being too busy and having listening ears to everyone else but You. Help me hear from You alone.

"I have set you aside for a season. You are preparing for a new place in the body of Christ. As a prayer warrior in the boiler room of your church. I will also send you to those still seeking me like Michael and Rick. You will be like a guidepost for those who are lost and are weary. Make disciples like Rose Anne. Encourage those who are hurt and broken like the girls at Dr Chandra's office who have been abused. Be a discerner for those who are confused. Be an evangelist for those who are lost and a leader for those who need my direction. I have prepared Christian Leaders Association for you to stand firm and be grounded in My Word and grow in Christ. Remember nothing is more important than eternal things. I will show you the things that will last."

May 12, 2013
Mother's Day

"Thank you for praying!" said Pastor Bruce, as he popped his head in the door of our Prayer Closet. I responded, "It is my pleasure to pray, Pastor." It is called the Boiler Room Ministry that meets in a conference room at church before the service. Many times I sit there alone. Prayer warriors come and go. But today was a special day. I felt tears well up in my eyes. I heard your voice tell me, *"You have found your place here in this body of believers. Prayer is the work I have called you to do. Your pastor understands the importance of this ministry, and now so should you. This is the new place for this new season I have called you to serve. You are not alone. You are in the war room doing battle against the enemy so My Word can go forth to bind up the bruised and broken and save the lost. I am here with you."*

Every woman was given a beautiful red rose today. Seeing all the women leaving church was a showstopper. A breathtaking, speechless beautiful sight. Each of us felt honored by our pastor and church family. Thank You Jesus for this special Mother's Day.

May 17, 2013
Codependent No More[39]

I felt you were reading the book again. You had even provided the twenty dollars in my purse. At the bookstore on the top shelf, I saw a new workbook to go with the book that I had already read several times. I heard you say I felt tears well up and start to flow from the emotional release and I heard you say. "Your lessons will come to you when it is time, one after another. You are being refined. You're becoming a new person! You are codependent no more, but healthy and well. You are recovering what has been lost. You are whole, nothing missing, nothing broken—by My grace."

May 19, 2013
Pentecost Sunday

Today is a special day. Pastor Walt from Abundant Life Church prayed for me. "Lord, I pray for a breakthrough in her mind, set her free from old patterns of thinking. Reveal yourself to her in a New Way. Baptize her in the Holy Spirit power again. Release your power in her life. In Jesus's name, amen.

"Bride of Christ, put on your robe of righteousness. Have no fear. The devil is under your feet."

Burning Inside

What is this, Lord? I excuse myself to the ladies' room. Praying, prepare me, Lord. Show me if this is what you want for me? It looks like a show. It sounds like a clanging cymbal, so loud. It feels like sandpaper on my skin, cold goosebumps, uncomfortable in my inward being physically, mentally, and emotionally. I feel vulnerable like a baby Christian again—watching the show of the Pentecostals. Their spirit and tongues are on display. They jump and dance and take off their shoes and fall to their knees and jump to the stage and rub bel-

---

[39] Melody Beattie, *Codependent No More* (Minnesota: Hazelden, 1986).

lies and lay hands to those who receive gifts of the Second coming—tongues. They pace the floors in the room and a young man saw a vision of five in the front with tongues of fire on their heads. Who are the five? Everyone in the room had come forward except Bob and I and the worship team. The microphones were on the pastor and the guest speaker. The tongues grew louder and louder and the chorus of those in the circle around them until I could no longer pray. I no longer felt the Spirit of the Lord but another spirit, the loud obnoxious chaotic noise of the satanic spirit. My husband said, "I can't take no more of this," and he left. It was the answer…flee from sin…I do not belong here! The people at the back table asked my husband, "You aren't going to buy anything?" He just walked away. I packed up my Bible and notebook. I put on my jacket and followed my husband. I had enough of the show. The Holy Spirit is a gentleman. Well, I never saw a gentleman yell or jump and rub bellies and ask people to buy his wares or push his opinion on other people. "The small quiet voice of the Holy spirit was echoed out by the loud and proud spirits of the Pentecostals. I felt the fire of the Holy spirit burning inside of me! Lord Why am I here? Are you teaching me to become a prophet, one who tells the truth?

Revelation 10:10: "I took the little scroll from the angel's hand and ate it. It tasted as sweet as honey in my mouth, but when I had eaten it, my stomach turned sour" (NIV).

I Timothy 4:1: "The Spirit clearly says that in later times some will abandon the faith and follow deceiving spirits and things taught by demons" (NIV).

June 24, 2013
The Hummingbird in My Hand

I felt like time stood still. I was frozen in awe, in awe of the awesome God who made us both. I felt the vibrations of her wings on my hand like a rushing wind. The humming sound filled my ears. It hovered at the feeder in my hands right before my eyes.

The Lord spoke to me in that moment just like he had at my first sighting many years ago. It was a red-letter Day I will never forget!

"See, I know the times and the seasons of all things. I hold your life in my hands. I am putting you in a new place. You will see how you fit into the body of Christ. You have been set aside for a time to grow into your calling. You are anointed to be sent forth with a word of truth. My word for those appointed to hear my will unfold in their lives. You had my prophets speak into your life so you could be and become a vessel I can use for my glory!"

Confirmation:

Rita Reyes said, "Be the Prophet, the Visionary for the Blind."

Be Anxious for Nothing
January 19, 2015

"Rose, you are anxious about many things. Let the main thing be the main thing. I brought you out of the darkness into my marvelous light so that you can bring others into My presence. Realize your purpose. Be ready. I have prepared you. Go and jump into action to see My Spirit works through you. You will see wonders before your eyes like the hummingbird in your hand. I placed it there in My perfect timing. Be anxious for nothing or no one. I am the Lord, Your God."

June 1, 2015
Seize the Divine Moments
Matthew 14:22–33

Come and get my feet wet! Get out of the boat!

Joshua 13 to 19: Strong and Courageous Faith
God told Joshua that he's old and there is more work to do.

When your feet step—actions to claim the land, obey today (from chapter 1)!

Become courageous, become courageous, become courageous (3×)!

Think of love as a weapon. Abe Lincoln said, "Love all and malice toward none."

June 26, 2015
Do Not Be Afraid

Supreme Court decision for gay marriage. "No longer the same America. Do not be afraid. I am with you till the end of the age." Church age? "Time for grace."

July, 2015
Red Carpet Treatment

First time in St. Louis at Herbalife Extravaganza. I went into the wrong door the wrong way. As I walked on the red carpet to be one of the first seated in the dome. I heard you say, "You are called here." My guilt was gone and I enjoyed the special treatment. My chair had a green seat cover for the Global Expansion Team. I sat and was in awe of you, Lord. The goose bumps, the lights in the darkness, the Christians on the stage and around me made me realize I am Home with my Herbalife Family. This is where I belong.

Walking in the Arch and hearing the history, I felt privileged to be here. Amazed by the structure, I peeked out the window and saw the beauty of the city below. Lord, show me your will and guide me in everything! I feel very creative after this trip!

Frank Capra "A Hunch Is Creativity
Trying to Tell You Something!"
July 24, 2015
"Keep Close and Rest in my Presence"
Secret of the Dragonfly

"Rest in my Presence and Abide in Me. Keep Close. Live in My Presence. That is the secret of all power, all peace, all purity, all influence in keeping very near to Me, your Source." Even dragonflies have to rest.

August 1, 2015
Tormenting Spirits

James 3:14: "But if you harbor bitter envy and selfish ambition in your hearts, do not boast about it or deny the truth" (NIV).

"Focus on what I have called you to do: Pray for the Sick, cast out demons. Do My will on the Earth. Jesus is the Author and Finisher of Your Faith. All is well."

September 27, 2015
The Blue Moon

I watched with my new friends from the shore like a drive-In movie to watch the blue moon and then the eclipse. I am in awe of you and Your presence! It puts everything into perspective. The eclipse piercing the darkness was an amazing sight. A red glow could be seen by the naked eye in the sky. Just beautiful! And the crazy thing is that it is called a blue moon! Always heard all my life about the blue moon and this is the first I have actually seen it.

After one hour, it began the process backward. Red is the color of royalty and the Blood of Jesus that pierced through the darkness and brought Light to the world. Signs and wonders in the sky—let it bring all to You! Lord, did something happen or change in the atmosphere? I pray for America and the world to be ready for your coming. Come Lord Jesus.

September 30, 2015
Wisdom from Above

"The same spirit that raised Jesus from the dead lives in you!" All wisdom and strength is given to me from my Abba Father for each task given to me. "No fear, no doubt."

October 1, 2015
The Dream Giver

Lord, you have given every dream in my heart. I heard a red cardinal at the bird feeder, the sound of her call, opened my heart to your voice. The Lord said, "Sit and Be Still and I will show you and teach you unsearchable things. You must learn to hear and discern my voice quickly and clearly. I am the Lord who comforts you and strengthens you and leads you into a New Day. I long to speak to you but you fail to listen. Open your heart and mind every morning as you open your eyes." Isaiah 61:1: "Morning by morning, He awakens me to the understanding of His will."

October 2, 2015
God Remembered Princess Rose

First Epistle of Peter 2:10: "Once you were not a people, but now you are the people of God; once you had not received mercy, but now you have received mercy" (NIV).

October 4, 2015
"Do Not Lose Your Courage"

Hebrews 10:35: "So do not throw away your confidence; it will be richly rewarded" (NIV).

Lord, Thank You for being my Best Friend of my Broken Heart. I know you are talking to me about specific things, my Herbalife Biz, my children, grandchildren and my homeschool efforts, political aspirations. Bob won. Is it time to push forward or to rest? Your answer to me-"Come unto me for everything."

Psalm 71:1–2: "In you, Lord, I have taken refuge; let me never be put to shame. In your righteousness, rescue me and deliver me; turn your ear to me and save me" (NIV).

First Corinthians 13:4: "Love is patient, love is kind. It does not envy, it does not boast, it is not proud" (NIV).

Hebrews 11:6: "And without faith it is impossible to please God, because anyone who comes to him must believe that he exists and that he rewards those who earnestly seek him" (NIV).

December 15, 2015
A Sad Day

Today I lost my good friend Mary Lou. She was a kindred spirit and a prayer partner. We met through Marriage Encounter and would get together with her and her husband.

My heart ached as I remembered many of the stories of faith she had shared with me. My favorite being the first.

They lived in an old home. She said she would hear voices when she first moved in, and the floorboards creaked like someone else was in the home with her. When she would tell her husband, who was a policeman, he told her, it was her imagination. The last night she had gone into her kitchen and saw all her butcher knives laid on her countertop very neatly. She asked her husband if he put them there. He said, "No, of course not. I thought it was you." So she went to her pastor to discuss what was happening. She went to the library and did some research too. She found out that a murder had happened in the house years ago. Some said it was haunted by the woman who had committed the murder. She stabbed her husband and his girl-friend to death in the upstairs bedroom.

Her pastor came and prayed through the house and blessed it and all the unusual noises and happenings came to an abrupt end. The power of prayer is amazing.

The favorite summer story was the fire story. Mary Lou son had been sick. As a nurse also she was very concerned as they could not seem to find out the problem. The night before it happened, she had prayed with a prayer partner from California. Her friend said, "The Lord is telling me to tell you, to trust in him and not the circumstances. Things are not as they seem. He will carry your son in the palm of my hand. Do not be afraid no matter what happens."

She was working the 3–11 shift at a local hospital. As she walked out to the parking lot, she felt a strong feeling of dread. She knew something was wrong at home with one of her children. She came home as fast as she could, praying for the Lord to protect her children. When she drove up to her home, she saw a burnt mattress on the front lawn.

All three of the children were up trying to tell her what had happened. Her oldest son was sleeping in her bed with the electric blanket. It caught on fire! Her husband was able to fold the mattress in halve and throw it out the window. Then put out the flames with the hose.

Her heart was racing as she thanked the Lord under her breath for his protection. As she put her oldest son to bed, she asked him what made him wake up? He said, "Dad's friend woke me up."

"Oh, thank God!" she said.

She asked her husband, "Who was the friend that was here tonight?"

He said, "No one was here tonight."

Then who woke our son up? They asked their son what he looked like. He said, "He was tall with blond hair like Daddy." She thought, *It must have been the angel I asked God to send to protect my children.*

Weeks later, her son still was not well. In the middle of the night, she heard banging on the pipes. What is that she thought?

She rang downstairs and saw her son on the floor in the bathroom with his head in the toilet, vomiting. He said, "Mom, I am too weak to get up."

She remembered what her friend had said earlier, "Things are not as they seem." So she called 911 for an ambulance. She worked in the emergency room and knew the doctor.

He met her and said, "The stomach flu is going around."

She said, "I want a CAT scan of his brain."

The doctor said, "Mary Lou, you are over-reacting. Your insurance will not cover it. But to make you feel better I will order it. Go get some coffee and relax."

So she went back to the waiting room.

About fifteen minutes later, the doctor came running out into the hall. He said, "How did you know? Your son has a bleeding brain tumor in the back of his head. We have to fly him to Pennsylvania Hospital. They will pick him up at the high school. You need to sign for his surgery now and can meet him there. He will be in surgery before you get there."

She was numb but praising the Lord for saving her son. "Please, Lord, give the surgeon wisdom and knowledge and heal my son." It was a long road to recovery but the Lord answered her prayer.

We always had lots to pray for. My five kids and her four. And the Lord watched over them all.

One day as I was leaving her house, my son locked his hand in the car door. He was screaming and I was crying. My friend came out and took authority in the name of Jesus. She said, "Open in Jesus's name!" It opened, and we all cried, "Praise You, Jesus!" I learned many things from my spiritual friend.

She was with me when my mom passed. My mother asked her to take care of me. And she did help me through my grief. I am forever thankful for a godly friendship. I look forward to seeing her in heaven someday. Thank you, my friend.

January 20, 2016
Your Will, Not My will

Philippians 4:9: "Whatever you have learned, received, heard or seen in Me—put into practice" (NIV).

Hebrews 10:23: "Hold unswervingly to the hope we profess, for He who promised is faithful" (NIV).

Hebrews 10:35: "Do not throw away confidence; it will be richly rewarded" (NIV).

Hebrews 10:36: "You need to persevere so that when you have done the will of God, you will receive what he has promised" (NIV).

"All is well. The time of the Lord's favor has come. My grace changes everything."

"You are being rooted and grounded. Do not try to plan. Rose is a builder, not an *architect*!"

Proverbs 27:1: "Do not boast about tomorrow, for you do not know what a day may bring" (NIV).

"Lessons from the Bad Girls of the Bible" was my new study this year. My favorite lesson was from the Woman at the Well. I found that true thirst can be a gift.

Thirst is a gift when I go to meet with God. I should accept no substitutes. My story can attract others to my Savior.

Psalm 42:2: "My soul thirsts for God, for the living God. When can I go and meet with God" (NIV).

James 1:5: "If any of you lacks wisdom, you should ask God, who gives generously to all without finding fault, and it will be given to you" (NIV).

Psalm 32:5: "Then I acknowledged my sin to you and did not cover up my iniquity. I said, "I will confess my transgressions to the Lord." And you forgave the guilt of my sin" (NIV).

Acts 20:24: "However, I consider my life worth nothing to me; my only aim is to finish the race and complete the task the Lord Jesus has given me—the task of testifying to the good news of God's grace" (NIV).

Lessons of the Sabbath

Sabbath is special communion with God. He restores the spirit and gives rest. Not physical but spiritual the heart of rest is living water. "Teach your daughters. Be not just relaxed but rested. Only I can give true rest to a weary soul. Come and receive. Be expectant.

When you see Me, stand on your feet. I will give you exactly what you need. Come with empty hands and an empty cup. I will fill your needs and your cup will overflow with joy and peace. You will be used to Bless others that I send to you. Be still, empty your hands to receive my blessings on the Sabbath day. I am the Lord of the Sabbath who restores your soul."

Become Fearless. Become un offend able. Seek truth with out compromise. You will be in my training for 70 to 80 years to prepare for Eternity. "Be not Afraid I am with you always even to the end of the age." I heard the Lord speak to my heart.

I feel release of my fear and stress. In its place I feel peace and assurance that my life is in your hands. You will fill my hands with what I need to fulfill my **destiny.** Your plan for my life!

August 1, 2016
The Lord Is Present in the Prayer Closet

Psalm 46:1: "God is our refuge and strength, an ever-present help in trouble" (NIV).

Psalm 46:10: "Be still and know I am God; I will be exalted among the nations, I will be exalted in the earth" (NIV).

Proverbs 16:22: "Prudence is a fountain of life to the prudent, but folly brings punishment to fools" (NIV).

The Water's Edge Hearing the Holy Spirit and Seeing Inner Beauty

"You moved close to the water's edge to hear My voice in the surf. But in Long Beach, California, you thought you heard the surf 2.5 blocks from the ocean. Only to find that I had provided a water garden outside of your window and you heard my voice day and night, My Holy Spirit blows over you like the warm breeze on your face, the aroma of your fragrance reminds you that your life and your praises, rise to me and I recognize your aroma. You had to think, 'What is this beautiful smell?' It is the inner beauty that you do not see. It is the essence of the real you. Reminder of the day at the beach when Bob found the inside of a conch shell. He handed it to you. You said, 'That is pretty—he picked it up for you because you are beautiful.' He has always seen your inner beauty!

Let me reveal it to you!"

Taco Night

"Did you see that, Ladies Taco Night, on the screen during the praise and worship at Christ Fellowship? You thought it was a mistake as it kept flashing onto the screen again and again. I wanted you to know that it was for you to go. Your test has become a testimony to lead others to me. My daughters who are struggling with hidden sin will be affected and effected to make the change to make a decision to turn their wills over to the care of their God as they understand. You must help them understand. My body of daughters will be strengthened and encouraged by your testimony. Do not be afraid-I am with you. I will speak to your husband. Be still and wait on Me. Be ready to share the hope that you have in your heart."

Four Months Later

Donna came up to me at the anniversary dinner. She said, "Rose, thank you for sharing your testimony. I want you to know I have been clean and sober since that night!" Praise you, Lord. You are an amazing God!

August 14, 2016
True Rest

Jesus gives true rest. I saw a dragonfly sitting on my bike handlebars. I started to take photos thinking he would fly away. But he didn't. He sat very still. I asked the Lord, *Why is he just sitting here?* You reply, "He is resting and that is what I want you to do today. The Sabbath is to rest! I have your life in my hands just like I put the hummer in your hand. Remember when you had to relocate the chimes to hear the music? You must recall your mind to focus on me and to hear my voice. Listen to your senses! You saw the dragonfly and mistaken him for a grasshopper. I sent the grasshopper to the beach yesterday to remind you of the blessings of the woods and the beach and that I will speak to you in every location. The dragonfly this morning reminded you of my message on rest last year and today my servant Pastor Andy spoke on Sabbath, and you received it. You will be blessed if you put My word into action in your life."

August 15, 2016
Restful Pondering

A full day in your presence—you spoke clearly through nature. The lesson you taught me, "Learn the lesson and forget the details." You see me as a learner. To learn and to unlearn and relearn the correct way according to your word, revealed to me each day. Your plan will unfold in my life. "Be diligent—stay on track. Remember a flawed diamond is more valuable than a perfect brick. You need to be cut! So you will shine forth in my presence."

Write the Book

"Shut the door of your prayer closet and finish the work."

Mathew 6:6: "But when you pray, go into your room, close the door and pray to your Father, who is unseen. Then your Father, who sees what is done in secret, will reward you" (NIV). And I am still writing.

August 21, 2016
Red-Letter Day
Personal Growth Leads to Promotion

Focus on El Shaddai, the Lord God Almighty.

Isaiah 50:1: "Where is your mother's certificate of divorce with which I sent her away? Or to which of my creditors did I sell you? Because of your sins you were sold; because of your transgressions your mother was sent away" (NIV).

"Higher Position requires less doing and more critical thinking and teaching!"

Psalm 2:10: "Therefore, you kings, be wise; be warned, you rulers of the earth" (NIV).

August 22, 2016
Red-Letter Day
Ocean of Mercy, Townsend Inlet Sea Isle City, New Jersey

Thank You for your grace and mercy with me all these years. For this is the day with the heart radio on my phone. For your words have drowned out the noises of the bridge, cars, boats, bells and sirens, overhead planes and squeaking sea gulls. The music opened my heart to praise and worship and your presence filled my heart mind and restored my spirit. The ocean of mercy has refreshed my soul today. I am surrounded by your love and mercy. Your presence blows over me like a sea breeze. Fill me with your Holy Spirit. I love you, Lord!

My fisherman is still catching no fish. The boat is still broken. Problems still try to fill my mind. A black mussel mother of pearl shell comes to my feet as I sit on the rock.

"Sit still, I will bring it to you! Sit a spell and rest in me and be refreshed. Stay firm on the rock and everything you desire will come to you. The water and sand will massage your feet." As I pick up the treasure at my feet, I realize that You are the treasure that I have sought. It is Your presence and Your peace that is my real treasure!

Psalm 23:2–3: "He makes me lie down in green pastures. He leads me beside the quiet water. He restores my soul. He guides me along the right paths for his name's sake" (NIV).

Thank You, Lord, for this quiet time at the beach today and for speaking to my heart and restoring my soul.

September 4, 2016
Labor Day Sunday at Mercer Red Bank Battlefield

"Pray for the Persecuted Church." I feel convicted and shallow. I cannot go to church because I am tired. Forgive me Lord! Above all the distractions and the walking dead at the park. A woman said," You have a poke man on you. She is so cute!" I thought Yikes! I rebuke you Satan in the name of Jesus. Lord, they do not know that this is a sacred place. A battle ground where blood was shed for our freedom. Lord help America! Help us to teach our children the true history of our country. Our godly roots that have blessed our nation. Please help the next generation to know the truth.

December 24, 2016
Red-Letter Christmas Day

As I have prayed for my grandchildren to know the Lord all year, today was the highlight. As we were acting out and telling the Christmas story, my youngest grandchild, Caleb, wanted to be Baby Jesus! My heart leaped within me for joy! You are calling each one to know you, even the baby! Even though he is four, he is beginning to understand. Thank You Lord for answering my prayers. "I hold your children, and grandchildren in the palm of my hand."

January 6, 2017
Epiphany, A Sudden Understanding

"You have received seven years of my favor and increase. It is time for you to release. Remember things come to pass not to stay. Keep moving forward. It is time to no longer read the devotionals, it is time to write the devotional. Dedicated one hour per day. I will direct you and help you put the words to paper. You will see your story come to life. I will reveal hidden things that you do not know. Trust Me."

Review of the Things the Lord has taught
me and spoke to me to Date

D = Daily
E = Everything
L = Leave
I = In
G = God's
H = Hands and
T = Trust!

You are of me!
Pray more do less.
Listen and learn.
Unlearn and relearn new habits.
Take it easy.
More will be revealed—when…I am ready.
Pray for yourself first—then others.
The Lord can use a broken vessel.
One day at a time. Every day for the rest of my life.
Let go and let God.
Turn it over—do not carry a burden.
Give it to Jesus—He gives true rest.
He will restore what the locust have eaten.
Wasted years are not wasted when you know the Lord.
The test creates the testimony.
I will overcome by the blood of the Lamb and the word of my
testimony,
Be strengthened and encouraged by the Lord of the Sabbath!
Be bold and courageous. I always go before you always!
Be audacious and fearless
Be not drunk with wine but filled with the spirit.

Acts 4:13: "When they saw the courage of Peter and John and
realized that they were unschooled, ordinary men, they were astonished and they took note that these men had been with Jesus" (NIV).

The Second Letter to the Corinthians 3:12: "Therefore, since we have such a hope, we are very bold" (NIV).

Philippians 1:20: "I eagerly expect and hope that I will in no way be ashamed, but will have sufficient courage so that now as always Christ will be exalted in my body, whether by life or by death" (NIV).

Hebrews 4:16: "Let us then approach God's throne of grace with confidence, so that we may receive mercy and find grace to help us in our time of need" (NIV).

Mother's Day

Four words from the Lord
Pray more, do less.
Let go, let God.
Take time for togetherness.
Put God's priorities first.
Put your husband first.
Reclaim family life from runaway activities.
Even children need quiet time alone for thinking, being creative, and using imagination.

Never Forget

God is love.
God answers prayers.
It is okay to be different.
God sees us in our pain.
Marriage is work.
Postpartum depression is real.
Crawl out of the pit to see the light.
You are not alone.
God's presence brings joy.
"How sad when someone comes looking for Jesus and all they see is you" (Mother Teresa, *The Joy in Loving*).

"To God be the glory for things He has done in my life" (Rosemarie Page Yerka).

Memories and Maturity

Reading about myself, I realize it could be any of my daughters or granddaughters or great granddaughters. The world has changed but the basic emotions of youth have not.

I invite you to become a "whosoever" too. In Revelation 3:20, Jesus says that He stands at the door and knocks. And if we open the door, He will come in and have fellowship with us.

Three Reasons to Read This Book

To overcome grief.
To overcome insecurity.
To overcome the "Cinderella complex."

Results: Fruit of the Spirit

Love
Joy
Peace
Patience
Kindness
Goodness

"On the Shore of Nature's Magic, I dreamed Summer knew no end." Angie Weiland Crosby[40]
Reflections of Summer
The Process of Being and Becoming

Psalm 90:12: "So Teach us to number our days, that we may gain a heart of wisdom." (NIV)

Becoming teachable over and over again one day at a time is step 1.

My life is unmanageable and out of control, I choose to turn it over to God.

Discovery of what I do not know.

Analogy of who is on the throne, me or Jesus? How do I know what it looks like?

Have you had a time when you were at the end of yourself and ready to let God intervene and change your life? Or to allow others to help you?

Have you or do you know anyone who was at the point of suicide? Did you pray for help?

What does becoming teachable look like in your life? How do we let go and let God have his way in our life?

Is it important to realize that there are things we do not know, so we are willing to learn new things?

Who do you say is in control of your life? Are you too afraid to be out of control?

Are you willing to let go so you can allow God to lead your life? What does it look like for you?

The puzzle of life continues to come together in each season with each step.

Adoration, the Second Part of the Fairy Tale
End Book 3

---

[40] Angie Crosby Welland, "On the shore of nature's magic, I dreamed that summer never ends."

PART 4

RECOVERY
FALL

Red-Letter Days of a Life Well Lived

How to Become Transparent and Overcome Fear

It reminds us that change can be beautiful.
October, November, to December, back to winter and step 1 again.
Full circle finding (love), faithfulness, gentleness
and self-control (consolation), acceptance.

The fall of life brings down the things that need to come to the
ground for the next season. Allowing the crushing to produce that
which allows the light of the Lord to shine through the broken
vessels. Let go, and let God instead of bargaining with God over the
pain and grief. There will be a harvest if I do not give up. Autumn
is the transition between summer and winter. For things to get
better I must get better. For things to change, I must change.
When I change everything changes and more will be revealed.
All things become beautiful in God's timing.

Introduction, Part 4

Being Consoled by the Lord…Intervention, the
Height of Fear, Becoming Fearless
Prologue

My son said, "Mom, I have a drug problem. The principal is going to call you today." My heart raced, my palms were sweating, and my eyes filled with tears. I said," It will be okay, we will get you help." The phone rang, and I heard the principal's kind voice, "Mrs. Yerka, you are a good mother!" I started to cry. He continued. "If every child was able to go to his denying mother and get help when they needed it, my job would be easy. Instead, I have to convince them that the child has a problem. They say, "No way, not my child!" Your son has a secure loving relationship with you. He knew he could come to you with his problem. Again, remember that you are a good mother." How did he know that that was what I needed to hear? Thank you, Lord, for consoling me through this man. I called my insurance company and found they did not cover rehabilitation. I called the Governor Christie's office. I asked, "What about the War on Drugs?" Where can my son get help? They told me to call the health department. They asked me if he started with alcohol. If so, they can help him. I think so probably. Then I felt a twinge of guilt and shame that I was a poor role model to my child. Alcoholism runs in my family. I should have known better as a nurse.

That day his friend came into my foyer asking for him. I felt a strong sense of evil that came into the door that day. It was like it came in my front door. How can I protect my son. Please, Lord, help us.

How to get help for my son, I prayed and asked the Lord what to do. That night, my son came into my room in the middle of the night crying with blood running down his arm from his wrist. He was crying for help. The doctor told us to go to Cherry Hill Medical Center for evaluation. They referred him to Hampton Hospital. I hear it is one of the best in our area. He was there for a couple of days and then transferred to a rehab. The Lord had answered my prayers.

My husband was late for work the next day. From all the upsetting things the night before, he had overslept. This never happens. As all the kids and he tried to get out the door, we heard a crash. We all stood at the top of the stairs and saw the hanging lamp had dropped to the floor right where my sons's friend had stood the day before. I had goosebumps. It did not even break. But it could have killed my husband. Thank you, Lord, for hearing my prayers for protection.

He was replacing my fear with courage. I was afraid to drive over the bridge or in Philly and now I was driving there at night by myself. Love had replaced Fear. It seemed like a mirror,

"My children, myself." But I was still in denial...until the second time. Many years later, 8 am phone call from my daughter-in-law, "You need to come over for an intervention."

The Fall
Prologue for Recovery
Becoming Transparent and Becoming Fearless

The phone rang, and the voice of Richard from the town political party chairman said, "Rose, how would you like to run for town council?"

I hesitated and asked, "Are you kidding me? No way, I do not have time for that!"

"Well, I think you would be a good leader and could do well," he said. "Will you think about it?" he asked. I answered a little sarcastically, that I would pray about it tomorrow at the National Day of Prayer ceremony and I did.

The councilman who was running it had worked with me for about ten years. He did not know my name. But he was able to offend me that day. He said, "Some lady last year mentioned abortion. We must be politically correct, and we cannot offend people."

I thought, *Really!* He just offended me and does not represent me or even know who I am.

I prayed, "Lord, do you really want me to run against him? No one can beat him. He has been in that position for over twenty years."

The Lord answered me by saying, "Yes, you will run against him, and I will humble him under My mighty hand! Run to win, and I will take care of the rest."

I told Richard my decision.

He asked, "Do you have any skeletons in your closet?" Nothing that I was afraid of, I answered. My drinking had not yet become a real problem to my knowledge. So I began my steps toward transparency and honesty.

Election day, a hundred-year-old woman was being honored at the fire department. My daughters and I were to go and serve the food. At lunch, I had two glasses of wine before we left. I ran out the door to the car parked on the street. At the curb, I fell into a hole covered with leaves, and I heard the loud *crack*! It seemed like slow motion as I hit the ground. I was in shock, and the pain was like childbirth but in my broken ankle. I screamed for the girls to call 911 and asked for two extra-strength Tylenol. I was hoping with the wine that it would give some relief. I waited for twenty minutes for the ambulance to arrive. As I lay there, I thought, *Did I fall because I was drunk? Or did I just not see the hole?* The latter, I am sure.

I was in a cast for six weeks. Now my husband was learning just how much I was drinking. The pain was my excuse because I did not want to become addicted to the pain medicine. Which was true, but now I need to learn to be really transparent. The whole town knew me now. I had ended the campaign with a bang, so to speak. And lucky I had nothing to hide.

CHAPTER 11

Being a Christian and Becoming a Disciple

An Influencer to the Next Generation
I Need a Friend

I want You and need You as my personal friend, confidant, and Savior. You are the only one who stays the same today, tomorrow, and always. I love you so much.

I am your slave. I praise you and thank you for coming after one of your lost sheep. I promise not to stray. I am sorry for the terrible sin I have committed against my own body, which does not even belong to me. It is yours. Please forgive me, Lord.

I love you.
Rose

The Answer

"I love you just the way you are. I made you just the way you are. I accept you just the way you are. you are of me."

Becoming teachable over and over again, one day at a time, step 1.[41]
Discovery of what I do not know.

Analogy of who is on the throne, me or Jesus? How do I know what it looks like? Are you real, God?

Consolation: The Third Part of a Fairytale

The third part of my fairy tale is consolation. Finally, I am able to see what I could not see before. The resolutions of the pain coming to console and comfort the insecure princess. By definition, insecurity means being subject to fears and doubts and exposed to risks and dangers. The changes that I see in myself shows me that I am now secure in Jesus Christ. Security is being free from danger or harm. Free also from anxiety, doubts and cares. Being protected and made safe. I feel Jesus all around me like a security blanket. Like a Royal Princess with bodyguards, I am no longer afraid. I realize the Sovereign Lord has kept watch over me and has his angels surrounding me to keep me safe. Not to continue to take precautions against crime or attack but I know I am not alone, and My God watches over everything that concerns me. I need not be afraid. My consolation is knowing and trusting

God's Plan for My Life

There are 365 days of the year, and the words "Do not be afraid" appear in the Bible 365 times. One for each day of the year. So the Lord knows we are all insecure. I have been changed to a secure princess.

The Second Epistle of Peter 2:9: "If this is so, then the Lord knows how to rescue the godly from trials and to hold the unrighteous for punishment on the day of judgment" (NIV).

---

[41] William Griffith Wilson, *The Twelve Steps and Traditions* (Alcoholics Anonymous World Services Inc., 1953).

Afterword and Answered Prayers

The Lord has answered my cry for help and answered my prayer like He did for my mother. This time he rescued me from me. Looking back, I now see postpartum depression was probably my problem. Despite the fact that I am a nurse, I missed it in myself. I went back to work too soon and was pushing myself too hard with two small children…and then continued to work after the next three children.

The Grief I Felt Not Knowing My Father Was Taken Away

Jesus introduced me to His heavenly Father. I realized I have value and purpose as a woman, wife and mother. Now I can do all things through Jesus Christ who strengthens me. Philippians 4:9: "Whatever you have learned or received or heard from me, or seen in me—put it into practice. And the God of peace will be with you" (NIV). I found a business to make $25.00 per hour as a Beauty Consultant. I feel beautiful and I can make my own hours around my family. I was lost and now I am found by Jesus and My Heavenly Father. Winter is gone. A new season of spring growth, and success for me, the Royal Princess has come. The Lord gave me True love, Joy and peace.

The New Us: The Joy of Being Changed

Everyone close to me noticed the new me. The unafraid new me. My mother especially noticed as I was a lot like her with my fears and insecurities. I was able to share my newfound faith with her. I encouraged her to read the Bible herself and to search for the truth. As she did that, I noticed changes in her too. She no longer badmouthed the TV ministers. Instead, she listened and supported them and got herself two new easy to read Bibles. She was praying for her sisters to come to know Jesus. My husband now checked with me before making major decisions. He said because we are married and one in the spirit, he wanted my opinion. Of course, this was years after he had bought a lemon without me! Now the Lord could provide everything we needed, and he did. My husband realized Jesus was our provider. It was a major shift and his mother and brother noticed. We were becoming testimonies to our loved ones. So we prayed for them all. And we saw the Lord draw many to Himself through us. We were blessed to see our loved ones come to know Jesus.

The Insecure Princess had found her security in Jesus Christ. This changed everything! I was able to overcome the grief, denial and anger about my unknown father. I was able to forgive him and my mother. I realized that my husband was a gift to me not a prince. I no longer needed to be rescued. Jesus was the one who rescued me. Now I was able to lead others to him to be rescued too. I now had brothers and sisters in Christ as part of his family. Again, the joy of the Lord flooded my soul. I was on fire and everyone saw the changes in me. My greatest joy is knowing many of my loved ones are now with Jesus because they saw Him in me.

Growing Pains

I Am Broken Like My Ankle
Wake-Up Call on My First Election Day as a Candidate

"This is your wakeup call again. For things to change you must change. For things to get better you must get better. Allow me to help you become transparent and I will take away your fear."

I was embarrassed when the fireman came and saw me this way. I am feeling transparent and vulnerable. And this pain has me wide awake!

After I got home Councilman Jake Jacobs called me to tell me I had run a good campaign. He said, "You made me work! I heard you are going out with a bang!" Small town news travels fast! I thought to myself, I will never run another campaign. Never say never to the Lord. Lord, heal me.

From my study of the Bible, I had been prepared my whole life from my mother's womb to do what he calls me to do. That there is a destiny for me, things to do, people to meet and lead to Christ. I can be and become what he wants me to be.

Along the way back, Retreats, Refreshments and Recommitments. Cape May at the Dunes, The Lord spoke to me, "I am with you, I will bring beauty for ashes. I love your children more than you do. You are of me, Trust Me. I am your All in All." Pennsylvania Dutch Black Rock Retreat, I heard. Be a writer. Ocean City with Rita I heard, "I am the only perfect One. Allow my Love to heal you and your marriage. Become a student of Bob. I will teach you how to love him. Your marriage is my testimony to your children. I will make it beautiful."

The snow on the Beach, which I had never seen before. Sheryl Sofia was speaking about the seasons of a woman's life. The Holy Spirit had fallen on the hotel that had three women's retreats that weekend. The Ocean City Fire Department was called by someone on the boardwalk who had seen smoke coming from the building. We all had to go outside in the cold. As I watched the fireman go in and out, I wondered what was happening. So I asked one of the firemen was what was happening. He said, "We saw smoke but cannot find a fire." I responded, "Maybe it is the Fire of the Holy Spirit from the prayers of the three hundred women inside.!" We both laughed. But I pondered that in my heart and remembered Azusa Street in California when the same thing had happened and people were being healed inside. Lord, heal me.

My whole life had prepared me for the writing of the *Joys of Being and Becoming*. Marriage, parenting, business, politics. They all revealed more of what was needed to be real and transparent. Failure was not an option. I had to run to win, even if I failed. Nothing to hide, nothing missing, nothing broken. Learning to leave the past behind and reverse the curse for the next generation! Passing the torch of faith to my family and leaving a legacy of love as a roadmap.

Nicole

My young second cousin came to visit us this summer. We were talking to her and her boyfriend about their plans and his intentions in the relationship. She turned to him and said, "I want what they have." Finally, she asked how did you do that and what should we do? We encouraged them to allow Jesus to be part of their relationship. He is the one who kept us together all these years. She smiled. "That is really cool!" I'm not sure if she understands but I pray for both of them. Open or close this door and lead her to yourself, Lord.

Ready to Teach—Teach Me, Lord, That I May Teach

Lord, I pray that you give me the right words to be effective to help others come to you personally and have an abundant life. Being and becoming all you desire by your grace and love. In my life, Lord, be glorified. Amen.

Season of Harvest and Blessing

Time to pass the torch of faith to my children and grandchildren and great grandchildren. So I can say it is well with my soul and my work here on earth is done. Fear is gone and faith has come full circle. I want to go over there where my mother, grandmother, and great-grandmother and all those who taught me well. This taught me to follow the way of love and the people of the way.

The beach is windy, and the surf is rough. But the peace within my soul as the sounds of the ocean speaks to my spirit, I heard the Lord call my name again! He is calling me to a closer walk with Him. He wants to give me life abundantly as He sets me free from the bondage of sin, past hurts and ancestral influences. He wants to renew and make new my born-again life! Praise the Lord.

Chapter 12

Being a Disciple, Becoming a Rose Filled and Fearless

DeSales, Francis: *"Doing little things with strong desire to please God makes them really great."*[42]

October 1, 2015
The Dream Giver

Lord, you have given every dream in my heart. I heard a red cardinal at the bird feeder, the sound of her call, opened my heart to your voice. The Lord said, "Sit and Be Still and I will show you and teach you unsearchable things. You must learn to hear and discern my voice quickly and clearly. I am the Lord who comforts you and strengthens you and leads you into a New Day. I long to speak to you but you fail to listen. Open your heart and mind every morning as you open your eyes." Isaiah 61:1: "Morning by morning, He awakens me to the understanding of his Will."

---

[42] Francis DeSales, "Doing little things with strong desire to please God makes them really great."

October 2, 2015 God Remembered Princess Rose

The First Letter of Peter 2:10: "Once you were not a people, but now you are the people of God; once you had not received mercy, but now you have received mercy" (NIV).

My Cinderella Story

I found true love in Christ
the hope that I can change
The cinders of a less than perfect life
Out of the ashes—He transformed me
He gave me beauty for ashes
He invited me to dance with Him and gave me His power and position.
Dancing in the arms of my God! Embraced by love and respect. Communicating intimacy and freedom. My Lord leads me to…
Become the woman He created me to be.

The First Epistle of Peter 3:15–16: "But in your hearts revere Christ as Lord. Always be prepared to give an answer to everyone who asks you to give the reason for the hope that you have. But do this with gentleness and respect, keeping a clear conscience, so that those who speak maliciously against your good behavior in Christ may be ashamed of their slander" (NIV).

Learning to be Humble
Psalm 71:1–2: "In you, Lord, I have taken refuge; let me never be put to shame. In your righteousness, rescue me and deliver me; turn your ear to me and save me.
First Corinthians 13:4: "Love is patient, love is kind. It does not envy, it does not boast, it is not proud" (NIV).

January 20, 2016
Your Will, Not My Will

Philippians 4:9: "Whatever you have learned, received, heard or seen in Me—Put into Practice" (NIV).

Hebrews 10:23: "Hold unswervingly to the Hope we profess for He who Promised is faithful" (NIV).

Hebrews 10:35: "Do Not throw away confidence; it will be richly rewarded" (NIV).

Hebrews 10:36: You need to persevere so that when you have done the will of God, you will receive what he has promised" (NIV).

"All is Well. The time of the Lord's favor has come. My grace changes everything."

"You are being rooted and grounded. Do not try to plan. Rose is a builder not an architect!"

Proverbs 27:1: "Do not boast about tomorrow, for you do not know what a day may bring" (NIV).

Lessons from the Bad Girls of the Bible was my new study this year. My favorite lesson was from the Woman at the Well. I found that true thirst can be a gift.

Thirst is a gift when I go to meet with God. I should accept no substitutes. My story can attract others to my Savior.

Psalm 42:2: "My soul thirsts for God, for the living God. When can I go and meet with God" (NIV).

James 1:5: "If any of you lacks wisdom, you should ask God, who gives generously to all without finding fault, and it will be given to you" (NIV).

Psalm 32:5: "Then I acknowledged my sin to you and did not cover up my iniquity. I said, "I will confess my transgressions to the Lord." And you forgave the guilt of my sin" (NIV).

Acts 20:24: "However, I consider my life worth nothing to me; my only aim is to finish the race and complete the task the Lord Jesus has given me—the task of testifying to the good news of God's grace" (NIV).

August 1, 2016
The Lord Is Present in the Prayer Closet

Psalm 46:1: " God is our refuge and strength, an ever-present help in trouble" (NIV).

Psalm 46:10: "Be still and know I am God; I will be exalted among the nations, I will be exalted in the earth" (NIV).

Proverbs 16:22: "Prudence is a fountain of life to the prudent, but folly brings punishment to fools" (NIV).

Blessings Years Later

The greatest compliment to a mother is when her daughters become mothers. Five children later and they all married. A great complement to me and my husband. Our marriage has endured to show how scary and beautiful it is to be intimate and vulnerable. Genuineness takes time and mature love is the payoff for investing in romantic love. Many, many grandchildren and great grandchildren later, I now appreciate the blessing of being a wife, mother and grandmother.

April 2020 History Repeats Itself Prayer in the Pandemic

The Lord woke me up in the middle of the night. I laid awake from 1:23 a.m. till 2:03 a.m. then decided to get up and pray for those who are serving on the frontline this morning in hospitals across the nation. I stood before the Lord and cried tears for those who are suffering and perishing. Lord let me be faithful to do my part and pray for those who are doing what needs to be done for others. Thank you for their courage, give them strength.

This is a surreal situation. Everywhere I go, I see others with gloves and masks and fear on their faces. It has become like a war zone out in the marketplace. Help me bring your love to a world that needs your hope. Let my light shine before others so they will see you, Lord.

Passover to Pentecost 2020, Hearing from God

The verse that hopped out to me was Galatians 4:12: "I plead with you, brothers and sisters, become like me, for I became like you. You did me no wrong" (NIV).

Psalm 25:4–5: "Show me your ways, Lord, teach me your paths. Guide me in your truth and teach me, for you are God my Savior, and my hope is in you all day long" (NIV).

We prayed to pursue God's presence for the next generation to return to the fear of the Lord. Baptize us in the fear of the Lord with fire. We turn our hearts to you, Lord.

Review 2020
Year of Grace

Words for the year 2020: gumption, fortitude, strength of mind to endure adversity with courage. Become whole hearted.

The Second Letter to the Chronicles 29:26: "So the Levites stood ready with David's instruments, and the priests with their trumpets" (NIV).

December 20, 2020
Happy Birthday Mom
Finished New Season

Rough Draft of the *Joys of Being and Becoming*. The pandemic gave me time to rethink my priorities and to focus on Being and Becoming and getting to see the light at the end of the tunnel. Thank you, Lord.

January 6, 2021

Epiphany—a sudden grasp of understanding. Help me not to succumb to fear of this day. 8:00 a.m.: Lord, as I read Hosea chapter 5, I knew you were calling me to pray for America. Lord, have mercy.

I pray that Congress does right in the electoral certification. Forgive our sin as a nation, I pray in Jesus's name. Amen.

3:15 p.m.: My heart raced as tears flowed from my eyes as I watched in unbelief of anarchy images in the Capitol in Washington, DC. I heard the gunshots and saw the woman bleed out and die, murdered on TV. Lord, have mercy. I feel sad and angry and broken-hearted. Lord, show me your will let me be able to rest and sleep after these horrible images in my mind. Show me your will in the morning. Give me the courage to meet with Claire about the NJFRW and Stacey to study Luke and Christian to study Romans.

Epiphany moment: I will not be distracted by discouragement any longer. I will press on and share the word, the Good News of Jesus Christ, my Lord! I will plan my Epiphany party on Saturday for my grandchildren and water seeds planted for years. May you have a harvest of your Word in their lives in your timing. Amen.

New Year 2021

His presence to be and become the person he designed me to be. I am redeemed, revived, restored and refreshed! Help me to be strong in the Lord and prepared for this new season. Let me win one in 2021, or more!

January 17, 2021
Red Letter Day
Spiritual Birthday—Forty-Four Years in the Lord

As I sit in the outside cathedral—now Calvary Chapel, then St. Matthew's play yard—I hear your voice again. "When you return to the beginning of your spiritual walk again, you will always find Me ready to listen and speak to you. Always remember your roots. It is where I planted seeds of faith for your spiritual walk with Me.

"The words you remember, 'You, my daughter, are of Me.' I am your Father, I love you and forgive you. Now forgive yourself. Do not blame Bob for your mistake. He is on his own journey. I will reveal myself to him in my time. Be patient with him and yourself.

"As you ponder the red-letter days, you will be reminded of a life well lived and that your red-letter days will never end. I am with you always. Many times, when you came here to hear My voice, I would meet you here at the Battleground on the river in National Park. This is hallowed ground. Young men shed their blood for your freedom. It brings tears to your eyes. Then you would thank me for the blood of my son Jesus shed for your freedom from sin. As a child you have memories of running and playing and picnics and swimming. As an adult you remember times with your new husband at the park. I saw you when you planned the two cousins' reunions for your family. Your desire for a close family was given as your heart was enlarged by all the new family you met. Your face light up when you were accepted as a McCleary and you found yourself on the family tree. I am continuing to show you where you fit into my plan. Your tears are healing.

The old oak tree reminds you of the time I spoke to you in the hospital room after your ruptured ovary. You were angry with me and complaining about your pain with tears in your eyes. On the wall was a painting of a large oak tree. I told you to let your roots go down deeper and you will grow strong like a mighty oak of righteousness. Your branches will be for others to rest. I will use this time together for good in your life and I will lead others to Myself through your testimony, and I did!

Younger mothers heard of you from their teenage daughters from the retreat. Where you shared your testimony with them. Many opened their hearts to me because of you. I appointed you to speak, and you did. Remember I put the words in your mouth. I appointed you from your mother's womb just like Jeremiah, to be a prophet to the nations. Speak the truth that I tell you and many shall be drawn to Myself by the power of my Holy Spirit. You read the monuments with the words of victory to gain courage for your spiritual battle over alcoholism."

"I give your freedom from all bondage. Be strong and courageous, be reminded that you are a daughter of a King and that your kingdom has overcome the world. Do not be afraid. Happy 44th Spiritual Birthday! As you see the tugboat come down the river you think of your stepfather Mike, remember that it is I who has provided all that you have needed since you were a child.

Do not worry about your children. You dedicated them to Me and I have them in the palm of My hand. I will speak to your grandchildren and great grandchildren because of your love and dedication to do My will. I will watch over them with the same care. The seeds and roots of your faith shall grow into the next generations. Do not fret for the future. Just trust in Me. I hold the future in My hand.

Only with the Holy Spirit do I move you forward to your destiny. The divine appointments will come each day and you will easily find your way. I have people attached to your destiny. Do not question what seems insignificant or an interruption of your plans.

Remember I orchestrate circumstances and bring people into your life for my purpose. Even those who are difficult or confused are assigned to meet you. I will use you to teach them the way. They will see Me in you. Let your heart stay open to embrace even a stranger. Remember the man on the bench in Israel at Peters Home Garden. Whatever you do to the least of these that you do for me. Treat others with love and respect and they will see my reflection in your eyes! The pain in your eyes as you trusted Dr. Friedburg is a reminder to keep the planks out of your own eyes and do not worry about the specs in others.

Religion is not important, only love will last. Love will draw many to myself. Open the eyes of your heart to see the people around you. Let me open your eyes to those assigned to you. Be ready to show them My love and give an answer of My salvation.

You are My daughter, you are of Me. Let your light shine from within. I will draw others to Myself. You will be My Missionary." Blessed are the feet of those who bring Good News

Growth

Measure life by the trees…only God can see our growth from above—trust him. Remember how far I have come. My roots have gone deeper. I am stronger by the storms of my life.

Will She Hide the Past Pain or Heal and
Find Consolation in the Truth?

With birth certificate in hand, will she introduce herself to her half-sister or close the door for the next generation? Because we are Christians, can we be reconciled with the mistakes of the last generation? Is it possible to find Joy for the next generation? Will they want to know the author, her husband, five children, sixteen grandchildren and two great grandchildren? This Secret finally reveals that God does not make mistakes. He has a Plan and a Purpose. And with His Attitude and Perspective, we find Joy even in our pain. We choose our own ending. Jesus is the Author and finisher of our faith. He makes all things Beautiful in His Time.

Psalm 23:3: "He refreshes my soul. He guides me along the right paths for his name's sake" (NIV).

Isaiah 49:15–16: "Can a mother forget the baby at her breast and have no compassion on the child she has borne? Though she may forget, I will not forget you! See, I have engraved you on the palms of my hands; your walls are ever before me.

Philippines 2:2–5: "Then make my joy complete by being like-minded, having the same love, being one in spirit and of one mind. Do nothing out of selfish ambition or vain conceit. Rather, in humility value others above yourselves, not looking to your own interests but each of you to the interests of the others. In your relationships with one another, have the same mindset as Christ Jesus:" (NIV).

Step 12
Choose Joy!
Reflections
The War in My Mind

I thank God that he provided what I needed through a man, my stepfather, who adored me and treated me like a little princess. He taught me how to be loved by a father. So I thought I had no need for this "Unknown Father." But a war started in my mind like an emotional roller coaster.

The Second Letter to the Corinthians 6:18 says, "And I will be a Father to you and you shall be my sons and daughters to me, says the Lord Almighty."

Philippians 4:19: "And my God will meet all your needs according to the riches of his glory in Christ Jesus" (NIV).

Becoming Real like the Velveteen
Rabbit.[43] *Knowing God's Plan.*

"If I speak in the tongues of men and angels but have not Love, I am a resounding cymbal. If I have the gift of prophecy and can fathom all mysteries and all knowledge and I have faith that can move mountains but do not have love, I am nothing. If I give all I have to the poor and give over my body to hardship that I may boast, but do not have love, I gain nothing. Love is patient, love is kind, it does not boast, it is not proud. It does not dishonor others, it is not self-seeking, it is not easily angered, it keeps no record of wrongs. Love does not delight in evil but rejoices with the truth. It always protects, always trusts, always hopes, always perseveres. Love never fails… And now these three things remain: Faith, Hope and Love. But the greatest of these is love" (1 Corinthians 13:1–8 NIV).

---

[43] Margery Williams, *The Velveteen Rabbit* (United Kingdom: George H. Doran Company, 1922).

Growing Pains

The Process of Being Processed
How to Stop …
The Struggle of The Wakeup Call and Cold Turkey

As I saw my reflection in the mirror after the intervention. I saw very clearly an alcoholic looking back at me. I had a round fat reddened face and swollen eyes that were glossed over. I looked unkempt, not like my old self. What I saw looking back at me woke me up! I was no longer true to the girl in the mirror. I had left her to slip the slippery slope into alcoholism, a place I swore I would never even visit. No, not me, I thought. Not my family. But here I was watching my children suffer and admit that they needed help. The struggle to stay hidden and above water was real every day and became a little harder. When would the craving go away? I cried out to the Lord, Help Me! I cannot do this alone. I give you my problem and ask for your help to overcome it. Please take it away and He did!

But much like Natural Childbirth and Natural Amnesia the follows so a woman is ready to do it again. So the struggle is real… It was easy to forget that like an allergy, I can never drink again. Instead, I thought now I can handle just a little wine. But then the whole bottle later. Then the bigger the bottle needed to last a couple of days. I started step 1 again. One day at a time! It was a personal struggle. My family saw it. I asked for no alcohol at family events for a while. After I learned the poison it can be for those of us predisposed, I did not want to add to it or tempt my struggling cousin or in-laws with the stumbling block. I had a plank in my own eye and could not help anyone else but myself. I was hoping as they saw me struggle, they would want to avoid the trap for themselves. And my son and I Became Clean and Sober together. I am so proud of the godly man he has become for himself and his family by the grace of the Lord. He was my cheer leader too. We encouraged each other. And The Lord gave us the victory!

Twenty-One-Day Challenge: Becoming *Undone* and Learning New Habits

At a women's retreat, the Speaker Anita Keggy gave the challenge to create a habit to feed ourselves spiritually. As I was still struggling to balance my carbs to avoid alcohol cravings, it was just what I needed. It takes twenty-one days to make a new habit. I understand that only the Lord could help me on my journey of recovery one day at a time. I needed soul food.

So I read one chapter of the book of John every day for twenty-one days. I started to look forward to hearing from the Lord each day. It was beautiful to hear His voice again. Even the elementary, John chapter 3 spoke to my soul again. I did not realize how hurt and unhealthily thinking had become. I was negative and depressed. But I began to notice the power in God's word the Bible to cut through the stinking thinking. Spiritual power for the day to change my thinking and my habits. It seemed every day I got what I needed for that day, a dose of spiritual power to change.

John chapter 15 reminded me that I was chosen. That verse humbled me to know that God had a plan for me, even in all this mess, and the painful process of recovery from my past. Anita soon asked, "Are there any writers in the room of these three hundred women?" Shyly, I raised my hand. She said, "See me afterward."

At that time, she asked, "What are you writing? How can I encourage you?" I told her my story. She said, "Wonderful! Don't stop until you get it finished. God will use your story to help others." And I am still writing…

Recovery Quote: "You can't keep it if you don't give it away."

Reflections
God Is Love

> What is your definition of love? How do you feel loved?
> When was the last time you thought about true love?
> Have you grieved the loss of a loved one?
> Did you ever go to a funeral for yourself? What is the difference?

Is forgiveness a form of Loving others and yourself?
Have you or someone you know experienced Recovery?

End of Part 4, Consolation

BEING AND BECOMING A WOMAN FOR ALL SEASONS BY GOD'S DESIGN

Life by Design

CHAPTER 13

Lessons of Godliness

As a Christian, these are the lessons I had learned and held dear to my heart. As I read the Bible, it taught me how to become spiritually mature. These are some of those lessons:

We must be weak to become strong.

We must be strong to become gentle.

We must be gentle to become powerful.

We must be powerful to become careful.

We must be careful to become sensitive.

We must be sensitive to become intentional.

We must be intentional to become attentive.

We must be attentive to become fruitful.

We must become fruitful to become spiritually mature.

So this is the story through each step, season, and storm. So ask God to help you see yourself in my account. Seek to be changed by the Word of God. Ask God to answer your prayers. Prepare yourself to become more and make yourself ready to become whole—nothing is missing, nothing is broken. Become all God has for you. It is like a masterpiece of value to the artist. There is a design for each of us, and it is beautiful.

Life by Design

It was after learning more about my maternal grandmother, Rose McCleary that I became a generational thinker. Someone who understands the value of each generation to the next generation. A life invested is an asset never lost. The value is an inheritance for the generations to come. Rose was a woman of faith and love. She gave of herself freely to others. She even put her own life in danger as she cared for her sick mother, who died from the flu. Her faith-filled, loving actions had enormous consequences for her daughter Agnes, after Rose also died along with her newborn son. Her father's mother and sister raised Agnes. Her father found a new Rose to marry and had six more children. It was difficult for young Agnes to share her father with many, especially living in a different home. She must have felt abandoned by her father even though he did his best to provide for and support his first-born child.

Learning about my grandmother Rose, helped me to understand my mother and the circumstances she found herself in. She found herself as an unwed mother. She was looking for love and the support of a man she did not find until after I was born. He would be a loving stepfather to her child. As I understood my mother, I began to understand myself. My anger and anxiety with men, my fears have been learned and rehearsed. It was now my goal as a generational thinker and mature woman to reverse this curse of anger and fear in my life, my marriage, and children. I wanted to become more like the woman I am designed to be. I wanted a life without fear, a life of faith that I could pass onto the next generation, life for my grandchildren that would make them proud, a life by God's design for each one of us. I was being and becoming all that he had designed me to be so that we could do all that he had assigned me.

My assignment as a person is to touch others for Jesus. It is an unfolding of God's will and design that makes life fulfilling and exciting. So this is the story of being and becoming by God's plan.

Step 1. "My life is unmanageable and out of my control. I chose to turn it over to my Designer."

Being at one stage and becoming the new creation by our Designer. Contained in this book are pictures that are worth a thousand words. But for every shot, there are a thousand other pictures that show the broken pieces and dreams that have created a beautiful mosaic of a life put back together by my Lord and Savior, Jesus Christ. The fruit of the spirit is a gift for my healing. They are available to anyone who believes in them.

Galatians 5:22–23: "But the fruit of the Spirit is love, joy, peace, forbearance, kindness, goodness, faithfulness, gentleness and self-control. Against such things there is no law (NIV).

The Second Epistle to Timothy 1:5: "I have been reminded of our sincere faith which first lived in your grandmother, Lois (Rose) and in your mother Eunice (Agnes), and I am persuaded that it now lives in you also (Me)" (NIV).

Titus 2:3–4: Likewise, teach the older women to be reverent in the way they live, not to be slanderers or addicted to much wine, but to teach what is good. 4 Then they can urge the younger women to love their husbands and children" (NIV).

This is the journal of the journey. The story of the grace to live soberly, righteously, and godly in this present age.

So this is the story through each step, season, and storm. So ask God to help you see yourself in my account. Seek to be changed by the Word of God. Ask God to answer your prayers. Prepare yourself to become more and make yourself ready to become whole—nothing missing, nothing broken. Become all God has for you. It is like a masterpiece of value to the artist. There is a design for each of us, and it is beautiful.

The Best for Last

Let me start again at the beginning with my grandmother's story.

The Final Part of the Three Generational Story

Rose McCleary's Story

Rose was the daughter of a tree farmer in Sewell, New Jersey, and Orange Grove in Ft. Lauderdale, Florida. She helped all year at the farm in New Jersey and went to Florida during school breaks to help her father. One year her father, John McCleary, stopped in Georgia. He was admiring the peaches there. He said, "I bet I can grow these in New Jersey." And he was the first to do so. His produce would travel by train to the market in Philadelphia. Rose was the oldest girl in her large family. She was a country girl.

John Thomas Page lived in Woodbury with his family. He had two brothers and two sisters. They walked to the Roman Catholic St. Patrick's Church. The Page family lived on Glover Street in Woodbury. The men worked at Saucony Oil Refinery, Mobil Oil in Paulsboro. John was the youngest of his family. He went boxing with his brothers in Camden on Saturday Night to make extra money. He was a city boy.

Rose and John met at St Patrick's Church in Woodbury. The McClearys arrived by horse and buggy and parked outside the beautiful church. The church still stands on Cooper Street in Woodbury near the train station.

John asked permission from Mr. John McCleary to court his daughter, Rose. It was love at first sight. John would catch the back of a train car after church to go courting in Rose's parlor on Sunday afternoons.

Rose had long light brown hair and was tall like a model. She was beautiful. The parlor was for special occasions, like courting, weddings, wakes, and funerals.

Research on courting from a hundred years ago. "In the 1900s, courtship was a public act. In other words, in the 1900s, a male suitor "courted" a potential woman mate in a private space (the woman's porch or living room or parlor) in front of a public audience (the family)." ~May 7, 2018 Reyerson, Lia, www.insider.com "What dating looked like the year you were born."

Courtship is an old-fashioned word that assumes two people who love each other will eventually get married. The word is indeed from the 16th century, when it meant "paying court to a woman with intention of marriage." So by definition, courting, which started in America around the time of the Civil War, is to be involved romantically, typically with the intention of marrying. To pay special attention to someone in the attempt to win their favor. It was the period wherein a couple get to know each other. Preceded by a proposal, courtship traditionally begins after a betrothal (promise to marry) and concludes with marriage. In due time Rose and John were married in a church wedding at St. Patrick's.

My Mother, Agnes' Story

On December 20, 1917, a cold, snowy winter night, Rose and John's first baby, Agnes Mary, was born too early. She only weighed about three pounds. She was placed in a high-top shoe box and put on the black-bellied stovetop to keep her warm. She was fed by mouth with a dropper. They had to buy a goat because Agnes was not tolerating the cow's milk. She grew healthy and thrived, thanks to the loving care of her family. Agnes was one of the first babies to be baptized at St. Patrick's Church. When Agnes was eight months old, she had a premature baby brother, just born in July 1918. He was named John Thomas Page. Rose's mother, Anna became very sick with the influenza virus. John told Rose, "Do not go near your mother. It is too dangerous for you and the baby."

Rose was one of the oldest daughters in her family. She must have felt obligated to help her mother and family. She was more familiar with the role of a daughter than a wife and mother. It was all new to her. She had to help her sister, Mary and her little sister, Gertrude. Gertrude could watch Agnes outside in the baby buggy while working inside with the baby. Anna died on August 20, 1918, and Rose and her baby died days later in the same week. They were all buried in Glassboro. A rose bush marks the location for Rose and baby John at St. Bridget's Cemetery. The family must have been overwhelmed with three deaths so close together.

For historical reference, in the early- to mid-1900s, everything happened in the homes; the births with midwives, the courting, and weddings. The dead were laid out in the parlor for the wake (hence, the term *funeral parlor*) and then the funeral service at church and then a family plot at the church you attended. The solitary historian journey of a lifetime, mourning the dead in 1870 and 1900.

I researched in the government archives on the flu epidemic to understand the impact of this sad time on my family. The flu epidemic of 1918 to 1920 carried an unusually deadly influenza virus to some 500,000,000 people worldwide killing 100 million people, with 675,000 deaths in the United States. World War I killed 16,000,000 people and lowered life expectancy in the United States. The flu epidemic affected one-fifth of the world's population and decreased the life expectancy down by twelve years. In 1917, female life expectancy was 54 years old and males, 48 years old. In 1918, it was females at 42 years old and males at 36 years old ("History of 1918 Flu Pandemic," Center for Disease Control (cdc.gov).

By late spring of 1918, the three-day fever occurred, and it was called that because most people died within three days of getting it. By fall, some were dying within hours of the first symptoms. Others would struggle a few days, then their lungs would fill with fluid and suffocate the victim. Photos show people wearing masks, like letter carriers, policemen, transit workers and military personnel. Fear gripped our nation.

In October 1918, 195,000 died in the Philadelphia area. Some 500 corpses were awaiting burial with cold storage plants used as temporary morgues. Trolley car companies were donating 200 packing crates to be used as coffins. Per *The Philly Voice*, the first person to die in New Jersey was a soldier from Fort Dix. He had just returned from the war in Europe. The irony is that he had survived the war and died within days of coming home. The flu had hit Philadelphia hard and then traveled over the Walt Whitman bridge to Gloucester City, New Jersey. It was reported that every doctor had several cases a day within weeks. Schools were closed to prevent the virus's spread, but many lives were lost in this Camden County city. Then it traveled to Gloucester County and the surrounding rural areas. The flu epidemic in full swing took hundreds of lives in Gloucester County and across the country, thousands of lives were lost. It was a sad time in America. It is known as the deadliest documented epidemic in human history as per government archives.

Agnes Gets a New Stepmother and Family Sorrow upon Sorrow

Both the McCleary and Page families must have been devastated by the loss. John and Agnes went to live with his parents in Woodbury. Agnes was cared for by her grandparents in Woodbury while John worked at the Mobil Oil refinery in Paulsboro.

John McCleary also later lost a son who was struck by lightning while working on the farm. Despite all the tragedy, John McCleary became the first mayor of Mantua, Sewell, New Jersey. He served many terms and was revered by his community.

Agnes grew bitter when her father, John, remarried. He married another Irish Rose. My mother did not like to go to the house with them in Gloucester. They had four more girls and one son. Agnes became angry with her father. My aunts said that my mother, Agnes, became a spoiled brat; that was how they saw it. But Agnes had another story. She felt left out and taken advantage of to help care for the younger half-siblings. She wanted to spend time with her father but as the family grew, there was less and less time for John to travel to Woodbury to visit Agnes.

A Historical Framework 1929 to the Late 1930s:

The Great Depression was a severe worldwide economic depression that took place mostly during the 1930s, beginning in the United States. The timing of the Great Depression varied around the world; in most countries, it started in 1929 and lasted until the late 1930's."

The Balance.com has an article by Kimberley Amadeo (updated January 27, 2022) titled, "How This Low Point in US History Still

Affects You Today." It includes a vivid description of the Great Depression of 1929 noting that it "devastated the US Economy." A third of all banks failed. Unemployment rose to 25%, and homelessness increased. Housing prices plummeted, international trade collapsed, and deflation soared. It took twenty-five years for the stock market to recover.

The Dust Bowl drought destroyed farming in the Midwest. It lasted ten years, too long for most farmers to hold out. As farmers left in search of work, they became homeless. Thousands of people gathered in "cardboard shacks" called Hoovervilles. Many people thought this was the end of the American dream (the idea of guaranteed rights to pursue one's vision of happiness). Instead, it changed the dream to include a right to material benefits.

During the Depression, things were bad for everyone. John had a fantastic job of fighting on Saturday nights in Camden to make extra money. He was a hero in the Irish ghetto of Gloucester City. Several men had to do the same. He also became a heavy drinker on the weekends with the boxers. I found after visiting Belfast and Dublin, Ireland that the garden row homes in Gloucester City even resembled the houses there. And the pride of the owners was much the same. There seemed to be a cultural similarity. And alcoholism is a big problem in Ireland. I found out this is part of my genetics on the Page side of my family.

Aunt Nellie, an Uncommon Teacher in a Common One-Room Schoolhouse

In the meantime, in Woodbury, John's family tried to make ends meet. They had all lost their jobs except for John's sister Nellie, a single schoolteacher, who worked at the one-room schoolhouse of Repaupo, she became the breadwinner.

An engaging description of early education in America, I have combined both Google and Wikipedia's profiles of the one room schoolhouse: In the nineteenth and early twentieth centuries, most American students attended a one-room schoolhouse. A single teacher would typically have students in the first through eighth grades, and she taught them all. The teacher usually taught reading, writing, arithmetic, history, and geography. Because there was more fluidity in the learning, the one-room schoolhouse became more of a community-based education where everyone had to pitch in to some extent. (November 7, 2020)

"Exploring the History of One Room Schoolhouses" by Diane Church of Reminder News, says this: "John Day did research and presentation on the one-room schoolhouses on June 11, 2015. Historically, generations of American youths were educated in one-room schoolhouses. The last one closed in 1967. 'The schoolhouses were originally established by the local church,' he explained. 'The whole point of education was to teach reading so students could read the Bible.' 'This went on until 1909 when the state had the towns take over the schools and establish Boards of Education.'" (June 16, 2015, at 2:23 p.m.)

Unfortunately, Nellie was being paid by script. She would have to go business to business in Woodbury to see who would buy her script, which is a promise to pay from the school. Cornell's in Westville became a benevolent business that helped many families in the area. Nellie became the hero even though I heard she was tough with the children.

Destitute and Frightening Times

My mother told me of the holes in her shoes and the fear in the hearts of even the children. One of her most frightful memories as a child living in Woodbury was when she saw a parade of men in white sheets with tall hats and torches. She was terrified! They rode on horses right down Broad Street in Woodbury. My mother noted that they were all men and wore dress shoes on horseback. She thought she recognized who they might be. She ran home to tell her grand-mother what she had seen. Her grandmother said, "Hush! Do not talk about that. They are the Ku Klux Klan and are very dangerous." So my mother never mentioned it to anyone or saw them again.

She lived with her cousins Jeanette and Bobby after their father had abandoned them in Florida after coming home from the war. Her aunt Elizabeth had a nervous breakdown and contracted a sexually transmitted disease from her husband and went mad. She spent the rest of her life in a mental hospital in Pennsylvania. So the household was a family of seven also. My mother remembers being very poor most of her life.

But there were happy memories of making cherry pies from the cherry tree in the yard of her Glover Street home. So I always remember that cherry pie was her favorite pie all of her life. And Jeanette became like a sister to Agnes. She would be my caretaker while my mother worked for years. She was my favorite aunt, as I called her, on my mother's side of the family.

After high school, Agnes decided to go to Taylor Business School in Philadelphia. She planned to become independent to care for herself and not have to be poor again. Agnes found a job right in Woodbury at Woolworth's Department store. She got an apartment in Thorofare. Jeanette lived with her.

It was not until she was 35 that she met my father, the love of her life, or so she thought. He had lied to her. He was married with three children. When she became pregnant with me, he offered to pay for an illegal abortion in New York City. My mother said a prayer that day, asking God for a sign to know what to do. She felt a new life that day. It was Rosemarie. She felt God's answer in her heart. He said, "I will take care of you and be the father to this child." My mother decided to love despite the cost to herself. It was not a popular choice in 1953. She had chosen to love just like her mother had loved her and her mother, even at the expense and her own life. My mother had to give much of herself to become my mother.

My mother does not remember her mother either. Only the Legend of Love as a hero in the McCleary family, was left behind. There is a void in the family history from the flu epidemic that has left many questions unanswered. With only one photograph and a blue china cup, my mother faced her future alone without a mother.

In her older years, she wondered what her life would have been like if her mother's family had raised her. She felt they were loving, caring, and she would have learned to be more like her mother, instead of bitter toward her father. But we do not change our past; we only can look forward to a better future. She introduced me to my aunt Mary, aunt Gertrude, and cousin Doris McCleary McFadden. They were all so happy to meet me. They say I look like aunt Gertrude, who in turn looked like Rose. At the family reunions, I was Rose McCleary's grand-daughter. My one cousin said, "I thought so. You are beautiful just like us." When I saw my name on the family tree, I started to cry. I realized I had found where I fit in. Doris is my favorite cousin. She has beautiful thick white hair like French vanilla ice cream, at age ninety-one. She is a strong woman of faith and love. I hope to be like her when I mature into a woman in my winter season.

One summer, we visited my cousin Mary Lynd in Florida. She showed us an old photo album, almost one hundred years old. My children and I were looking through it when they yelled, "Look, Mom, it is Charity!" I was astonished and felt the chills go down my spine. The picture looked just like my daughter, who was about three years old at the time. To my surprise, I found out it was Rose McCleary! Genetics do not lie. I am thankful that I look like my mother's family as I do not know my father's family. We were given the photo and tried to dress Charity the same and make the photo look alike. It was surreal! You ask how do I know all the things about a woman I have never met? It is because I do know of the time and the season and those she left behind and what they have said about her.

She had a short life but left a legacy of love behind that has stretched for generations to my great-grandchildren. I hope to do the same someday. To live a life by God's design and leave a legacy of love and values for the next generations.

My prayer is that my journey empowers you. May you hear the voice of the Holy Spirit of God for yourself. He is always speaking, if we are listening. He guides, teaches, and corrects us. We need to engage our mind, will, and emotions to be who God calls us to become. It takes a broken heart to be humble. Then you find rest for your weary soul.

Joys of Being and Becoming: Directions from the Lord

The Bible is filled with promises and guidance for every challenge life presents us with.

Jeremiah 33:3 the Lord promises, "Call to me and I will answer you and tell you great and unsearchable things you do not know" (NIV).

Ephesians 6:18 tells us to, "And pray in the Spirit on all occasions with all kinds of prayers and requests. With this in mind, be alert and always keep on praying for all the Lord's people" (NIV).

Revelation 12:11 explains how Christians triumph through trials, telling us, "They triumphed over him by the blood of the Lamb and by the word of their testimony; they did not love their lives so much as to shrink from death" (NIV).

Romans 12:6: speaks to using the different gifts we have each been given, "We have different gifts, according to the grace given to each of us. If your gift is prophesying, then prophesy in accordance with your faith;" (NIV).

Romans 12:8 says, "If it is to encourage, then give encouragement; if it is giving, then give generously; if it is to lead, do it diligently; if it is to show mercy, do it cheerfully" (NIV).

Acts 2:28: encourages us to rejoice in God saying, "You have made known to me the paths of life; you will fill me with joy in your presence' (NIV).

In Acts 20:24, the Apostle Paul his "all in" commitment to Christ and the gospel as he declares that, "However, I consider my life worth nothing to me; my only aim is to finish the race and complete the task the Lord Jesus has given me—the task of testifying to the good news of God's grace" (NIV).

Prepare for Rain

As I am writing at my summer home, I am praying for you. I have been coming to this place in the woods at the Jersey shore for over thirty-five years. It is a camping resort in the woods that has a lake, pool and amenities. This is the first time ever that I have been here alone for over a week without family. I would think I would be lonely, but as I look back over my life, I realize that I have never been alone. Jesus my Lord has always been with me every step of my journey. I felt His presence and heard His voice the first time in the whirlwind of a hummingbird's wings. I was in awe. I didn't even know what it was. He had to remind me that, "You do not know everything." My first sighting of a majestic bird is a time I will never forget. And it is raining almost every day, so I will not be distracted from my work. Hurricane Ida is heading our way. I felt compelled to pray for the safety of my children at 5:30 p.m. that night. My husband called and told me two tornadoes touched down in both towns that my family lives in. They were shaken but protected. I thank the Lord for reminding me to pray at all times. I listened to the radio with Christian music to focus myself, I sat under the awning and wrote in the RV and typed with the Wi-Fi in the members lounge for hours upon hours, ninety minutes at a time for sixteen days and over forty hours. It was amazing for someone like myself, with attention deficit disorder. It was a blessing from the Lord for me.

Just as a farmer prepares his fields for rain, be prepared for what the Lord Jesus will say to you personally. My prayer for you is that this would not just be another memoir of a self-help book, but a God Help Book. I pray He reveals himself to you personally through His presence and my testimony.

God Is an Ever-Present Help in Times of Troubles

This is what I heard spoken in my heart while preparing for this book:

"You need to face your giants of fear and ignore your distractions. You need to prepare for the rain of My Holy Spirit. Your prayers are being answered. I will give you undisturbed time to finish book 1. Discipline yourself every day. Be prepared to see My hand in every area of your life. Be ready to give Me the glory! Just like Nehemiah rebuilt the walls of Jerusalem in only fifty-two days with little help from men, I will help you complete the work and be ready for the publisher. Let me guide and direct your words and your work. Be diligent and faithful. Prepare for Rain…

Nehemiah 6:15: "So the wall was completed on the twenty-fifth day of Elul in fifty-two days" (NIV).

Luke 24:45: "Then he opened their minds so they understood the Scriptures" (NIV).

Second Letter to Timothy 3:16: "All Scripture is God-breathed and is useful for teaching, rebuking, correcting and training in righteousness" (NIV).

John 15:15–17: "I no longer call you servants, because a servant does not know his master's business. Instead, I have called you friends, for everything that I learned from my Father I have made known to you. You did not choose me, but I chose you and appointed you so that you might go and bear fruit—fruit that will last—and so that whatever you ask in my name the Father will give you. This is my command: Love each other" (NIV).

I pray for you my readers, prepare for rain. May the Lord refresh, redeem and restore you so that you too will water others who are thirsty to be and become more. And you will!

I count you among the many blessings in every season as the Lord has been so good to me. Counting it all Joy and to God be all the Glory!

Love of Jesus,
Rosemarie Page Yerka

Always Remember:

> There is a design and a Designer
> We are designed to know God
> God knew you before you were born
> Overcome insecurity by seeking truth
> Learn to listen for God's voice
> Seek truth, pray, and find Joy
> There is a secret formula for Joy

Be and become all you are designed to be.
Not self-help but God-help
Everything in life can change by a moment in time.

In Closing
My Prayer for You

Holy Spirit, Let Jesus be seen in my story. Help me shed your light on the path that would lead them to You in these pages and to God be the Glory! Amen.

"How sad when someone comes looking for Jesus and all they see is you."

~ Mother Teresa.

"To God be the Glory for things He has done in my life."

~Rosemarie Page Yerka

End of Part 5, Becoming a Woman for All Seasons by Design

The Gift of a Second Chance

The Pitch

"I would like you to come to 'Pioneer Girl Camp,' you'll get three days off and you won't have to cook, just teach the same Bible lesson all day on Saturday. It will be a nice getaway for you!" said Anita. She is a godly older woman with five older children who used to be a missionary. I immediately answered, "No, I cannot go. It will be too much for my husband and mother to look after the other four children. My baby is only nine months old." She insisted that the Lord had told her I am the one to teach the children. "I'll ask my husband," I replied. To my surprise, my husband agreed and told me to go.

I was excited to be a part of the camp, my daughter Tara had just accepted the Lord in her heart as personal Savior two years before, at age eight. I had the privilege to lead her to my Jesus. The next day, she observed, "Mommy, I feel different!" I thought, "Oh no, is she getting sick." Until, she followed up with, "I feel Jesus in my heart!" Yes, I told her, "He will never leave you. He will be your best friend!" Now Tara would have a chance to get away and grow in her knowledge of His Word, it would be a good experience for both of us. On the way to Strasberg, Pennsylvania, I was hit right between the eyes with the truth and discovered that my role at the camp was just a tiny bit different than what I had been told. "You will be in charge of the teenagers at camp, all you have to do is do devotions with them at night," said Anita.

As I processed this new "job description," I became painfully aware of a growing headache and an intensifying pain in my side that seemed to be getting worse. Even my Tylenol is not touching it—Great, it must be that time of the month I thought. This is going to be anything but a restful weekend, I'm afraid as I navigated the mounting sense of apprehension that I may have made the wrong decision. "Oh well, too late now," I murmured beneath my breath as I wondered what in the world I could share with the teenagers. The sole semi-relevant frame of reference I had was my ten-year-old-daughter, which shifted my prayer life into overdrive, "Lord, show me what you want me to do, please!"

The Drama Unfolds

The pain in my side was growing worse by the minute. When I got there, it was very cold, but I was freezing and shaking uncontrollably. The staff offered me hot chocolate, an extra blanket, and more Tylenol. I went to bed with my clothes on and thought, is it my time of the month again? When was the last time—I could not remember.

The teens were not church kids but instead were from the neighborhood and more familiar with street corners than pews. They spoke of guns, hiding in closets, abuse, drugs, and fear... I thought and prayed, "How can I get these girls to *want* to do devotions?" I desperately wanted to go to sleep but the pain I was in cut like a knife in my side, causing any hope of slumber to flee from me.

As the night wore on, I listened to all their stories staying as still as possible in an effort to control the pain. I knew I would not be able to sleep, so I just listened until the right moment finally presented itself and I said, "My turn to tell you my story, come in and sit down." Every girl who was still awake throughout the whole camp entered the bunkhouse and found room anywhere they could, from the bunks to the floor. It was about 2 a.m. and you could hear a pin drop as they sat with legs hanging off the bunks, just looking at me. I estimated some 20-to-25 young ladies, from middle school to high school as I shared my dramatic conversion experience with them. I assured them that Jesus knew and loved each one of them and had a plan for their individual lives. That He wanted them to invite Him into their hearts this very weekend—and then I prayed for all of them. I was convinced it had been a divine appointment as I dismissed them to return to their bunks and go to sleep.

Later, about 5 a.m. as I tried to get up, I found myself doubled over in agony. I was a nurse, and as strange as it sounds, I was familiar with various "smells" that would provide a warning and clue me in to different medical conditions in my patients. As I made my way to the bathroom, my radar lit up upon discovering the distinct smell of blood. A glance into the commode confirmed my worst fear revealing murky black water instead of bright red blood—that's when I realized I was in big trouble. Guessing that my appendix had burst, I immediately woke up one of the older girls and told her to get Miss Anita and tell her to call an ambulance. "Miss Rose has to go to the hospital," she breathlessly told Miss Eleanor, a beautiful Black Christian woman. She took my daughter, Tara, by the hand and under her wing as the tears streamed down her face and she sobbed in her squeaky voice, "Mommy are you going to die?" "No, your mommy will be okay, we will pray for her. I will bring you to the hospital with me," Miss Eleanor replied.

The Emergency Medical Technicians (EMTs) arrived with a stretcher. As they carried me over the icy sidewalk and hills of the camp, I saw little girls crying, their drawn faces etched with looks of fear, tears glistening across their cheeks. I felt so angry with God! "Why am I here? Am I not here to do your work? Why are you allowing this to happen in my life and the lives of these children? Tell me why," I demanded!

As I got a hold of my thoughts, I asked some questions of my transport team. "Do you know the name of a good surgeon at this hospital?" They replied, "No!" Then I asked, "Do you know the name of the bad surgeon?" They laughed and said, "Sorry we are not from around here!" My thinking drifted to the Great Physician, and

I decided it was a good time to drop His name. "I guess I will have to trust the Great Physician," I proclaimed boldly. "Who is that" they wondered? "Jesus," I said, silently shooting up another SOS prayer, "Please help me, Lord Jesus!"

When I arrived at the hospital, I listened as carefully as possible to the assessment which didn't leave much to the imagination, "We need prep and a surgical team ready… Probably appendix," the ER physician said unflinchingly. "Let us know if the pain stops." I guess I was right, this is not good. "We are taking some blood in one arm and starting an IV in the another," the team noted matter-of-factly. "We have to tape your ring and do you have any foreign objects in your body?" "Yes," I admitted. "I have an intrauterine device. It is good for four years."

I had decided that after my last baby, "Charity," was born, that I was too young to have my tubes tied. "I have five kids," I reasoned, "if something happened to my husband, I would not be able to raise them alone. And if I found someone, it would probably be a man without kids and would want one with me. So now I have four years to make that decision. I am safe and it is under my control. We cannot afford another baby and my husband would not get a vasectomy. So it was up to me to come up with a plan."

"Sorry lady, it has to come out! It is a foreign object. It has to go for surgery. I replied, "Oh no, you don't," I protested, "I paid $200 for it and it is good for four years. Can you put it back when you are done? I cannot believe this!" My complaints were interrupted by, "Blood test results are in Mrs. Yerka, I want you to know it is not your appendix." "What is it then," I asked? "You are pregnant!" he answered. I started to cry! "We have to do an ultrasound. It is probably an ectopic tubal pregnancy."

They set my stretcher up to move me. "Are you okay?" "I feel faint," I heard myself murmur, "but the pain has gone away!" They all looked at each other, unplugged the bed, got the IV and Oxygen on wheels and started maneuvering me down the hall. "There's no time for an ultrasound. You have ruptured and we need to open you up now!" Against the backdrop of Tara's sobs, Miss Eleanor said,

"Goodbye, Mommy will be okay. Jesus is with her. We will pray for her." I heard them say, "Call her husband and tell him to get here ASAP." I thought, "Bob is bad with directions, I hope he finds me!"

I was faint, nauseous, and scared, feeling myself grow weaker and weaker as if my life was leaving my body. I could no longer answer the questions I was being peppered with, nor could I speak. I saw a bright light and felt like my body was rising above the gurney… "Lord, am I dying? Please, I want to see my kids again."

A wake-up call barged into my prayer, "Mrs. Yerka! Wake up, your brother is her to see you. He even gave blood for you. You are a new woman with all the new blood you have received!" As I awoke in the intensive care unit against the cacophony of all the wires and beeping sounds, I asked, "You said what, my brother? I thought, I do not have a brother. I am an only child. This is very strange. A young minister named Dave, from the camp walked in. He said, "I am your brother in Christ. Your husband is on the way!" I cried, "Thank you for being with me." He said, "You gave us a scare, we all prayed for you!"

Little Less Pregnant

The doctor came in to see me explaining, "You had an ovarian pregnancy. These are very rare. I had never seen one, myself… So it ruptured, and you lost your tube and we tied the other like you asked." I had a vague memory about that and said, "Do whatever you have to do to save my life and that I do not get pregnant again. I cannot do this again. I cannot believe I am pregnant again." I asked, "Am I still pregnant?" He answered, "You are less pregnant today than you were yesterday!" Thank you, Lord." After being transferred to a real room, my husband made it to see me. I was so happy to see him. "How are you doing," he asked? "Good," I said, "less pregnant than yesterday." We laughed, enjoying a nice visit. I was good as long as the pain medicine was working. He left as I felt the pain beginning to return along with feeling lonely and sad and still angry with God.

This must be all His fault… Or maybe it is Bob's fault, I cannot be that fertile, I am an only child. He would not fix this.

Grow Stronger

I started to cry out in pain, "Why Lord? What is the purpose of this?" There was a painting of a large oak tree on the wall in front of me. Through my tears, it looked so real.

I heard the Lord's voice speak in my ear, "I want your roots to go down deeper. When the storms of life come, the tree stretches its roots down deeper to hold onto the earth and grows stronger. You will become stronger like a mighty oak. Your branches will provide a resting place for those who are weary. You will become a strong woman for My Name's sake. Do not be afraid, I am with you always, I will carry you through this and you will become strong in your faith. Do Not be afraid I am with you."

Here I go Again

The nurse came in with a cheerful voice. "Okay time to get up dear," she said. "I can't get up. I am in too much pain. I feel dizzy and weak." "No problem," she said. "Nurses do make the worst patients. You will be fine!" "No, I feel the same way I felt when I first got to the emergency room. I feel like my blood pressure is dropping. Please check it for me." I asked. She took it and the number read 60/40. She lowered my head of the bed and pressed the button for the desk. "Code Blue" she said. I heard people running down the hall with the crash cart again. "Get her prepped. We need to go now! Call, get her husband on the phone for a verbal consent. She is bleeding again! Get the surgical team here now!"

Smacking my face, calling my name… "Rosemarie, open your eyes!" Smelling salts at my nose. Can you hear me?" I felt needles and pinching, but I could not speak. I saw the bright light again and felt such peace—I was completely unafraid. "Lord, is that you? Am I dying again? How can this be? Are they too late to save me this time? Please let me live again to see my children."

ICU Again

I woke up to the bright lights and beeping of the ICU again. "Mrs. Yerka, you gave us a scare. It was very strange, I have never seen anything like it before," the doctor said. "You had all the active signs of bleeding. I looked for almost an hour to find it but I could not. When I opened you up, you were filled with clots. Very unusual that it seemed to have stopped on its own. I have never seen anything like this. You gave me a real scare!"

"I know what happened," I answered the doctors' questions. "The Great Physician had got there before you. You were too late." "Who?" the doctor asked with a puzzled look on his face. "Jesus Christ, my Lord and Savior. He is the Great Physician. To him be all Glory and praise for sparing my life." I explained. "Well, I cannot explain what happened. I am just happy that you are alive." the doctor replied. "Thank you for your good care," I said.

Second Chances

I now have a second chance to be a good mother, and to tell others about my Jesus—He has saved me three times. From the abortionist knife, my suicide attempt, and a ruptured ovary. I will never be the same, I will never take life for granted again.

Level 1 Emergency Room

My friend Mary Lou came to pick me up with my husband. We even had to make a stop at the Pennsylvania State Troopers headquarters for me to rest. They were so kind because of Tom, Mary Lou's husband, who was a Trooper. On the way home she told me that God had sent me to this particular hospital Emergency Room to save my life. "If you were at our local hospital, you would have died while they attempted to obtain a diagnosis. I know I work there. They are not equipped for your kind of emergency. You are a lucky woman. God must have a special plan for you. He sent you to one of the best emergency rooms on the east coast. Yes, he was with you. He planned everything. He has got His hand on you."

Becoming Fearless

On the last day of Pioneer Girls, I was invited to be the guest speaker. All the girls and their mothers had sent me flowers and cards, while the ladies from church visited, watched my kids and cleaned my house. I was embarrassed by how dirty my house was and busied myself trying to clean before they came. As I did, I lost my footing and fell down my stairs seeing stars and grimacing in pain. I thought, "Have I torn out my stitches?" The Lord spoke to me as I sat on the foyer floor, saying, "You must learn to receive and not just be a giver. This is harder but it is for My purpose so you will understand how to minister to others."

The church ladies were so generous and caring that it seemed like they were my real sisters, making me feel wonderfully blessed to be in a church family. The last day finally came and as the time arrived for me to speak, I found my shyness front and center. "I do not think I can do this Lord," I thought. "You can do all things. I will strengthen you. You will become fearless to share the good things I will do in your life. Do not be afraid. I am with you. I will put the words in your mouth"

I shared my testimony with the girls and their mothers to some fifty-to-seventy people who had come to hear me speak. One of the mothers came up to me afterward and said she would like to receive Jesus in her heart like me and her daughter. Her daughter was one of the girls in my room that awful night. I prayed for her and all in the room to know my Jesus! I had a test and a testimony, feeling stronger with my fear completely gone. In Jesus's name. I am not shy anymore, I am fearless.

Repression

Postpartum depression had set in again. I had repressed the sad feeling and grief about losing baby 6 and realized that it was my IUD that caused the baby not to be able to implant inside the uterus wall, so it anchored to the ovary. I repressed the grief. After all, I needed to get on with my life and take care of my children.

Many years later, I was working as the manager of "Choices of the Heart Women's Resource Center," having been trained for post abortion counseling. My first client named her aborted baby after me and her grandmother which left me so humbled. That night the Lord spoke to my heart about my repressed grief concerning my lost child and told me his name was David John. The tears started to flow and I found inner healing along with my client as I faced the truth about what had happened for the first time. I almost died with him like my grandmother Rose, and look forward to seeing my baby in heaven someday.

Full Circle

Like my grandmother Rose McCleary who died at age twenty-three, I also could have died prematurely, at age thirty-four. She left my mother and lost a son while I lost a son and would have left five children behind. At least I had already had a good life and now have a second chance to not only come out of this alive, but to come back to my born again, life from age twenty-three.

I had almost *forgotten* my first love, Jesus. He met me and carried me through this near-death experience, teaching me how precious life really is. Thankfulness is the royal road to joy. I serve an amazing God who is available to all who call upon His name. Ephesians 2:8–9 explains, "For it is by grace you are saved through faith. Not of yourselves. It is a gift of God, not by works, so that no one can boast." Second Corinthians 9:15 tells us, "Thanks be to God for his indescribable gift" (NKJV), while Psalm 95:2 says, "Let us come before His Presence with thanksgiving. Let us shout to him with praise."

He gave me my life back as a gift and put a ribbon around me so I could share my story with you. He trusted me to learn the lesson and would not hear me until I was right with Him. He wanted me to stop complaining and see the gifts my children were to me—that I could not do parenting on my own without Him. My born-again life came full circle until it doubled back to the basics. Jesus does not just want to be Savior. He wants to be Lord of every area of my life. Doing things my way wears me out, and I have learned that apart from Him I can do *nothing*. The Lord loves my children more than I do. He knows what is best for them, and will guide me if I ask for His help, the same way He provides what I need when I ask Him. He provides all I need and I can trust Him to watch over me. Love is a circle. Give more love and it comes back full circle. Thank God for second chances!

The fruit of the Spirit is love, joy, peace, patience. kindness, goodness, faithfulness, gentleness and self-control (Galatians 6:22–23). These are many virtues of the Proverbs 31 godly woman, a woman for all seasons.

Introduction

Merriam-Webster defines an "heirloom" as, "Something of special value handed down from one generation to another." The Christmas song, "Heirlooms," by Amy Grant, is a vivid rendering of my story in countless ways. Among the more touching and meaningful lines tucked into its lyrics is, "A box from the attic, tags that contain yellowed letters, photographs, trinkets, diaries and calendars that tell the story of the Spring and Summer of my life." In this spirit, I have broken down my life's circle into the following seasons:

> **The Joy of Winter:** My Mother's Story
>
> **The Joy of Spring:** The Story of Love with the Love of My Life
>
> **The Joy of Summer:** A Story of a Loving Dysfunctional Family
>
> **The Joy of Autumn:** The Joy of Red-Letter Days and Recovery
>
> **The Joy of the Circle of Life by Design:** A Legacy for the Next Generation

These reflections, from pondering, to passages, to perspectives, while not something that can be held in the hand, are heirlooms, nonetheless. They are held in the heart and passed on from the deepest recesses of my soul, hopefully, to the depths of yours. It is my hope that as you explore the heirlooms unique to each season of my life through these reflections, you will take the time to savor each thought, each dream, each tear, and each triumph as a wine connoisseur would savor a rare, celebrated, and cherished vintage. Thus, they are offered to you, the reader, in the hope that their universal value and significance are taken to heart, treasured, lived out, and paid forward.

—Rosemarie Page Yerka

I. *Heirlooms of Joy in Winter*

A. Ponder the Word
1. Jeremiah 1:5 "I knew you before you were in your mother's womb…"
2. Jeremiah 31:3 "I loved you with everlasting love."
3. Psalm 46:10 "Be Still… "
4. Galatians 5:22 "The fruit of the Spirit is love, joy, peace…"

B. Quotation to Consider

"In Winter the days seem long but the years are short, making ready for Spring." Author Unknown

C. Reflective Questions
1. What would you do if you were Rose?
2. Would you forgive your aunt and mother?
3. Would you want to meet your father?
4. What has made you feel insecure?
5. How did you find Joy in the Winter of your life?

II. *Heirlooms of Joy in Spring*

A. Ponder the Word
1. Jeremiah 1:5 "I set you apart…"
2. Psalm 46:10 "and know…"
3. Psalm 13:5 "Take your questions to God."
4. Ecclesiastes 3:3 "a time to plant…"
5. Galatians 5:22 "patience, kindness, goodness…"

B. Quotation to Consider

"The Becoming process is an exciting possibility for a dreamer like me." Rosemarie Page Yerka

C. Reflective Questions
1. What would you do if you were Rose?
2. Would you follow your original plans?
3. Would you marry young?
4. How did you become lovable?
5. How did you find joy in the spring of your life?

III. *Heirlooms of Joy in Summer*

A. Ponder the Word
1. Jeremiah 1:5 "I appointed you…"
2. Psalm 46:10 "I am God…"
3. Galatians 5:22 "Faithfulness, gentleness…"
4. Philippians 2:12 "Continue to work out your own salvation with fear and trembling…"
5. Romans 8:28 (NIV) "And we know in all things God works for the good of those who love him, who have been called according to his purpose."

B. Quotation to Consider

"The battle is in your mind." (Joyce Meyers, *Battlefield of the Mind*)

C. Reflective Questions
1. What would you do if you were Rose?
2. Are you afraid of change?
3. Have you done the "dysfunctional dance?"
4. How did you overcome fear?
5. How did you find joy in the summer of your life?

IV. Heirlooms of Joy in Autumn

A. Ponder the Word
1. Jeremiah 1:5 "as a prophet to the nations"
2. Psalm 46:10 "I will be exalted in the nations"
3. Jeremiah 29:11 "I know the plans I have for you says the Lord…"
4. Ecclesiastes 3:2 "a time to uproot and a time to heal…"
5. Galatians 5:22 "and Self-Control…"

B. Quotation to Consider

"Second Chances are a gift." Unknown
"The ground of liberty must be gained by inches." ~Thomas Jefferson

C. Reflective Questions
1. What would you do if you were Rose?
2. Have you experienced recovery or a second chance?
3. Have you heard God's voice?
4. How did you come to unshakeable faith?

V.   Heirlooms Circle of Love

A.   Ponder the Word
1.   John 15:9–11 "My Joy will remain with you. Your Joy will be complete."
2.   Philippians 1:6 "God is not finished with me yet."
3.   Philippians 4:13 "I can do all things through Christ who strengthens me."
4.   1 Corinthians 13:13 "And now these remain: Faith Hope and Love. But the greatest of these is Love."

B.   Quotation to Consider

"Whatever does not kill you makes you stronger." Unknown
"The harder the conflict, the more glorious the triumph." Thomas Paine

C.   Reflective Questions
1.   What would you do if you were Rose?
2.   What would you do if you were Agnes?
3.   What heirlooms were given to your family?
4.   What do you want to leave as a legacy heirloom for your family?
5.   What do you want to give the next generation?

Heirlooms of Joy for A Woman for All Seasons

"For such a time as this?" Esther 4:14b (NIV)
"There is a time for everything and a season for every activity under the heavens" Ecclesiastes 3:1(NIV)

Many years ago, the Lord gave me the theme, the Bible verses and two of the songs the last two weeks of the study.

He has reminded me of the power of my testimony. And he told me I was to give my testimony at the Ladies Tea. He wants me to sing the song that He gave me. Amy Grant, Heirlooms.

I briefly told Him of my inadequacy but He reminded me that" I can do all things through Christ who strengthens me." Praise the Lord! What a Joyful noise and memory!

Labor of Being and Becoming More Like Jesus
A Woman for All Seasons

Ecclesiastes 2:25–26: "For without him, who can eat or find enjoyment? To the person who pleases him, God gives wisdom, knowledge and happiness, but to the sinner he gives the task of gathering and storing up wealth to hand it over to the one who pleases God. This too is meaningless, a chasing after the wind.

I Strive to Be and Become a Woman for All Seasons

My mother's birthday is December 20, and was at the very end of fall and then the first day of winter begins. Life is a circle like love. It becomes bigger and bigger and includes so many people and generations of children, grandchildren and great grandchildren. A legacy of love.

My mother had a hundred people at her funeral. Her priest blessed her body and her coffin and Pastor Bruce reminded us that she is no longer there. "To be absent from the body is to be present with the Lord." She prays for all of us now. She knew where she wanted to go.

Her priest told her it was time to let go because the dialysis was no longer working. One of last words were, "I want to go over there with my sister Ann." And she told my friend Mary Lou, "Take care of my Rose Marie."

A life well lived is prepared for the last season. Trusting the Lord to complete the circle of love left behind, so I write her legacy to us.

Leaving a Legacy

Romans 1:2: "The gospel he promised beforehand through his prophets in the Holy Scriptures" (NIV).

Acts 20:24: "However, I consider my life worth nothing to me; my only aim is to finish the race and complete the task the Lord Jesus has given me—the task of testifying to the good news of God's grace" (NIV).

One hundred and five years ago, on December 20, 1917, Agnes was born. Her life made a difference to all who knew her. She passed the torch of faith from her grandmother who passed it to her mother and father. She passed it to her only daughter, Rose, named after her mother, a mother she never knew, who was taken in the flu epidemic of 1918. Rose showed loving care to her mother fearlessly. Both her mother and son also died. Her mother's love became the consolation to Agnes, who was left behind as a baby and who lost her mother.

Her memory lived on as a legend in Agnes' heart. She carried on the love to her daughter, Rose, her brother and five sisters and their children, which brings it full circle today.

Being loving helps one become a blessing to others. Then the legacy lives on from one generation to the next. It is time for Rose to become more like Jesus, loving, kind, gentle, patience, joyful, peaceful and merciful, meekness, faithfulness and have self-control. She will become a woman for all seasons. A fairy tale of the woman within and the journey to wholeness is now complete. *A woman for all seasons.*

Proverbs 31 Woman: The Epilogue of a Wife of Noble Character

Lord, I know You want me to become a woman for all seasons. A Proverbs 31 woman is what I hope to become for my family to leave a legacy of love for my children and grandchildren and great grandchildren too. A Proverbs 31 woman lives her entire life out of a desire to honor and serve the Lord. Proverbs 31:30: "Charm is deceptive, and beauty is fleeting; but a woman who fears the Lord is to be praised." (NIV).

Ecclesiastes 7:1 *"A good name is better than fine perfume and the day of death better than a day of birth"* (NIV).

Lord, I pray to live well like my mother and grandmother. So that my day of death will be a celebration of the life you have given to me for others.

Rose, a giver of love for the next generations

A legacy wrapped in truth brings love, joy, peace, patience, kindness, goodness, faithfulness, gentleness, and self-control. The secret of joy revealed through the stages and the struggles of a life well-lived. She is learning to seek joy and not happiness for her children, grandchildren, great-grandchildren, and the next generation. I am becoming a generational thinker and living life by design as a story from a hundred years ago lived backward and as an answer to prayer.

"As the Father has loved me, so have I loved you. Now remain in my love. If you keep my commands, you will remain in my love, just as I have kept my Father's commands and remain in his love. I have told you this so that my joy may be in you and that your joy may be complete" (NIV).

A Three-Braided Cord Is Not Easily Broken

"It is said that some lives are linked across time. Connecting an ancient calling that echoes through the ages." I never met Rose McCleary, my grandmother. But I am named Rose after her. *Rose* means "giver of love." My mother does not remember her mother either. Only the legend of love as a hero in the McCleary family was left behind.

A three-braided cord is not easily broken. My story, my mother's story, and my grandmother's story have left an unbreakable bond of love to leave as a legacy for the next generation. The Lord himself is the glue that has created a story of love to be passed on to my children and great grandchildren. He is the unseen character in your story too.

He answered my prayer for me, and now my prayer for you is that you too would come to know Jesus personally as your Lord and Savior. He is the best friend you will ever know. May your journey of faith begin for the next generation.

My Testimony

I own no religious pride. I used to think I had a ticket to heaven based on my religion. No, Jesus is the Way, the Truth, and the Life. No more daily devotions—it is a minute-by-minute devotion to hear His voice and His word for me today. Speak, Lord. Your servant listens. I will pray until my heart sings, "Hosanna!" The joy of the Lord is my strength. I seek to be taught by you, my Lord. Intimate knowledge of who You are and who You want me to be, Your unique creation. Philippians 1:6—developing…perfecting…full completion in You. Isaiah 30:15: "In quietness and in confidence shall be my strength."

My goal to silence, my whole attention toward my God. Focus on the Lord Himself.

Isaiah 40:31 (NIV): "But those who hope in the Lord will renew their strength. They will soar on wings like eagles; run and not grow weary, they will walk and not faint."

Zechariah 9:9: "Rejoice, daughter—see, your king comes to you."

My thoughts on love and how it can change your life.

The First Letter to the Corinthians 13:8: "Love never fails." Verse 13: "And now these three remain: faith, hope, and love. But the greatest of these is love" (NIV).

Dear Lord, help me grow in love, more and more in love with you, to show others your love. *Thank You, Jesus!*

Amen.

THE SECRET REVEALED

I hope this multigenerational story has uplifted and inspired you. The secret is that you are not alone. You are not an accident. God has a plan for everyday of your life. Life can shake you but not stir your faith. Allow joy to become part of your life as you be and become more like the person you are created to become.

Luke 2:19: "But Mary pondered up all these things and pondered up all these things in her heart." *Ponder* according to Oxford Dictionary is "to improve thinking and become self-aware. To think carefully before making a decision or reaching a conclusion. To contemplate, meditate, think deeply." This positive practice links between the heart and the mind.

Romans 8:28–29: "We know that for those who love God all things work together for good, for those called according to his purpose. For whom he foreknew he also predestined to be conformed to the image of his son."(NIV)

There is a different future for you when God shows up in your life! Refined to the likeness of Christ. We become graceful; in growth becoming more mature and find joy in the process.

Ecclesiastes 3:11: "God makes all things beautiful in His time" (NIV).

He has the ability to complete the plan he has for me and you. Trust Him!

Psalm 94:19: "When anxiety was great within me, your consolation brought me joy!" (NIV).

Praise has the power to lighten the burdens of life and bring Joy, God's presence in your mind.

Becoming More Like Jesus

This book is about change and hope. It is not about me. The chief purpose in life is to be like Jesus. He is our identity. This life is a vapor and goes so quickly!

Life explodes with faith, hope and love, which brings joy!

Transformation

How to live well and finish well? Continue to listen and follow the Holy Spirit. Tell your story of how God intersects with you and changes you. Be a truth teller. Develop transformational friendships. These are covenant relationships that cover you and prayer and help to carry your burdens. Be a friend. A friend loves at all times.

Always remember that Jesus is your best friend you will ever know.

He will lead guide and direct your path.

The Secret

Jesus is real. He is the unseen character in this book. He wrote my story.

He answered my mother's prayer for me almost seventy years ago. He answered my grandmother Rose's prayer for Agnes a hundred and four years ago.

He also answered my great-grandmother Anna's prayer for Rose, my grandmother, the same day she died of the flu in 1918.

My story is about answered prayers that will still be important one hundred years from now because it will be about how God is answering my prayers for my five children.

He saved my life from destruction after I made many mistakes and lost my footing or fell asleep at the wheel. He was the supernatural fifth dimension of every memory. I finally realized His presence and who He really was, when I accepted Him as my Lord and Savior. He came into my heart and was always with me even before—past, present, and future. He is with me even now as I write these last words. In his presence is fullness of joy.

The Secret Formula to Joy Is Found for Me in These Scriptures Philippians 2:2–5 (NIV)

"Then make my Joy complete by being like minded, having the same love, being one in the spirit and purpose. Do nothing out of selfish ambition or vain conceit, but in humility consider others better than yourselves. Each of you should look out not only to you own interests, but also to the interest of others. Your attitude should be the same as that of Christ Jesus."

Psalm 16:11 (NIV): "You made known to me the path of life: you will fill me with joy in your presence, with eternal pleasures at your right hand."

The Secret Revealed to Me

Colossians 2:2–3 (TLB) "This I have asked God for you; that you will be encouraged and knit together by strong ties of love, and that you will have the rich experience of knowing Christ with real certainty and clear understanding. For God's secret plan, now at last made known, is Christ himself. In him lie hidden all the mighty untapped treasure of wisdom and knowledge."

His presence is the secret for joy in every season and stage of life. His joy is what gives strength. He gave my life back to me as a gift. Now I write my story to you, my readers, as an invitation to receive the same gift of new life—real life filled with the joy of his presence. Jesus is the best friend you will ever find. He was always there. I was the one who was lost on my way. He is the way, the truth and the life. I belong to him and will spend eternity with him when my earthly life is over.

I will get to see my mother Agnes, grandmother Rose, and great-grandmother Anna. Now in this season, it's back to winter. I pray for my children, grandchildren, and great-grandchildren, and someday, great-great-grandchildren a hundred years from now. Because love is a circle. God is love, and love never fails. Winter is where love begins—choose life and love. Faith, hope, and love, but the greatest is love. They will bring joy in your life.

John 15:16 (NIV): "You did not choose me I chose you."

Revelation 3:20 (NIV): "Here I am! I stand at the door and knock. If anyone hears my voice and opens the door, I will come in and have eat with that person and they with me."

Psalm 100:1–2: "Shout for joy to the Lord, all the earth. Worship the Lord with gladness, come before him with joyful song."

Wishing you, my reader, the joy of the Lord!

Afterword

History has repeated itself this year, 2023. The *Jesus Revolution* movie[44] came out about the Jesus Movement in 1970s. It is a multigenerational movie just like my book. It is the story of Lonnie Frisbee, Chuck Smith and Greg Laurie.

The night before it was released, a revival was being aired on TBN from Asbury Theological College. It appears that what the Lord did fifty years ago, he plans to do again.

The Jesus movement in 1970s was a countercultural movement that became the greatest spiritual awakening in American history. Now we desperately need another move of God for the next generation. The quest for meaning and hunger and thirst for truth is always a precursor for revival. That describes me in 1970s. The movie was a walk down memory lane with happy memories of meeting a real-life Jesus experience. I considered myself a Jesus freak from then on.

Come, Holy Spirit, come. Tears for those we love and our nation. Raise up an army of prayer warriors. Let us be a part of what you are doing. Let us be faithful.

Lord, do it again! It is our fiftieth wedding anniversary this year. As we celebrate, revive us again to remember our first love, You, and then each other. May Bob and I both become the people you have created us to become.

May my story be part of what you use to bring others to yourself. Let others become part of the new story of the Jesus Revolution of 2023. Be glorified and rescue those who are lost, I pray. In Your name.

---

[44] Jon Erwin and Kevin Downes (producers), Greg Laurie and Ellen Vaughn (writers), *Jesus Revolution* (Lionsgate, February 24, 2023)

ACKNOWLEDGMENTS

To My Husband

Bob, thank you for your patience and love. You are my soulmate and best friend. Thank you for your support for all my dreams. We have shared many adventures and hold many extraordinary memories. I am forever grateful for your love in our marriage and your love that helped me become a mother to our children. You are in my heart forever.

A Life of Love Invested in Eternity

Proverbs12:27: "The substance of a diligent man is precious." Verse 13: "A wise son hears his father's instructions."

Genesis 2:8: "The Lord said, 'It is not good for man to be alone. I will make him a companion and helper.'"

My husband gave me unconditional acceptance and love while I was still in process. I am reminded of his godly traits that have blessed my life. he has enhanced my personhood and allowed me to be and become more myself by his love.

Psalm 25:12: "Who is the man who trusts in the Lord?" (Robert Michael Yerka).

This man shall have a legacy to pass on for generation to generation. I am thankful for my godly husband.

To My Children

It has been quite the journey, and God has been so good to our family. As an only child, I am blessed to have many children. To my older children, thank you for your patience with me as I was becoming a mother and developing a mother's heart full of love. I love all of you and respect the unique people you have become. You are all strong, kind and wonderful. You are my favorite people in the whole world. You each made me become a better mother and gave meaning and purpose to my life. I am forever grateful that you didn't hold my dysfunction against me. I am thankful for your forgiveness and love. I pray it ends with me and not to continue in your families by God's grace and mercy. I am also grateful for all the added children by law. You have blessed my heart with your love for my children. May God continue to bless your love and marriages.

To My Grandchildren and Great-Grandchildren

You are the hope for the future. You bring joy and love. May you remember where it comes from, God is Love. He is the invisible character in your lives and the answer to my prayers for you. May you each be blessed. I am so proud of each of you. May you become all that God has designed you to be.

To My Becoming Team

Thank you for your prayers and encouragement to "get it done!" I am grateful for each and every one of you. You are in my heart and are a part of my journey and my life's story. You know who you are. You continue to impact me, shape me, and believe in me. You help me to become stronger. Thank you for your love, prayers, and many kindnesses.

This has truly been like birthing a baby. This writing process is similar, but it is long past the nine-month mark. My friendships and family have expanded with many marriages and births. My circle has become larger, and I am ever thankful for each one who has enriched my life with love and joy!

I thank my God every time I remember each one of you. John Robert Yerka, thank you for the beautiful rose artwork. You are the artist in our family. Nicole Garcia and Mary Versaggi, thank you for your technical support. You are my blessings!

Special thank you to my pastor Joseph Bruce Sofia for his support. For allowing me to use the ABCs and for recommending Rick and Kim Kern, comprehensive editor. I would also like to thank Brenda Gilliland, publishing specialist, and Christian Faith Publishing for your patience with me as I stumbled to the finish line. You are truly a Christian company. Your patience and mentoring made this book possible and better. I thank God for all of you.

This Is the End Before ABCs

Do You Know Your ABCs?[45]

Let's Start Here

No one would deny that knowing the ABCs is one of life's essentials. In fact, trying to get through life without them is extremely difficult. To be quite honest, knowing the ABCs is, in actuality, a matter of life and death. Let me show you what I mean, answering the following questions, will determine how well you know your ABCs:

> Question 1: If you were to die today do you know for certain that you would go to heaven?
>
> Question 2: Suppose you were to die today and stand before God, and He should ask you, "Why should I let you into heaven?" what would you say?

If you had trouble answering the first question, you are not alone. Most people are not sure they will go to heaven when they die. Second, most believe they will enter heaven because they are "good enough." Nothing could be further from the truth. However, knowing your ABCs will not only guarantee that when you die you *will* go to heaven, it will also help you live a life of purpose and abundance today while living on planet earth.

Here's the *A*. This first part is tough but necessary and the foundation for B, C, and D: God is holy, and we are not, so…

---

[45] J. Bruce Sofia, "Do you know your ABCs?"

A. Admit the Truth About Yourself

- You have done things that are wrong. God calls these wrongs "sin."
- Therefore, acknowledge that you are a sinner: Psalm 14:1–3 and Romans 3:23 tell us, "For all have sinned and fall short of the glory of God."

You may ask, "What is sin?" First, it is breaking the law of God, and second, it's failing to do what we are supposed to do. Isaiah 56:3 tells us, "We have all gone our own way," and James 4:17 tells us, "Therefore, to one who knows the right thing to do, and does not do it, to him it is sin." Simply put, that means we're all sinners.

With that in mind, God's Word tells us we cannot *earn* eternal life or a relationship with Him. Other religions may propose a way of achieving some state of goodness where their "god" will grant you salvation, heaven or eternal life. That is the distinction between Christianity and all other faiths, the God of the Bible tell us, "For it is by grace you have been saved through faith and that not of yourselves; it is a gift of God, not of works, lest anyone should boast" (Ephesians 2:8–9).

Think it through! If a person could be good enough in him/herself to *earn* salvation, there would have been no need for Jesus. There would be no Virgin Birth, no crucifixion, and no resurrection.

Now here's the *ouch!* Because of your sin, you cannot dwell in the presence of a holy God, you are separated from Him. Furthermore, because He is holy, He must judge sin. This means when you die you will go to hell *unless* you receive God's *gift* of forgiveness for your sins, Jesus Christ. Romans 6:23 tells us, "For the wages of sin is death" (Romans 6:23a). This is why all men die physically (Hebrews 9:27) and spiritually (Colossians 2:13). Do you understand this? Good, let's go on! Now here's the "good news!" This takes the *ouch* away.

B. Believe the Truth about God

- God loves you and does not want you or anyone else to perish. Romans 5:8 tells us, "But God demonstrates His own love toward us, in that while we were yet sinners, Christ died for us."

- God is entirely just and must punish sin. Exodus 34:7b tells us, "[God] does not leave the guilty unpunished."
- God sent His only Son, Jesus, to die on our behalf. John 3:16 tells us, "For God so loved the world that he gave his one and only Son, that whoever believes in Him shall not perish but have eternal life."

Here's the truth about God: Jesus died on the cross to pay the penalty for your sin and He arose from the dead to purchase a place for you in Heaven. Romans 6:23b tells us, "…the free gift of God is eternal life through Christ Jesus our Lord." Do you believe this about God? Good, let's continue!

C. Commit Yourself to God

- Begin by receiving God's free gift, Jesus Christ, by faith. Ephesians 2:8 tells us, "For it is by grace you have been saved, through faith and that not of yourselves; it is a gift of God."
- Trust God and not yourself. John 1:12 tells us, "Yet to all who received him, to those who believed in his name, he gave the right to become children of God."
- Receive Christ as Lord and Savior. Romans 10: 9–10 gives us the promise and guarantee: "That if you confess with your mouth, 'Jesus is Lord,' and believe in your heart that God raised him from the dead, you will be saved. For it is with your heart that you believe and are justified, and it is with your mouth that you confess and are saved."

Grasp this! Jesus took your place for the punishment of sin (death) and arose from the dead to give you eternal life and an eternity in Heaven. Now that you believe this about God, repent of your sins. Acts 3:19 instructs us to "Repent, then, and turn to God, so that your sins may be wiped out, that times of refreshing may come from the Lord." Be more than sorry; repent (turn from trusting your own righteousness and abide in His). Make a decision today to turn from those things that displease God to those things that please Him; the difference is *life vs. death.* Obeying God brings life while disobeying God brings death. And although after you've received Christ sin cannot remove your relationship with the LORD, it will certainly mess up your fellowship.

You may say, "I can't I've already tried!" When you give your life to Christ, He will give you the strength to change. Philippians 4:13 tells us, "I can do all things through Christ who strengthens me," and Philippians 6:1 assures us that what God began in you He will complete. Okay, now that you understand our ABCs, you're ready for the *D.*

D. Do It Today!

Why is the *D* so important? Two reasons.

First, none of us are guaranteed tomorrow. I have officiated the funeral services of far too many children, teenagers, healthy young men and women, husbands and wives who everyone thought would outlive the rest of us, but they are not here today. James 4:14 tells us, "Why, you do not even know what will happen tomorrow. What is your life? You are a mist that appears for a little while and then vanishes." Second, you can begin living in true *joy* right now! No need to merely exist from one day to the next, or wonder why you are here, Jesus said, "The thief [Satan] comes to kill, steal, and destroy, but I have come that you may have life, and have it more abundantly" (John 10:10b).

You say, "Okay, I believe the ABCs and D, *what do I do next?*" Say a short prayer to God that expresses your desire to commit your life to Him. Please understand, the words in this prayer do not save you; rather they simply express your heart. What you believe in your heart is what God hears, and then God does the "saving." Romans 10:9–10 tell us, "If you confess with your mouth Jesus as Lord and believe in your heart that God raised Him from the dead, you shall be saved; for with the heart man believes, resulting in righteousness, and with the mouth he confesses, resulting in salvation."

Pray something like this:

> Father in Heaven, I'm sorry for the things I've done that are wrong: I am a sinner; forgive me. Thank you for loving me and sending your Son, Jesus, to pay the penalty for my sins. Holy Spirit, come into my heart. Jesus, be my Lord and Savior. I give You my life. Amen!

If you just prayed that prayer, or one like it, *welcome to the family of God!* You are now a child of God and a citizen of Heaven. Now that you are a child of God this promise is yours: "I tell you the truth, he who believes has everlasting life" (John 6:47).

What's Next?

Consider giving these five steps to knowing God a significant place in your life:

1. Read God's Word. This is God speaking to you.
2. Pray. This is you speaking to God.
3. Attend church. Find a church where the Bible is taught as God's Word (all of it). Hebrews 10:23–25 tells us God has established the church as a canopy for those who believe.
4. Fellowship with other Christians. Find Christian friends who will help you grow in your relationship with the Lord as well as hold you accountable for your actions, and don't select friends who want you to be "just like them." True godly friends want you to be like Christ. It is impossible to grow as a Christian without this interaction. Look at the life of Christ. He had a close circle of twelve and within that circle He had an inner circle of three: Peter, James, and John.

5. Tell others. Tell someone about what God has done, is doing, and will do. There is no greater joy.

Here are a few *final reminders* worth memorizing:

Salvation *is not*:

- in the church
- in the sacraments
- in our own goodness

Salvation *is*:

- in a person, Jesus the Christ

If salvation is in what we could achieve or what the church could do for us, we would have no need of Jesus. Furthermore, although the sacraments, the church, and our good deeds are important for our fellowship with God, our salvation is in Jesus—that's the relationship, and in Jesus alone. Relationship is God's doing, fellowship is our doing.

Bob in Uniform 1970

Bob and Rose Dating 1971

Rose Graduation Photo 1972

Grandpa Page

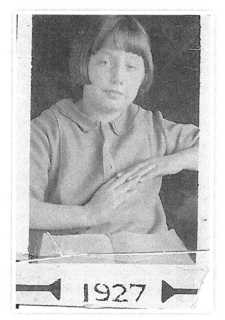

Agnes Fourth Grade Woodbury New Jersey

Agnes in Bloomers in Atlantic City age 13.

Aunt Rose Page in her Nursing scrub uniform
Thomas Jefferson Hospital Philadelphia

Agnes and her Sister Marge on the Atlantic City
Boardwalk(race horses on the beach)

Marko (Mike) Mudrinic Rose's Stepfather

Bob and Rose Wedding Day 11-3-1973

Rose and Doris McCleary McFadden

Baby Rose McCleary

Baby Charity Joy Yerka

Rose McCleary Graduation Photo

Rose and her little sister Gertrude McCleary

John Robert Yerka

Rose before and After Herbalife
Results not typical but possible

Rose Family Photo

Bob and Rose 50th Anniversay
11-3-2023

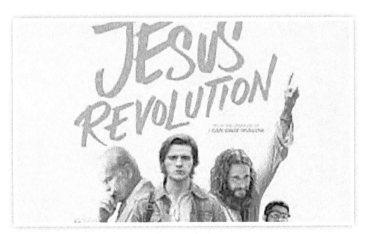

Jesus Revolution.

Jesus by Joseph Bruce Sofia

Aunt Gerry Page Keegan with Page cousins

ABOUT THE AUTHOR

Rose Marie Page Yerka is a wife, homeschool mother, grandmother and great-grandmother.

Her career background is nursing and business, and she is also a Herbalife personal wellness coach.

Rose is National Day of Prayer coordinator and Child Evangelism Good News club teacher. She is actively involved and serving in her church community prayer ministry and circle of friends and a caring ministry leader at Gloucester Community Church. She is an active member serving in her community with National Federation of Republican Women, chapter leader, and chaplain for New Jersey.

She is presently working on her first book and enjoys time with family camping in her motorhome and traveling.

Life in a Nutshell for Rose

After a fifty-year journey…

The secret of being and becoming finally revealed to me that I am not a mistake. There is a plan and a purpose for all things. With this attitude and perspective, I can find joy even in my pain. I write to share my secret with others. Pay it forward. Life is a gift. Handle with prayer. May you experience the joy of being and becoming. The best is yet to come.

Choose joy!